Lecture Notes in Computer Science

Commenced Publication in 1973
Founding and Former Series Editors:
Gerhard Goos, Juris Hartmanis, and Jan van Leeuwen

Dieter Gollmann   Jean-Louis Lanet
Julien Iguchi-Cartigny (Eds.)

Smart Card Research and Advanced Application

9th IFIP WG 8.8/11.2 International Conference
CARDIS 2010
Passau, Germany, April 14-16, 2010
Proceedings

 Springer

Volume Editors

Dieter Gollmann
Hamburg University of Technology
Institute for Security in Distributed Applications
21071 Hamburg, Germany
E-mail: diego@tu-harburg.de

Jean-Louis Lanet
Julien Iguchi-Cartigny
University of Limoges, XLIM
87000 Limoges, France
E-mail: {jean-louis.lanet, julien.cartigny}@unilim.fr

Library of Congress Control Number: 2010924121

CR Subject Classification (1998): E.3, C.2, K.6.5, D.4.6, H.4, J.1

LNCS Sublibrary: SL 4 – Security and Cryptology

ISSN   0302-9743
ISBN-10   3-642-12509-3 Springer Berlin Heidelberg New York
ISBN-13   978-3-642-12509-6 Springer Berlin Heidelberg New York

springer.com

© IFIP International Federation for Information Processing 2010
Printed in Germany

Typesetting: Camera-ready by author, data conversion by Scientific Publishing Services, Chennai, India
Printed on acid-free paper   06/3180

Preface

These proceedings contain the papers selected for presentation at CARDIS 2010, the 9th IFIP Conference on Smart Card Research and Advanced Application hosted by the Institute of IT-Security and Security Law (ISL) of the University of Passau, Germany. CARDIS is organized by IFIP Working Groups WG 8.8 and WG 11.2. Since 1994, CARDIS has been the foremost international conference dedicated to smart card research and applications. Every second year leading researchers and practitioners meet to present new ideas and discuss recent developments in smart card technologies.

The fast evolution in the field of information security requires adequate means for representing the user in human–machine interactions. Smart cards, and by extension smart devices with their processing power and their direct association with the user, are considered the first choice for this purpose. A wide range of areas including hardware design, operating systems, systems modelling, cryptography, and distributed systems contribute to this fast-growing technology.

The submissions to CARDIS were reviewed by at least three members of the Program Committee, followed by a two-week discussion phase held electronically, where committee members could comment on all papers and all reviews. Finally, 16 papers were selected for presentation at CARDIS.

There are many volunteers who offered their time and energy to put together the symposium and who deserve our acknowledgment. We want to thank all the members of the Program Committee and the external reviewers for their hard work in evaluating and discussing the submissions. We are also very grateful to Joachim Posegga, the General Chair of CARDIS 2010, and his team for the local conference management.

Last, but certainly not least, our thanks go to all the authors who submitted papers and all the attendees. We hope you find the proceedings stimulating.

March 2010

Jean-Louis Lanet
Dieter Gollmann

Organization

General Chair

Joachim Posegga   University of Passau, Germany

Program Chairs

Jean-Louis Lanet   Université de Limoges, France
Dieter Gollmann   Hamburg University of Technology, Germany

Program Committee

Liqun Chen	Hewlett-Packard, UK
Christophe Clavier	XLIM, France
Wolfgang Effing	Giesecke & Devrient, Germany
Benoit Feix	Inside Contactless, France
Benedikt Gierlichs	COSIC Leuven, Belgium
Louis Goubin	Université de Versailles, France
Gilles Grimaud	Université de Lille, France
Marc Joye	Technicolor, France
Josef Langer	CDE Hagenberg, Austria
Cédric Lauradoux	INRIA Rhône-Alpes, Equipe SWING, France
Kostas Markantonakis	Royal Holloway, UK
Vaclav Matyas	Masaryk University, Czech Republic
Bernd Meyer	Siemens AG, Germany
Wojciech Mostowski	University of Nijmegen, The Netherlands
Pierre Paradinas	INRIA, France
Emmanuel Prouff	Oberthur Technology, France
Jean-Jacques Quisquater	Université Catholique de Louvain, Belgium
Jean Marc Robert	Ecole de technologie supérieure Montréal, Canada
Jean-Jacques Vandewalle	Gemalto, France

Additional Reviewers

Lejla Batina	Junfeng Fan
Samia Bouzefrane	Lars Hoffmann
Guillaume Dabosville	Jan Krhovjak
Elke De Mulder	François-Xavier Marseille
Simon Duquennoy	Nathalie Mitton
Hermann Drexler	Kenny Paterson

Michael Roland
Martin Seysen
Petr Svenda
Hugues Thiebeauld

Vincent Verneuil
Colin Walter
Marc Witteman

Local Organization

Arne Bilzhause
Sigline Böck
Bastian Braun
Agnes Grützner
Peter Häring
Daniel Hausknecht
Michael Kaeufl

Markus Karwe
Guido Lenk-Blochowitz
Simon Niechzial
Henrich Pöhls
Daniel Schreckling
Martin Steininger
Marita Ward

Table of Contents

The Polynomial Composition Problem in $(\mathbb{Z}/n\mathbb{Z})[X]$

Marc Joye[1], David Naccache[2], and Stéphanie Porte[3]

[1] Thomson R&D, Security Competence Center
1 avenue de Belle Fontaine, 35576 Cesson-Sévigné Cedex, France
marc.joye@thomson.net
[2] Ecole normale supérieure, Département d'informatique
45 rue d'Ulm, 75230 Paris Cedex 05, France
david.naccache@ens.fr
[3] Smart Consulting
2 rue Louis Vignol, 13600 La Ciotat, France
stef.porte@gmail.com

Abstract. Let n be an RSA modulus and let $\mathscr{P}, \mathscr{Q} \in (\mathbb{Z}/n\mathbb{Z})[X]$. This paper explores the following problem: Given polynomials $\mathscr{Q}$ and $\mathscr{Q}(\mathscr{P})$, find polynomial $\mathscr{P}$. We shed light on the connections between the above problem and the RSA problem and derive from it new zero-knowledge protocols suited to smart-card applications.

Keywords: Polynomial composition, zero-knowledge protocols, Fiat-Shamir protocol, Guillou-Quisquater protocol, smart cards.

1 Introduction

Smart cards play an active role in security systems. Their salient features make them attractive in numerous applications, including — to name a few — the areas of banking, telephone, health, pay TV, home computers, and communication networks.

One of the primary use of smart cards resides in authentication. There exist basically two families of methods currently used for authenticating purposes. The first family relies on secret-key one-way functions while the second one makes use of public-key techniques. Both families have their own advantages. This paper focuses on the second family. In particular, we study zero-knowledge techniques. In a typical scenario, the smart card, characterized by a set of credentials, plays the role of the proving entity.

The first practical zero-knowledge protocol is due to Fiat and Shamir [3]. Remarkably, the protocol is rather efficient, computation-wise. It amounts to at most two modular multiplications per interaction. However, in order to reach a level of confidence of $(1 - 2^{-k})$, the basic protocol has to be repeated k times — a typical value for k is $k = 40$. In order to reduce the communication overhead, there is also a multiple-key protocol, at the expense of more key material. Another zero-knowledge protocol well suited to smart-card applications is the

D. Gollmann, J.-L. Lanet, J. Iguchi-Cartigny (Eds.): CARDIS 2010, LNCS 6035, pp. 1–12, 2010.
© IFIP International Federation for Information Processing 2010

Guillou-Quisquater protocol [4] (a.k.a. GQ protocol). The GQ protocol features small storage requirements and needs a single interaction.

In this paper we introduce a new problem, the *Polynomial Composition Problem*, which can be stated as follows.

> Let $\mathscr{P}$ and $\mathscr{Q}$ be two polynomials in $(\mathbb{Z}/n\mathbb{Z})[X]$ where n is an RSA modulus. Given polynomials $\mathscr{Q}$ and $\mathscr{S} := \mathscr{Q}(\mathscr{P})$, find $\mathscr{P}$.

Most public-key cryptographic schemes base their security on the difficulty of solving a hard mathematical problem. Given that the number of hard problems harnessable to cryptographic applications is rather limited, the investigation of new problems is of central importance in cryptography. To understand the Polynomial Composition Problem and its variants, we explore in the following sections the way in which the PCP relates to the celebrated RSA problem.

The Polynomial Composition Problem in $(\mathbb{Z}/n\mathbb{Z})[X]$ does not imply the RSA Problem, that is, the computation of roots in $\mathbb{Z}/n\mathbb{Z}$. Nevertheless, we exhibit a related problem that we call *Reducible Polynomial Composition Problem* (RPCP) and prove that RPCP $\Leftrightarrow$ RSA. In particular, we prove that when $\mathscr{Q}(X) = X^q$ then the Polynomial Composition Problem is equivalent to the problem of extracting q^{th} roots in $\mathbb{Z}/n\mathbb{Z}$.

These new problems allow us to broaden the view of existing cryptographic constructions. Namely, we describe a general PCP-based zero-knowledge protocol of which the Fiat-Shamir and the Guillou-Quisquater protocols are particular instances. As will be seen later, if s denotes the secret, they respectively correspond to the cases $\mathscr{Q}(X) = vX^2$ and $\mathscr{Q}(X) = vX^v$ ($v \geq 3$), with $\mathscr{Q}(s) = 1$.

The rest of this paper is organized as follows. In Section 2, we formally define the Polynomial Composition Problem and introduce the notations used throughout this paper. The hardness of the problem and its comparison with RSA are analyzed in Section 3. Finally, in Section 4, we show that the PCP allows one to generalize several zero-knowledge protocols.

2   The Polynomial Composition Problem

We suggest the following problem as a basis for building cryptographic protocols.

Problem 1 (Polynomial Composition Problem (PCP)). Let $\mathscr{P}$ and $\mathscr{Q}$ be two polynomials in $(\mathbb{Z}/n\mathbb{Z})[X]$ where n is an RSA modulus. Given polynomials $\mathscr{Q}$ and $\mathscr{S} := \mathscr{Q}(\mathscr{P})$, find $\mathscr{P}$.

Throughout this paper p and q denote the degrees of $\mathscr{P}$ and $\mathscr{Q}$, respectively. Let

$$\mathscr{P}(X) = \sum_{i=0}^{p} u_i X^i$$

where the u_i's denote the unknowns we are looking for. We assume that

$$\mathscr{Q}(Y) = \sum_{j=0}^{q} k_j Y^j$$

is known. Hence,

$$\mathscr{S}(X) = \sum_{j=0}^{q} k_j \left(\sum_{i=0}^{p} u_i X^i \right)^j .$$

If, given polynomials $\mathscr{2}'(Y) := \mathscr{2}(Y) - k_0$ and $\mathscr{S}'(X) := \mathscr{2}'(\mathscr{P}(X))$, an attacker can recover $\mathscr{P}$ then the same attacker can also recover $\mathscr{P}$ from $\{\mathscr{2}, \mathscr{S}\}$ by first forming polynomials $\mathscr{2}'(Y) = \mathscr{2}(Y) - k_0$ and $\mathscr{S}'(X) = \mathscr{S}(X) - k_0$. Therefore the problem is reduced to that of decomposing polynomials where $\mathscr{2}$ has no constant term, i.e., $\mathscr{2}(Y) = \sum_{j=1}^{q} k_j Y^j$. Similarly, once this has been done, the attacker can divide $\mathscr{2}$ by a proper constant and replace one of the coefficients k_j by one. Consequently and without loss of generality we restrict our attention to monic polynomials $\mathscr{2}$ with no constant term, that is,

$$\mathscr{2}(Y) = Y^q + k_{q-1} Y^{q-1} + \cdots + k_1 Y . \tag{1}$$

Noting that $q = 1$ implies that $\mathscr{S} = \mathscr{2}(\mathscr{P}) = \mathscr{P}$, we also assume that $q \geq 2$.

3   Analyzing the Polynomial Composition Problem

As before, let $\mathscr{P}(X) = \sum_{i=0}^{p} u_i X^i$ and let $\mathscr{2}(Y) = Y^q + \sum_{j=1}^{q-1} k_j Y^j$. Generalizing Newton's binomial formula and letting $k_q := 1$, we get

$$\mathscr{S}(X) = \sum_{j=1}^{q} k_j \left(\sum_{i=0}^{p} u_i X^i \right)^j$$

$$= \sum_{t=0}^{pq} \underbrace{\left(\sum_{\substack{1 \leq i_0 + \cdots + i_p \leq q \\ i_1 + 2i_2 + \cdots + p i_p = t}} k_{i_0 + \cdots + i_p} \frac{(i_0 + \cdots + i_p)!}{i_0! \dots i_p!} u_0^{i_0} \cdots u_p^{i_p} \right)}_{:= c_t} X^t , \tag{2}$$

where the second sum is extended over all nonnegative integers i_j satisfying $1 \leq \sum_{j=0}^{p} i_j \leq q$ and $\sum_{j=0}^{p} j i_j = t$.

3.1   RSA Problem $\Rightarrow$ Polynomial Composition Problem

We define polynomials $\mathscr{P}_0, \dots, \mathscr{P}_{pq} \in (\mathbb{Z}/n\mathbb{Z})[U_0, \dots, U_p]$ as

$$\mathscr{P}_t(U_0, \dots, U_p) := \sum_{\substack{1 \leq i_0 + \cdots + i_p \leq q \\ i_1 + 2i_2 + \cdots + p i_p = t}} k_{i_0 + \cdots + i_p} \frac{(i_0 + \cdots + i_p)!}{i_0! \dots i_p!} U_0^{i_0} \cdots U_p^{i_p} - c_t . \tag{3}$$

Note that $\mathscr{P}_t(u_0, \dots, u_p) = 0$ for all $0 \leq t \leq pq$.

Proposition 1. *For all $0 \leq r \leq p$, $\mathscr{P}_{pq-r} \in (\mathbb{Z}/n\mathbb{Z})[U_{p-r}, \dots, U_p]$. Furthermore, for all $1 \leq r \leq p$, $\mathscr{P}_{pq-r}$ is of degree exactly one in variable U_{p-r}.*

Proof. For $r = 0$, we have $\mathscr{P}_{pq}(U_0, \ldots, U_p) = U_p{}^q - c_{pq}$. For $r = p$, the condition $\mathscr{P}_{pq-r} \in (\mathbb{Z}/n\mathbb{Z})[U_{p-r}, \ldots, U_p]$ is trivially satisfied.

Fix r in $[1, p)$. By contradiction, suppose that $\mathscr{P}_{pq-r} \notin (\mathbb{Z}/n\mathbb{Z})[U_{p-r}, \ldots, U_p]$. So from Eq. (3), there exists some $i_j \neq 0$ with $0 \leq j \leq p-r-1$. Since $1 \leq i_0 + \cdots + i_p \leq q$, it follows that $i_1 + 2i_2 + \cdots + pi_p \leq j \cdot 1 + p \cdot (q-1) < pq - r$; a contradiction because $i_1 + 2i_2 + \cdots + pi_p = pq - r$ for polynomial $\mathscr{P}_{pq-r}$.

Moreover, for all $1 \leq r \leq p$, $\mathscr{P}_{pq-r}$ is of degree one in variable U_{p-r} since we cannot simultaneously have $1 \leq \sum_{j=0}^{p} i_j \leq q$, $\sum_{j=0}^{p} j\, i_j = pq - r$, and $i_{p-r} \geq 2$. Indeed, $i_{p-r} \geq 2$ implies $i_1 + 2i_2 + \cdots + pi_p \leq (p-r) \cdot 2 + p \cdot (q-2) < pq - r$, a contradiction. When $i_{p-r} = 1$, $i_1 + 2i_2 + \cdots + pi_p = pq - r$ if $i_p = q - 1$ and $i_j = 0$ for all $0 \leq (j \neq p - r) \leq p - 1$. This implies that the only term in U_{p-r} appearing in polynomial $\mathscr{P}_{pq-r}$ is $qU_{p-r} U_p{}^{q-1}$, whatever the values of variables k_i's are.   □

Corollary 1. *If the value of u_p is known then the Polynomial Composition Problem can be solved in time $O(p)$.*

Proof. Solving for U_{p-1} the relation $\mathscr{P}_{pq-1}(U_{p-1}, u_p) = 0$ (which is a univariate polynomial of degree exactly one in U_{p-1} by virtue of the previous proposition), the value of u_{p-1} is recovered. Next, the root of $\mathscr{P}_{pq-2}(U_{p-2}, u_{p-1}, u_p)$ gives the value of u_{p-2} and so on until the value of u_0 is found.

Note that the running time of the resolution process is $O(p)$ and is thus exponential in the bit-length of p.   □

This means that for low degree polynomials, the Polynomial Composition Problem in $\mathbb{Z}/n\mathbb{Z}$ is easier than the problem of computing q^{th} roots in $\mathbb{Z}/n\mathbb{Z}$ because if an attacker is able to compute a qth modular root (*i.e.*, to solve the RSA Problem) then she can find u_p from $\mathscr{P}_{pq}(u_p) = u_p{}^q - c_{pq} = 0$ and then apply the technique explained in the proof of Corollary 1 to recover $u_{p-1}, \ldots, u_0$. In other words,

Corollary 2. *RSA Problem $\Rightarrow$ Polynomial Composition Problem.*   □

There is a proposition similar to Proposition 1. It says that once u_0 is known, $u_1, \ldots, u_p$ can be found successively thanks to polynomials $\mathscr{P}_1, \ldots, \mathscr{P}_p$, respectively.

Proposition 2. *For all $0 \leq r \leq p$, $\mathscr{P}_r \in (\mathbb{Z}/n\mathbb{Z})[U_0, \ldots, U_r]$. Furthermore, for all $1 \leq r \leq p$, $\mathscr{P}_r$ is of degree exactly one in variable U_r.*

Proof. We have $\mathscr{P}_0(U_0) = \sum_{j=1}^{q} k_j U_0{}^j - c_0$.

For $r \in [1, p]$, suppose that $\mathscr{P}_r \notin (\mathbb{Z}/n\mathbb{Z})[U_0, \ldots, U_r]$. Therefore, $i_1 + 2i_2 + \cdots + pi_p \geq (r+1) \cdot 1 > r$; a contradiction since $i_1 + 2i_2 + \cdots + pi_p = r$. Moreover, we can easily see that $\mathscr{P}_r(U_0, \ldots, U_r) = qU_0{}^{q-1}U_r + \sum_{j=1}^{q-1} k_j j U_0{}^{j-1}U_r + \mathscr{Q}_r(U_0, \ldots, U_{r-1})$ for some polynomial $\mathscr{Q}_r \in (\mathbb{Z}/n\mathbb{Z})[U_0, \ldots, U_{r-1}]$.   □

3.2   Reducible Polynomial Composition Problem $\Rightarrow$ RSA Problem

The Polynomial Composition Problem *cannot* be equivalent to the RSA Problem. Consider for example the case $p = 2$ and $q = 3$: we have $\mathscr{P}(X) = u_2 X^2 + u_1 X + u_0$ and $\mathscr{Q}(X) = X^3 + k_2 X^2 + k_1 X$, and

$$\mathscr{S}(X) = c_6 X^6 + c_5 X^5 + c_4 X^4 + c_3 X^3 + c_2 X^2 + c_1 X + c_0$$

with
$$
\begin{cases}
c_0 = k_1 u_0 + k_2 u_0^2 + u_0^3, \\
c_1 = k_1 u_1 + 2k_2 u_0 u_1 + 3u_0^2 u_1, \\
c_2 = k_2 u_1^2 + 3u_0 u_1^2 + k_1 u_2 + 2k_2 u_0 u_2 + 3u_0^2 u_2, \\
c_3 = u_1^3 + 2k_2 u_1 u_2 + 6u_0 u_1 u_2, \\
c_4 = 3u_1^2 u_2 + k_2 u_2^2 + 3u_0 u_2^2, \\
c_5 = 3u_1 u_2^2, \\
c_6 = u_2^3.
\end{cases}
$$

We define the polynomials $\mathscr{P}_0(U_0) := k_1 U_0 + k_2 U_0^2 + U_0^3 - c_0$, $\mathscr{P}_1(U_0, U_1) := k_1 U_1 + 2k_2 U_0 U_1 + 3U_0^2 U_1 - c_1$, and $\mathscr{P}_5(U_1, U_2) := 3U_1 U_2^2 - c_5$. Now we first compute the resultant of $\mathscr{P}_0$ and $\mathscr{P}_1$ with respect to variable U_0 and obtain a univariate polynomial in U_1, say $\mathscr{R}_0 = \mathrm{Res}_{U_0}(\mathscr{P}_0, \mathscr{P}_1)$. Next we compute the resultant of $\mathscr{R}_0$ and $\mathscr{P}_5$ with respect to variable U_1 and get a univariate polynomial in U_2, say $\mathscr{R}_1 = \mathrm{Res}_{U_1}(\mathscr{R}_0, \mathscr{P}_5)$. After computation, we get

$$
\begin{aligned}
\mathscr{R}_1(U_2) = {} & 27c_1^3 U_2^6 + (27c_1^2 c_5 k_1 - 9c_1^2 c_5 k_2^2)U_2^4 \\
& + (-4c_5^3 k_1^3 + c_5^3 k_2^3 b^2 - 18c_0 c_5^3 k_1 k_2 + 4c_0 c_5^3 k_2^3 - 27c_0^2 c_5^3).
\end{aligned}
$$

Since u_2 is a root of both $\mathscr{R}_1(U_2)$ and $\mathscr{P}_6(U_2) := U_2^3 - c_6$, u_2 will be a root of their greatest common divisor in $(\mathbb{Z}/n\mathbb{Z})[U_2]$, which is given by

$$
\begin{aligned}
& (27c_1^2 c_5 k_1 - 9c_1^2 c_5 k_2^2)c_6 U_2 \\
& + (27c_1^3 c_6^2 - 4c_5^3 k_1^3 + c_5^3 k_1^2 k_2^2 - 18c_0 c_5^3 k_1 k_2 + 4c_0 c_5^3 k_2^3 - 27c_0^2 c_5^3),
\end{aligned}
$$

from which we derive the value of u_2. Once u_2 is known, the values of u_1 and u_0 trivially follow by Corollary 1.

We now introduce a harder problem: the *Reduced* Polynomial Composition Problem in $(\mathbb{Z}/n\mathbb{Z})[X]$.

Problem 2 (Reduced Polynomial Composition Problem (RPCP)). Let $\mathscr{P}$ and $\mathscr{Q}$ be two polynomials in $(\mathbb{Z}/n\mathbb{Z})[X]$ where n is an RSA modulus. Given $\mathscr{Q}$ and the $\deg(\mathscr{P}) + 1$ most significant coefficients of $\mathscr{S} := \mathscr{Q}(\mathscr{P})$, find $\mathscr{P}$.

Definition 1. *When the Polynomial Composition Problem is equivalent to the Reduced Polynomial Composition Problem, it is said to be* reducible.

Equivalently, the Polynomial Composition Problem is reducible when the values of $c_0, \ldots, c_{p(q-1)-1}$ can be derived from $c_{p(q-1)}, \ldots, c_{pq}$ and $k_1, \ldots, k_{q-1}$. This is for example the case when $p = q = 2$, that is, when $\mathscr{P}(X) = u_2X^2 + u_1X + u_0$, $\mathscr{Q}(X) = X^2 + k_1X$, and

$$\mathscr{S}(X) = c_4X^4 + c_3X^3 + c_2X^2 + c_1X + c_0$$

with
$$\begin{cases} c_0 = k_1u_0 + u_0^2, \\ c_1 = k_1u_1 + 2u_0u_1, \\ c_2 = k_1u_2 + 2u_0u_2 + u_1^2, \\ c_3 = 2u_1u_2, \\ c_4 = u_2^2. \end{cases}$$

An astute algebraic manipulation yields:

$$c_1 = \frac{4c_2c_3c_4 - c_3^3}{8c_4^2} \pmod{n} \quad \text{and} \quad c_0 = \frac{4c_1^2c_4 - c_3^2k_1^2}{4c_3^2} \pmod{n}.$$

If follows that we can omit the first two relations (the information included therein is anyway contained in the remaining three as we had just shown) and the problem amounts to solving the Reduced Polynomial Composition Problem:

$$\begin{cases} c_2 = k_1u_2 + 2u_0u_2 + u_1^2, \\ c_3 = 2u_1u_2, \\ c_4 = u_2^2. \end{cases}$$

Theorem 1. *Reducible Polynomial Composition Problem $\Rightarrow$ RSA Problem.*

Proof. Assume that we are given an oracle $O^{\mathrm{PCP}}(k_1, \ldots, k_{q-1}; c_0, \ldots, c_{pq})$ which on input polynomials $\mathscr{Q}(X) = X^q + \sum_{j=1}^{q-1} k_jX^j$ and $\mathscr{S}(X) = \sum_{t=0}^{pq} c_tX^t$ returns the polynomial $\mathscr{P}(X) = \sum_{i=0}^{p} u_iX^i$ such that $\mathscr{S}(X) = \mathscr{Q}(\mathscr{P}(X))$. When the polynomial composition is reducible, oracle O^{PCP} can be used to compute a qth root of a given $x \in \mathbb{Z}/n\mathbb{Z}$, i.e., compute a y satisfying $y^q \equiv x \pmod{n}$.

1. choose $p + q - 1$ random values $k_1, \ldots, k_{q-1}, c_{p(q-1)}, \ldots, c_{pq-1} \in \mathbb{Z}/n\mathbb{Z}$;
2. compute $c_0, \ldots, c_{p(q-1)-1}$;
3. run $O^{\mathrm{PCP}}(k_1, \ldots, k_{q-1}; c_0, \ldots, c_{pq-1}, x)$;
4. get $u_0, \ldots, u_p$;
5. set $y := u_p$ and so $y^q \equiv x \pmod{n}$.

Note that Step 2 can be executed since the composition is supposed to be reducible. Furthermore, note that the values of $c_{pq-1}, \ldots, c_{p(q-1)}$ *uniquely* determine the values of $u_{p-1}, \ldots, u_0$, respectively. Indeed, from Proposition 1,

$$\mathscr{P}_{pq-r}(U_{p-r}, u_{p-r+1}, \ldots, u_p) \in (\mathbb{Z}/n\mathbb{Z})[U_{p-r}]$$

is a polynomial of degree exactly one of which u_{p-r} is root, for all $1 \le r \le p$. $\square$

3.3   A Practical Criterion

In this section, we present a simple criterion allowing to decide if a given composition problem is reducible.

During the proof of Proposition 1, we have shown that there exists a polynomial $\mathcal{Q}_{pq-r} \in (\mathbb{Z}/n\mathbb{Z})[U_{p-r+1}, \ldots, U_p]$ such that

$$\mathcal{P}_{pq-r}(U_{p-r}, \ldots, U_p) = qU_{p-r}U_p^{q-1} + \mathcal{Q}_{pq-r}(U_{p-r+1}, \ldots, U_p)$$

for all $1 \le r \le p$. From $c_{pq} = (u_p)^q$, we infer:

$$u_{p-r} = \frac{-\mathcal{Q}_{pq-r}(u_{p-r+1}, \ldots, u_p)}{q\,c_{pq}}\,u_p, \quad (1 \le r \le p) . \tag{4}$$

Using Eq. (4), for $r = 1, \ldots, p$, we now iteratively compute $u_{p-1}, \ldots, u_0$ as a polynomial function in u_p. We let Υ_{p-r} denote this polynomial function, i.e., $u_{p-r} = \Upsilon_{p-r}(u_p)$ for all $1 \le r \le p$. We then respectively replace $u_0, \ldots, u_{p-1}$ by $\Upsilon_0(u_p), \ldots, \Upsilon_{p-1}(u_p)$ in the expressions of $c_0, \ldots, c_{pq-p-1}$. If, for each c_i ($0 \le i \le pq - p - 1$), the powers of u_p cancel thanks to $(u_p)^{q-1} = c_{pq}$ then the problem is reducible.

We illustrate the technique with the example $\mathcal{P}(X) = u_3 X^3 + u_2 X^2 + u_1 X + u_0$ and $\mathcal{Q}(Y) = Y^3$. Then $\mathcal{S}(X) = \sum_{t=0}^{9} c_t X^t$ with

$$\begin{cases} c_0 = u_0^3, \\ c_1 = 3u_0^2 u_1, \\ c_2 = 3u_0^2 u_2 + 3u_0 u_1^2, \\ c_3 = 3u_0^2 u_3 + 6u_0 u_1 u_2 + u_1^3, \\ c_4 = 6u_0 u_1 u_3 + 3u_0 u_2^2 + 3u_1^2 u_2, \\ c_5 = 6u_0 u_2 u_3 + 3u_1^2 u_3 + 3u_1 u_2^2, \\ c_6 = 3u_0 u_3^2 + 6u_1 u_2 u_3 + u_2^3, \\ c_7 = 3u_1 u_3^2 + 3u_2^2 u_3, \\ c_8 = 3u_2 u_3^2, \\ c_9 = u_3^3 . \end{cases}$$

From the respective expressions of c_8, c_7 and c_6, we successively find

$$\Upsilon_2(u_3) = \frac{c_8}{3c_9}\,u_3, \quad \Upsilon_1(u_3) = \frac{3c_7 c_9 - c_8^2}{9c_9^2}\,u_3, \quad \text{and}$$

$$\Upsilon_0(u_3) = \frac{27c_6 c_9^2 - 6c_8(3c_7 c_9 - c_8^2) - c_8^3}{81c_9^3}\,u_3 .$$

Since $c_0, \ldots, c_5$ are homogeneous in u_0, u_1, u_2, u_3 and of degree three, they can be evaluated by replacing u_0, u_1, u_2 by $\Upsilon_0(u_3), \Upsilon_1(u_3), \Upsilon_2(u_3)$, respectively, and then replacing $(u_3)^3$ by c_9. Consequently, the composition is reducible: the values of

$c_0, \ldots, c_5$ can be inferred from $c_6, \ldots, c_9$ and the problem amounts to computing cubic roots in $\mathbb{Z}/n\mathbb{Z}$.

This is not fortuitous and can easily be generalized as follows.

Corollary 3. *For $\mathcal{Q}(Y) = Y^q$, the Polynomial Composition Problem in $\mathbb{Z}/n\mathbb{Z}$ is equivalent to the RSA Problem, i.e. to the problem of extracting q^{th} roots in $\mathbb{Z}/n\mathbb{Z}$.*

Proof. From Eq. (2), it follows that $\mathscr{S}(X) = \sum_{t=0}^{pq} c_t X^t$ with

$$c_t = \sum_{\substack{i_0 + \cdots + i_p = q \\ i_1 + 2i_2 + \cdots + pi_p = t}} \frac{q!}{i_0! \cdots i_p!} u_0{}^{i_0} \cdots u_p{}^{i_p},$$

which is homogeneous in $u_0, \ldots, u_p$ and of degree $i_0 + \cdots + i_p = q$. Moreover since by induction, for $1 \le r \le p$, $\Upsilon_{p-r}(u_p) = K_{p-r} \cdot u_p$ for some constant K_{p-r}, the corollary follows. $\qquad\square$

4   Cryptographic Applications

Loosely speaking, a zero-knowledge protocol allows a prover to demonstrate the knowledge of a secret without revealing any useful information about the secret. We show how to construct such a protocol thanks to composition of polynomials.

4.1   A PCP-Based Zero-Knowledge Protocol

A trusted third party selects and publishes an RSA modulus n. Each prover $\mathcal{P}$ chooses two polynomials $\mathcal{P}, \mathcal{Q}$ in $(\mathbb{Z}/n\mathbb{Z})[X]$ and computes $\mathscr{S} = \mathcal{Q}(\mathcal{P})$. $\{\mathcal{Q}, \mathscr{S}\}$ is $\mathcal{P}$'s public key given to the verifier $\mathcal{V}$ so as to ascertain $\mathcal{P}$'s knowledge of the secret key $\mathcal{P}$.

Execute ℓ times the following protocol:

- $\mathcal{P}$ selects a random $r \in \mathbb{Z}/n\mathbb{Z}$.
- $\mathcal{P}$ evaluates $c = \mathscr{S}(r)$ and sends c to $\mathcal{V}$.
- $\mathcal{V}$ sends to $\mathcal{P}$ a random bit b.
- If $b = 0$, $\mathcal{P}$ reveals $t = r$ and $\mathcal{V}$ checks that $\mathscr{S}(t) = c$.
- If $b = 1$, $\mathcal{P}$ reveals $t = \mathcal{P}(r)$ and $\mathcal{V}$ checks that $\mathcal{Q}(t) = c$.

PCP-Based Protocol

4.2   Improvements

Efficiency can be increased by using the following trick:

$\mathcal{P}$ chooses v polynomials $\mathcal{P}_1, \ldots, \mathcal{P}_{v-1}, \mathcal{Q}$ in $(\mathbb{Z}/n\mathbb{Z})[X]$, with $v \ge 3$. Her secret key is the set $\{\mathcal{P}_1, \ldots, \mathcal{P}_{v-1}\}$ while her public key consists of the set $\{\mathscr{S}_0 = \mathcal{Q}, \mathscr{S}_1 = \mathcal{Q}(\mathcal{P}_{v-1}), \mathscr{S}_2 = \mathcal{Q}(\mathcal{P}_{v-1}(\mathcal{P}_{v-2})), \ldots, \mathscr{S}_j = \mathcal{Q}(\mathcal{P}_{v-1}(\ldots(\mathcal{P}_{v-j}))), \ldots, \mathscr{S}_{v-1} = \mathcal{Q}(\mathcal{P}_{v-1}(\ldots(\mathcal{P}_1)))\}$.

The protocol is shown below:

- $\mathcal{P}$ selects a random $r \in \mathbb{Z}/n\mathbb{Z}$
- $\mathcal{P}$ evaluates $c = \mathscr{S}_{v-1}(r)$ and sends c to $\mathcal{V}$.
- $\mathcal{V}$ sends to $\mathcal{P}$ a random integer $0 \leq b \leq v - 1$.
- If $b = 0$, $\mathcal{P}$ reveals $t = r$ and $\mathcal{V}$ checks that $\mathscr{S}_{v-1}(t) = c$.
- If $b \neq 0$, $\mathcal{P}$ reveals $t = \mathscr{P}_b(\ldots(\mathscr{P}_1(r)))$ and $\mathcal{V}$ checks that $\mathscr{S}_{v-b-1}(t) = c$.

Nested PCP Protocol

4.3 Relations with Other Zero-Knowledge Protocols

It is interesting to note that our first protocol coincides with the (simplified) Fiat-Shamir protocol [3] (see also [5, Protocol 10.24]) when $\mathscr{P}(X) = sX$ and $\mathscr{Q}(X) = vX^2$ where $vs^2 \equiv 1 \pmod{n}$.

The nested variant may be seen as a generalization of the Guillou-Quisquater protocol [4] by taking $\mathscr{P}_1(X) = \mathscr{P}_2(X) = \cdots = \mathscr{P}_{v-1}(X) = sX$ where s is a secret value and $\mathscr{Q}(X) = vX^v$ so that $vs^v \equiv 1 \pmod{n}$. Indeed, in this case we have $\mathscr{P}_{v-1}(\ldots(\mathscr{P}_{v-j}(X))) = s^j X$ and hence $\mathscr{S}_j(X) = v^{1-j}X^v$.

An interesting research direction would be to extend the above protocols to Dickson polynomials.

5 Conclusion

This paper introduced the Polynomial Composition Problem (PCP) and the related Reducible Polynomial Composition Problem (RPCP). Relations between these two problems and the RSA Problem were explored. Further, two concrete zero-knowledge protocols suited to smart-card applications were given as particular instances of PCP-based constructs.

Acknowledgments. We are grateful to Jesper Buus Nielsen (ETHZ) for attracting our attention to an important detail in the proof of Corollary 1. We are also grateful to the anonymous referees for useful comments.

References

1. Cohen, H.: A Course in Computational Algebraic Number Theory. In: GTM 138. Springer, Heidelberg (1993)
2. Coppersmith, D., Franklin, M., Patarin, J., Reiter, M.: Low-exponent RSA with related messages. In: Maurer, U.M. (ed.) EUROCRYPT 1996. LNCS, vol. 1070, pp. 1–9. Springer, Heidelberg (1996)
3. Fiat, A., Shamir, A.: How to prove yourself: Practical solutions to identification and signature problems. In: Odlyzko, A.M. (ed.) CRYPTO 1986. LNCS, vol. 263, pp. 186–194. Springer, Heidelberg (1987)

4. Guillou, L.C., Quisquater, J.-J.: A practical zero-knowledge protocol fitted to security microprocessor minimizing both transmission and memory. In: Günther, C.G. (ed.) EUROCRYPT 1988. LNCS, vol. 330, pp. 123–128. Springer, Heidelberg (1988)
5. Menezes, A.J., van Oorschot, P.C., Vanstone, S.A.: Handbook of Applied Cryptography. CRC Press, Boca Raton (1997)

A   Mathematical Background

Let $\mathcal{R}$ be an integral domain with quotient field $\mathbb{K}$.

Definition 2. *Given two polynomials $\mathcal{A}, \mathcal{B} \in \mathcal{R}[X]$, the resultant of $\mathcal{A}$ and $\mathcal{B}$, denoted by $\mathrm{Res}(\mathcal{A}, \mathcal{B})$, is defined as*

$$\mathrm{Res}(\mathcal{A}, \mathcal{B}) = (a_m)^n (b_n)^m \prod_{1 \le i \le m, 1 \le j \le n} (\alpha_i - \beta_j) \tag{5}$$

if $\mathcal{A}(X) = a_m \prod_{1 \le i \le m}(X - \alpha_i)$ and $\mathcal{B}(X) = b_n \prod_{1 \le j \le n}(X - \beta_j)$ are the decompositions of $\mathcal{A}$ and $\mathcal{B}$ in the algebraic closure of $\mathbb{K}$.

From this definition, we see that $\mathrm{Res}(\mathcal{A}, \mathcal{B}) = 0$ if and only if polynomials $\mathcal{A}$ and $\mathcal{B}$ have a common root (in $\overline{\mathbb{K}}$); hence if and only if $\mathcal{A}$ and $\mathcal{B}$ have a (non-trivial) common factor. Equivalently, we have

$$\mathrm{Res}(\mathcal{A}, \mathcal{B}) = (a_m)^n \prod_{1 \le i \le m} \mathcal{B}(\alpha_i) = (b_n)^m \prod_{1 \le j \le n} \mathcal{A}(\beta_j) \ .$$

The resultant $\mathrm{Res}(\mathcal{A}, \mathcal{B})$ can be evaluated without knowing the decomposition of $\mathcal{A}$ and $\mathcal{B}$. Letting $\mathcal{A}(X) = \sum_{1 \le i \le m} a_i X^i$ and $\mathcal{B}(X) = \sum_{1 \le j \le n} b_j X^j$, we have

$$\mathrm{Res}(\mathcal{A}, \mathcal{B}) = \det \begin{pmatrix} a_m & a_{m-1} & \cdots & a_0 & 0 & \cdots & 0 \\ 0 & a_m & a_{m-1} & \cdots & a_0 & \cdots & 0 \\ \vdots & \vdots & \ddots & \ddots & \cdots & \ddots & \vdots \\ 0 & 0 & 0 & a_m & a_{m-1} & \cdots & a_0 \\ b_n & b_{n-1} & \cdots & b_0 & 0 & \cdots & 0 \\ 0 & b_n & b_{n-1} & \cdots & b_0 & \cdots & 0 \\ \vdots & \vdots & \ddots & \ddots & \cdots & \ddots & \vdots \\ 0 & 0 & 0 & b_n & b_{n-1} & \cdots & b_0 \end{pmatrix} \begin{array}{l} \left.\begin{array}{c} \\ \\ \\ \\ \end{array}\right\} n \text{ rows} \\ \left.\begin{array}{c} \\ \\ \\ \\ \end{array}\right\} m \text{ rows} \end{array} \ .$$

This clearly shows that $\mathrm{Res}(\mathcal{A}, \mathcal{B}) \in \mathcal{R}$.

A *multivariate polynomial* $\mathcal{A} \in \mathcal{R}[X_1, \ldots, X_k]$ (with $k \ge 2$) may be viewed as a univariate polynomial in $\mathcal{R}[X_1, \ldots, X_{k-1}][X_k]$. Consequently, it makes sense to compute the resultant of two multivariate polynomials with respect to one variable, say X_k. If $\mathcal{A}, \mathcal{B} \in \mathcal{R}[X_1, \ldots, X_k]$, we let $\mathrm{Res}_{X_k}(\mathcal{A}, \mathcal{B})$ denote the resultant of $\mathcal{A}$ and $\mathcal{B}$ with respect to X_k.

Lemma 1. *Let $\mathscr{A}, \mathscr{B} \in \mathcal{R}[X_1, \ldots, X_k]$ (with $k \geq 2$). Then $(\alpha_1, \ldots, \alpha_k)$ is a common root (in $\overline{\mathbb{K}}$) of $\mathscr{A}$ and $\mathscr{B}$ if and only if $(\alpha_1, \ldots, \alpha_{k-1})$ is a root of $\mathrm{Res}_{X_k}(\mathscr{A}, \mathscr{B})$.*

B   Additional Examples

B.1   The Case $p = 3$ and $q = 2$

Using the previous notations and simplifications, we write $\mathscr{P}(X) = u_3 X^3 + u_2 X^2 + u_1 X + u_0$ and $\mathscr{Q}(Y) = Y^2 + k_1 Y$. Expressing the c_i's we get:

$$
\begin{cases}
c_0 = k_1 u_0 + u_0^2, \\
c_1 = k_1 u_1 + 2u_0 u_1, \\
c_2 = u_1^2 + k_1 u_2 + 2u_0 u_2, \\
c_3 = 2u_1 u_2 + k_1 u_3 + 2u_0 u_3, \\
c_4 = u_2^2 + 2u_1 u_3, \\
c_5 = 2u_2 u_3, \\
c_6 = u_3^2.
\end{cases}
$$

Now using the criterion of §3.3, we find $u_2 = \frac{c_5}{2c_6} u_3$, $u_1 = V u_3$, and $u_0 = -\frac{k_1^2}{4} + L u_3$ with $V := \frac{4c_4 c_6 - c_5^2}{8c_6^2}$ and $L := \frac{8c_3 c_6^2 - c_5(4c_4 c_6 - c_5^2)}{16c_6^3}$. Hence, we derive:

$$
c_2 = c_6 V^2 + c_5 L, \quad c_1 = 2c_6 L V, \quad \text{and } c_0 = -\frac{k_1^2}{4} + L^2 c_6 .
$$

Being reducible, this proves that solving the PCP for $p = 3$ and $q = 2$ amounts to computing square roots in $\mathbb{Z}/n\mathbb{Z}$.

B.2   The Case $p = 3$ and $q = 3$

We have $\mathscr{P}(X) = u_3 X^3 + u_2 X^2 + u_1 X + u_0$ and $\mathscr{Q}(X) = X^3 + k_2 X^2 + k_1 X$. Defining polynomials $\mathscr{P}_i$ as in Eq. (3), we successively compute $\mathscr{R}_0 := \mathrm{Res}_{U_0}(\mathscr{P}_0, \mathscr{P}_1)$, $\mathscr{R}_1 := \mathrm{Res}_{U_1}(\mathscr{R}_0, \mathscr{P}_7)$, and $\mathscr{R}_2 = \mathrm{Res}_{U_2}(\mathscr{R}_1, \mathscr{P}_8)$ wherefrom

$$
\begin{aligned}
\mathscr{R}_2(u_3) = {}& 19683 c_1^3 u_3^{18} + (-6561 c_1^2 c_7 k_2^2 + 19683 c_1^2 c_7 k_1) u_3^{16} \\
& + (2187 c_1^2 c_8^2 k_2^2 - 6561 c_1^2 c_8^2 k_1) u_3^{13} \\
& + (2916 c_0 c_7^3 k_2^3 + 729 c_7^3 k_1^2 k_2^2 - 13122 c_0 c_7^3 k_2 k_1 - 2916 c_7^3 k_1^3 \\
& \quad - 19683 c_7^3 c_0^2) u_3^{12} \\
& + (-2916 c_0 c_7^2 c_8^2 k_2^3 - 729 c_8^2 c_7^2 k_2^2 k_1^2 + 13122 c_8^2 c_7^2 c_0 k_2 k_1 + 2916 c_8^2 c_7^2 k_1^3 \\
& \quad + 19683 c_8^2 c_7^2 c_0^2) u_3^9 \\
& + (972 c_8^4 c_7 c_0 k_2^3 + 243 c_8^4 c_7 k_1^2 k_2^2 - 4374 c_8^4 c_7 c_0 k_1 k_2 - 972 c_8^4 c_7 k_1^3 \\
& \quad - 6561 c_8^4 c_7 c_0^2) u_3^6 \\
& + (-108 c_8^6 c_0 k_2^3 - 27 c_8^6 k_1^2 k_2^2 + 486 c_8^6 c_0 k_1 k_2 + 108 c_8^6 k_1^3 + 729 c_8^6 c_0^2) u_3^3 \\
= {}& 0 .
\end{aligned}
$$

So, we obtain the value of u_3 by exploiting the additional relation $c_9 = u_3^3$ and hence the values of u_2, u_1, and u_0.

Note that if we choose $k_1 = k_2^2/3$ then the terms in u_3^{16} ($= c_9^5 u_3$) and in u_3^{13} ($= c_9^4 u_3$) disappear and consequently the value of u_3 cannot be recovered. In this case, the criterion shows again that the problem is equivalent to that of computing cubic roots in $\mathbb{Z}/n\mathbb{Z}$.

Enhance Multi-bit Spectral Analysis on Hiding in Temporal Dimension

Qiasi Luo

Shanghai Fudan Microelectronics Co., Ltd
Building 4, 127 Guotai Road, Shanghai 200433, China

Abstract. Random delays and dynamic frequency switching are widely adopted in smartcards and embedded systems as temporal hiding countermeasures to side channel attack.Temporal hiding is regarded as efficient to enhance the security of cryptographic devices. However, spectral analysis with Fast Fourier Transform is a powerful method to defeat temporal hiding countermeasures. Spectral analysis shares the same merit with integration different power attack. Multi-bit spectral analysis is enhanced with partitioning power analysis, which is much more effective than the correlation power analysis in the spectral domain. Multi-bit spectral analysis effectively defeats temporal hiding countermeasure with floating-mean dynamic frequency switching countermeasure. It is suggested cryptographic devices should employ other countermeasures together with hiding to ensure side channel security.

Keywords: Side channel attack, spectral analysis, differential power analysis, correlation power analysis, partitioning power analysis.

1 Introduction

Nowadays symmetric block ciphers are widely adopted in smartcards and embedded systems to provide security confidence to sensitive data. The implementation of the cryptographic algorithm may leak out side-channel information such as power consumption [1] , electromagnetic emanation [2], etc. These leakage information can be utilized by side channel attack (SCA) to retrieve the key of cipher. Masking, power-balanced logic and Hiding are main countermeasures to SCA [3]. Hiding in the temporal dimension is regarded as an efficient countermeasure in practice, since it is easy to implement together with masking and power-balanced logic to reinforce the security of cryptographic devices.

Hiding is usually implemented by inserting random delays or dummy operations which are called random process interrupts (RPIs) [4]. The RPIs de-synchronize the traces of side-channel signals, therefore the leakage information is concealed by noises in the classic SCA. More traces are need to distill the signal out of noise. Random delays can also be inserted at gate-level [5]. Dynamic frequency switching (DFS) [6] is another effective approach of hiding in the temporal dimension. Re-synchronize the random clocks of DFS is

D. Gollmann, J.-L. Lanet, J. Iguchi-Cartigny (Eds.): CARDIS 2010, LNCS 6035, pp. 13–23, 2010.

very difficult in practice. More effective way to generate the random delays or frequency switchings is the floating-mean method [7].

Several analysis methods were proposed to attack hiding in temporal dimension. Integration DPA (IDPA) [4] substantially reduces the number of traces with RPIs. Phase-Only Correlation (POC) technique [8] evaluates the displacements between traces, realigns traces or removes bad traces, and defeats countermeasure of random delays [9].

Differential frequency analysis (DFA) [10] is a powerful method against hiding, since the amplitude of Fast Fourier Transform (FFT) is time-shift invariant. To retain leakage position information, differential spectrogram analysis (DSA) [11] uses spectrogram traces generated with short-time Fourier transform. DEMA with DFA technique against HF and UHF tag prototype [12] proved the effectiveness and advantage of DFA over filtering and integration techniques [4] at the presence of noise and hiding both in amplitude and timing dimensions.

In this paper, we propose a significantly more efficient multi-bit spectral analysis method to attack hiding in the temporal dimension. The method avoid large random correlation noise and have much better performance. The method is also capable to attack DFS.

First, We introduce the basic concepts about spectral analysis and generalize the methodology. Analysis of its efficiency on hiding is presented. Then we compare different multi-bit spectral analysis methods both analytically and empirically. Finally, multi-bit spectral analysis method is carried out on two different DFS strategies and the results conform to the analysis.

2   Spectral Analysis Methods

2.1   Differential Power Spectral Analysis

Consider a cryptographic device that carries out encryption with secret key k. Let $d = \{d_1, \ldots, d_{N_d}\}$ be the intermediate data related to k which an adversary attacks, and N_d be the number of data bits. The side-channel measurement such as power consumption or EM trace is $w = \{w_1, \ldots, w_{N_w}\}$, where N_w is the total number of points. Multiple traces are $W = \{w^1, \ldots, w^{N_W}\}$, where N_W is the number of traces. The leakage information in w usually resides within a particular time interval T_l. Let $l = \{l_1, \ldots, l_{N_l}\}$ be the leakage trace during T_l, where N_l the number of sample points of l and $N_l < N_w$. The portion other than l in w is regarded as non-leakage trace and random to the intermediate data, and is denoted as $n = \{n_1, \ldots, r_{N_n}\}$. Thus, the full trace can be written as $w = \{n \bigcup l\} = \{n_1, \ldots, n_i, l_1, \ldots, l_{N_l}, n_{i+1}, \ldots, n_{N_n}\}$.

The original single bit DPA [1] computes difference of means (DOM) as

$$\Delta_w = \frac{\sum_{d_i=1} w^j}{N_{d_i=1}} - \frac{\sum_{d_i=0} w^j}{N_{d_i=0}}$$

where $N_{d_i=1}$ is the number of traces with $d_i = 1$, and $N_{d_i=0}$ the number of traces with $d_i = 0$, both under a particular key hypothesis $\hat{k}$. For the correct key, the correlation ε_l during T_l indicates the leakage correlation. Theoretically, ε_l converges to the ideal DOM ε with N_w, i.e. $\varepsilon_l \to \varepsilon$ when $N_w \to \infty$. The correlations ε_n at other places are random correlations which converge to zero, i.e. $\varepsilon_n \to 0$ when $N_w \to \infty$. So if we separate l and n in w, then

$$\varepsilon_l = \frac{\sum_{d_i=1} l^j}{N_{d_i=1}} - \frac{\sum_{d_i=0} l^j}{N_{d_i=0}} \to \varepsilon$$

$$\varepsilon_n = \frac{\sum_{d_i=1} n^j}{N_{d_i=1}} - \frac{\sum_{d_i=0} n^j}{N_{d_i=0}} \to 0$$

ε_l of different keys are used for hypothesis test with the maximum likelihood method, i.e. the correct key hypothesis has the maximum ε_l.

Applying the principles of DPA to spectral signals in frequency domain leads to differential power spectral analysis (DPSA). Let the power spectral density (PSD) of l be $\mathbf{L} = \{L_f, f = 1, \cdots, N_f\}$, where N_f is the number of points in FFT and also indicates corresponding sample frequency. DOM of DPSA at each frequency is computed as follow:

$$\varepsilon_{\mathbf{L}} = \frac{\sum_{d_i=1} \mathbf{L}^j}{N_{d_i=1}} - \frac{\sum_{d_i=0} \mathbf{L}^j}{N_{d_i=0}} \to \varepsilon' \tag{1}$$

$$\varepsilon_{\mathbf{N}} = \frac{\sum_{d_i=1} \mathbf{N}^j}{N_{d_i=1}} - \frac{\sum_{d_i=0} \mathbf{N}^j}{N_{d_i=0}} \to 0 \tag{2}$$

where ε' is the theoretical DOM of DPSA when $N_w \to \infty$.

After computation of $\varepsilon_{\mathbf{L}}$, all frequency components of $\varepsilon_{\mathbf{L}}$ are summed up (SumAll) as the overall evaluation $\hat{e} = \sum_f \varepsilon_{\mathbf{L}}$, to test key hypotheses with maximum likelihood method.

2.2 Generic Spectral Analsyis

Generic spectral analysis method is illustrated in Fig. 1. Two additional steps (in white box) are inserted into the temporal analysis method procedure. The two steps, spectral signal generation and evaluation metrics, are symmetric operations. The former is analytical and the latter synthetical.

The spectral signal generation decomposes original temporal signal into linearly independent components at different frequencies. The evaluation metric accumulates leakage at all frequencies to get the overall evaluation for hypothesis test. There are various PSD estimation methods in digital singal processing. Periodgram is a simple yet effective method, which is employed in this paper.

The straightforward evaluation metric is summation of all frequencies (SumAll), i.e. the leakage at all frequencies are added up to get the overall evaluation. In [13], the side-channel leakage information distributes along a very wide frequency rang from 10 MHz to 400 MHz almost uniformly. The

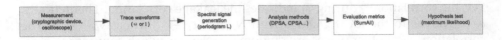

Fig. 1. Spectral analysis method

evaluation metric employed in [10] [11] is summation of significance (SumSig), i.e. only correlations larger than a certain significant level are accumulated. This approach helps to diminish the influence of noise. There are also various forms of noise in SCA such as electronic noise, data dependent switching noise etc [3]. The random correlations of wrong key hypotheses are also considered as noise while distinguishing keys. The standard deviation of evaluations of all keys is regarded as the threshold level to distinguish leakage correlation and random correlations, and is usually set as the significance threshold. Practical experience shows that the SumAll metric is of good balance between efficiency and robustness.

The sliding-window spectrogram analysis approach can be adopted [11], when the leakage position is not known. A window is set to include a portion of the trace to generate PSD. The window slides along the trace with specified step length to generate the spectrogram with temporal information. Separated spectral analyses are performed on corresponding PSD signals from the same window. As a result, the position of window where the largest correlation rises indicates the leakage position.

3   Spectral Analysis on Hiding

Hiding in temporal dimension is of great practical importance. RPIs increase the amount of traces needed for DPA quadratically, yet integration DPA reduce the quadratical redundancy into linear [4]. In embedded software implementation, RPIs are inserted by integer values. Integration DPA on RPIs adds points of fixed cycle intervals in the traces, which is easy to carry out. However, on DFS [6], this integration operation is not so easy to implement, since the cycles lengths are variant and the positions of leakage in different traces do not align with fixed clock edges.

Spectral analysis has inherent integration property thanks to time-shift invariance of FFT. This makes spectral analysis a natural method against hiding in temporal dimension. A typical DFS scenario is investigated as follow.

Suppose the trace $w = \{n \bigcup l\} = \{n_1, \ldots, n_i, l_1, \ldots, l_{N_l}, n_{i+1}, \ldots, n_{N_n}\}$ is randomly shifted with DFS. For different traces, the positions of l are floating randomly. Suppose the floating range of l falls into a particular interval I called as leakage interval. Let the lower and upper bounds of the leakage interval I be i_l and i_u, i.e. the positions of l_1 and l_u. The bounds i_l, i_u are random variables with mean values u_l, u_u and standard deviations σ_l, σ_u respectively. The statistics of I depend on how many cycles it contains:

- If I contains exact one cycle, then N_l is constant because the leakage information resides within a small interval right after the clock edge. So i_l and i_u have identical statistics.
- If I contains multiple cycles, N_l is variant with different traces. i_l and i_u are independent.

For spectral signal generation, only the portion of waveform falling in the leakage interval is of interest. Denote this portion of waveform as w_I. For simplicity and without confusion, rewrite w as w_I by discarding the portion of waveform out of I. Then $w_I = \{n \bigcup l; n \in I\} = \{n_1, \ldots, n_i, l_1, \ldots, l_{N_l}, n_{i+1}, \ldots, n_{N_n}\}$. Let $\mathcal{F}(\cdot)$ denote the FFT operator.

$$
\begin{aligned}
|\mathcal{F}(w_I)| &= |\mathcal{F}(\{n_1, \cdots, n_i, l_1, \cdots, l_{N_l}, n_{i+1}, \cdots, n_{N_n}\})| \\
&= |\mathcal{F}(\{n_1, \cdots, n_i, 0, \cdots, 0, 0, \cdots, 0\})| + \\
&\quad |\mathcal{F}(\{0, \cdots, 0, l_1, \cdots, l_{N_l}, 0 \cdots, 0\})| + \\
&\quad |\mathcal{F}(\{0, \cdots, 0, 0, \cdots, 0, n_{i+1}, \cdots, n_{N_n}\})| \\
&= |\mathcal{F}(\{n_1, \cdots, n_i, \})| + |\mathcal{F}(\{l_1, \cdots, l_{N_l}\})| + |\mathcal{F}(\{n_{i+1}, \cdots, n_{N_n}\})| \\
&= |\mathcal{F}(\{n_1, \cdots, n_i, n_{i+1}, \cdots, n_{N_n}\})| + |\mathcal{F}(\{l_1, \cdots, l_{N_l}\})| \\
&= |\mathcal{F}(n_I)| + |\mathcal{F}(l)|.
\end{aligned}
$$

Then the PSD of w_I is

$$
\begin{aligned}
\mathbf{W_I} &= |\mathcal{F}(w_I)|^2 \\
&= |\mathcal{F}(n_I)|^2 + |\mathcal{F}(l)|^2 + 2|\mathcal{F}(n_I)| \cdot |\mathcal{F}(l)| \\
&= \mathbf{N_I} + \mathbf{L} + 2N_I L.
\end{aligned}
$$

According to formula (1) and (2),

$$
\begin{aligned}
\varepsilon_{\mathbf{L}} &\rightharpoonup \varepsilon', \\
\varepsilon_{\mathbf{N_I}} &\rightharpoonup 0, \\
\varepsilon_{N_I L} &\to o(\varepsilon_L) \to 0.
\end{aligned}
$$

Thus

$$
\varepsilon_{\mathbf{W_I}} = \varepsilon_{\mathbf{N_I}} + \varepsilon_{\mathbf{L}} + 2\varepsilon_{N_I L} \to \varepsilon'.
$$

The formulas shows the integration process of spectral analysis method on the shifted leakage intervals. Although leakage positions in different traces are variant, they are all included in, thanks to the time-shift invariance of FFT. Besides, the linearity of FFT helps to eliminate noise and accumulate signal simultaneously.

In practical spectral analysis, the leakage interval is usually set as $I_S = [\mu_l - \sigma_l, \mu_u + \sigma_u]$ to include most of the leakage information and avoid too much noise. If the σ_l and σ_u of the particular DFS are larger, more noise should be included in spectral signal generation, then the signal-noise-ratio (SNR) of the spectral analysis is less, and the DFS is more resistant to attack.

Consider two DFSs with same mean values u_l and u_u, but different standard deviations σ_l, σ_u and σ'_l, σ'_u respectively. The delay penalties are the same, but the resistances to spectral analysis are different. The leakage interval I_s may contain only one cycle or multiple cycles:

- **One cycle.** The lower and upper bounds of leakage intervals have identical statistics, $\sigma_l = \sigma_u = \sigma$ and $\sigma'_l = \sigma'_u = \sigma'$. To successfully retrieve the key with spectral analysis, the amount of traces needed for DFS with σ is σ'/σ times as much as DFS with σ'.
- **Multiple cycles.** The lower and upper bounds of leakage intervals are independent. Each bound introduces noise independently. The noise level is proportional to the length of I. To successfully retrieve the key with spectral analysis, the amount of traces needed for DFS with σ_l and σ_u is $(\sigma'_l + \sigma'_u + u'_u - u'_l)/(\sigma_l + \sigma_u + u_u - u_l)$ times as much as DFS with σ'_l and σ'_u.

4 Enhance Multi-bit Spectral Analysis

4.1 Correlation Power Spectral Analysis

To improve DPA SNR, analysis methods make use of multi-bit leakage information. The most widely adopted multi-bit power analysis method is correlation power analysis (CPA) [14]. The Hamming distance model of CPA is written as

$$l = ah(d) + b \tag{3}$$

where $h(\cdot)$ is Hamming distance function, a is scalar gain, and b is the overall noise effect independent with $h(d)$.

The Pearson correlation coefficient between the power consumption and Hamming distance is

$$\rho_l = \frac{N_T \sum l^j h^j - \sum l^j \sum h^j}{\sqrt{N_T \sum l^{j2} - \left(\sum l^j\right)^2} \sqrt{N_T \sum h^{j2} - \left(\sum h^j\right)^2}}.$$

CPA has its corresponding spectral form. Rewrite formula (3) in the frequency domain,

$$\mathbf{L} = ah(d) + \mathbf{B}$$

where $\mathbf{B}$ is the PSD of b and is also independent with $h(d)$.

Pearson correlation coefficients are computed at all frequencies of $\mathbf{L}$ for correlation power spectral analysis (CPSA):

$$\rho_{\mathbf{L}} = \frac{N_T \sum \mathbf{L}^j h^j - \sum \mathbf{L}^j \sum h^j}{\sqrt{N_T \sum \mathbf{L}^{j2} - \left(\sum \mathbf{L}^j\right)^2} \sqrt{N_T \sum h^{j2} - \left(\sum h^j\right)^2}}. \tag{4}$$

Afterward all frequency components of ρ_L are summed up to get the overall evaluation $\hat{e} = \sum_f \rho_L$. Evaluation $\hat{e}$ is served for key hypothesis test.

Simple CPSA without evaluation metric synthesis has already been employed in [12] [15]. Here in this paper, a CPSA is exemplified on the data set of DPA contest [16]. The Pearson correlation coefficients of all frequencies of the CPSA with 5000 traces are shown Fig. 2(a), and the result along with number of traces are shown in Fig. 3(a). The evaluation metric is SumAll. One major problem with CPSA is the random correlations at higher frequencies. After FFT, the signals at the same frequency are already linear correlated. The Pearson coefficients of CPSA give large values even there are only random correlations at higher frequencies. If these random correlations are summed up with the SumAll metric, it will reduce the efficiency of CPSA.

4.2 Partitioning Power Spectral Analysis

Random correlations at higher frequencies in CPSA mainly originate from the normalization of standard deviations in the denominator of formula (4). The partitioning power analysis (PPA) [17] [18] without standard deviation normalization, has the same even better efficiency compared with CPA.

PPA attacks on multi-bit intermediate data $d_p = \{d_1, \cdots, d_{N_p}\}$, where N_p is the number of data bits PPA attacks and $N_p \leq N_d$. The traces are partitioned into groups by Hamming weights $g = h(d_p) = \{0, \cdots, N_p\}$ under different key hypotheses. Then means of groups are computed and they are summed up with different weights a_g to get the overall correlation ε_l^P.

$$\varepsilon_l^P = \sum_{g=0}^{N_p} a_g \frac{\sum_g l^j}{N_g}$$

where N_g is number of traces partitioned in group g and $\sum_g a_g = 0$. For $N_p = 4$, $a_2 = 0, -2a_0 - -a_1 = a_3 = 2a_4$, or $a_g = \{-1, -2, 0, 2, 1\}$.

The corresponding partitioning power spectral analysis (PPSA) computes correlations at different frequencies as

$$\varepsilon_L^P = \sum_{g=1}^{N_p} a_g \frac{\sum_g L^j}{N_g}.$$

Then all frequency components of are summed up (SumAll) as the overall evaluation $\hat{e} = \sum_f \varepsilon_L^P$ for hypotheses test.

A PPSA is performed on the same data set with the same order of traces as CPSA in Section 4. The correlations of PPSA with 5000 traces are shown in Fig. 2(b), and the results with number of traces are shown in Fig. 3(b). Compared to CPSA, there are no large random correlations at the higher frequencies. The characteristic frequencies where the correlation of correct key begins to sink into the random correlations of CPSA and PPSA are the same, which indicates that the leakage signals extracted by both methods are the same. The difference is

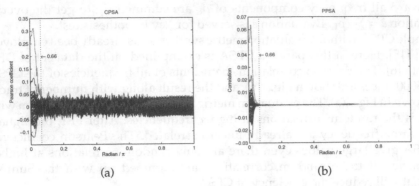

Fig. 2. (a) Pearson correlation coeffient of CPSA . (b) Correlation of PPSA. The red curves are for correct key and blue curves for wrong keys.

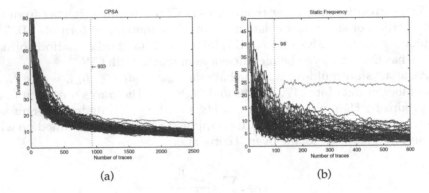

Fig. 3. Results of (a) CPSA. (b) PPSA. The red curves are for correct key and blue curves for wrong keys.

about the noise. The results in Fig. 3 show that amount of traces needed to get the same SNR level with CPSA is nearly 10 times as much as PPSA.

5   Experimental Results

The original data set is from DPA contest [16], which contains power consumption traces of an unprotected DES crypto-processor on a SoC in ASIC with static frequency. In general ASICs or micro-controllers, the power consumption leakage information all resides within a short time interval right after the clock edges. To generate traces with DFS, random delays of zero values are inserted into the original trace before the clock edges. DFS traces generated by this method share the same characteristic of randomly shifted leakage with actual DFS traces. The only difference is the actual DFS traces have very small power consumption for the random delays between shifted clock cycles, while the generated DFS traces have zero values. However, the signal, i.e. the leakage information residing right after the clock edges is the same.

Data sets for two kinds of random DFS are generated. The first DFS employs the most commonly used uniform distribution. The random delays follow independently uniform distribution with mean value μ_0 and standard deviation σ_0. For one single trace with 32 frequency switchings, the overall delay is the accumulation of 32 independent uniform delays. So the standard deviation of the overall delay σ_Σ is much less than σ_0, which leads to efficiency degeneration. The second DFS employs more efficient floating mean method [7] with parameters a and b. The standard deviation of the overall delay with the floating mean method does not diminish with accumulation.

The parameters used for random delay generation in this paper is as follow. Clock cycle length of the original traces is $T = 625$. The statistics of one single random delay of the uniform DFS are mean value $\mu_0 = 625$, and standard deviation $\sigma_0 = 360$. Parameters for floating mean DFS are $a = 1250$ and $b = 250$. The standard deviations of lower and upper bounds of leakage interval I for uniform DFS and floating mean DFS are shown in Table 1. Floating mean DFS has larger standard deviations than the uniform DFS, thus is more resistant to spectral analysis.

Table 1. Parameters of DFSs

	Uniform		Floating Mean	
	i_l	i_u	i_l	i_u
μ	14376	16253	14353	16244
σ	1730	1838	6653	7520

One trace from the original DPA contest data set and the DPA leakage positions are shown in Fig. 4(a). The red curve is for DOM of correct key and blue for wrong keys. One trace with uniform DFS and one with floating mean DFS are shown in Fig. 4(b). The red lines indicates the positions of lower and upper bounds of leakage interval I in spectral analysis on the DFSs. The range of leakage interval with floating mean DFS is much wider than uniform DFS.

The temporal analysis methods including CPA and PPA on the DFS traces all fail to retrieve the correct key with up to 81000 traces. PPSAs are performed on the original data with static frequency, generated data with uniform DFS and floating mean DFS. The PPSAs attack on the first S-Box of the 16th round in DES. The PPSAs process the data set with the same orders. Evaluation metric is SumAll. The results are shown in Fig. 5(a) and 5(b). According to the analysis in section 3, the ratio of amount of traces needed to retrieved the correct key for spectral analysis on two DFSs is $(\sigma'_l + \sigma'_u + u'_u - u'_l)/(\sigma_l + \sigma_u + u_u - u_l) =$ $(7520+6653+16244-14353)/(1730+1838+16253-14376) = 2.95$. While in Fig. 5, the ratio is $48663/6138 = 7.92$. The empirical value does ont fit the theoretical value very well, because more leakages are not included in the leakage interval

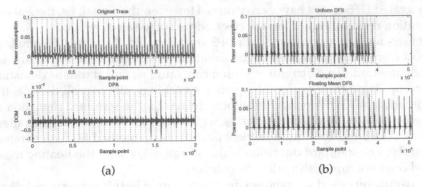

(a)   (b)

Fig. 4. (a) Up: original trace with static frequency; Down: DPA leakage positions. (b) Up: generated trace with uniform DFS; Down: generated trace with floating mean DFS. The dashed lines are nominal clock edges.

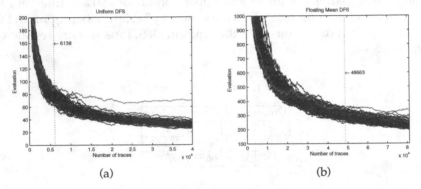

(a)   (b)

Fig. 5. PPSA on (a) uniform DFS and (b) floating mean DFS. The red curves are for correct key and blue for wrong keys.

I with the floating mean DFS than uniform DFS. Compared to results in [7] with DPA where the ratio is $45000/2500 = 18$, the PPSA gives much better results.

6   Conclusions

We proposed the spectral analysis method with evaluation metric on hiding in temporal dimension such as RPIs and DFS. The spectral analysis has inherent integration property thanks to shift-invariance of FFT. We proposed PPSA method to enhance the multi-bit spectral analysis. PPSA does not generate large random correlations at higher frequencies, and is much more efficient than CPSA. Experimental results show PPSA break down DFS. Hiding as a countermeasure can increase the amount of traces needed for successful attacks, but it is not always safe and should be implemented together with other countermeasures such as masking to ensure security.

References

1. Kocher, P.C., Jaffe, J., Jun, B.: Differential power analysis. In: Wiener, M. (ed.) CRYPTO 1999. LNCS, vol. 1666, pp. 388–397. Springer, Heidelberg (1999)
2. Agrawal, D., Archambeault, B., Rao, J., Rohatgi, P.: The EM side channel(s). In: Kaliski Jr., B.S., Koç, Ç.K., Paar, C. (eds.) CHES 2002. LNCS, vol. 2523, pp. 29–45. Springer, Heidelberg (2003)
3. Mangard, S., Oswald, E., Popp, T.: Power Analysis Attacks: Revealing the Secrets of Smart Cards (Advances in Information Security). Springer, New York (2007)
4. Clavier, C., Coron, J.S., Dabbous, N.: Differential power analysis in the presence of hardware countermeasures. In: Paar, C., Koç, Ç.K. (eds.) CHES 2000. LNCS, vol. 1965, pp. 252–263. Springer, Heidelberg (2000)
5. Bucci, M., Luzzi, R., Guglielmo, M., Trifiletti, A., AG, I., Graz, A.: A countermeasure against differential power analysis based on random delay insertion. In: IEEE International Symposium on Circuits and Systems, ISCAS 2005, pp. 3547–3550 (2005)
6. Yang, S., Wolf, W., Vijaykrishnan, N., Serpanos, D.N., Yuan, X.: Power attack resistant cryptosystem design: a dynamic voltage and frequency switching approach. In: Proceedings of the Design, Automation and Test in Europe, vol. 3, pp. 64–69 (2005)
7. Coron, J., Kizhvatov, I.: An efficient method for random delay generation in embedded software. In: Clavier, C., Gaj, K. (eds.) CHES 2009. LNCS, vol. 5747, p. 170. Springer, Heidelberg (2009)
8. Homma, N., Nagashima, S., Sugawara, T., Aoki, T., Satoh, A.: A high-resolution phase-based waveform matching and its application to side-channel attacks. IEICE Trans. Fundam. Electron. Commun. Comput. Sci. E91-A, 193–202 (2008)
9. Nagashima, S., Homma, N., Imai, Y., Aoki, T., Satoh, A.: DPA using phase-based waveform matching against random-delay countermeasure. In: IEEE International Symposium on Circuits and Systems, ISCAS 2007, pp. 1807–1810 (2007)
10. Gebotys, C., Tiu, C., Chen, X.: A countermeasure for EM attack of a wireless PDA. In: International Conference on Information Technology: Coding and Computing, ITCC 2005, vol. 1, pp. 544–549 (2005)
11. Gebotys, C.H., Ho, S., Tiu, C.: EM analysis of Rijndael and ECC on a wireless Java-based PDA. In: Rao, J.R., Sunar, B. (eds.) CHES 2005. LNCS, vol. 3659, pp. 250–264. Springer, Heidelberg (2005)
12. Plos, T., Hutter, M., Feldhofer, M.: Evaluation of side-channel preprocessing techniques on cryptographic-enabled HF and UHF RFID-tag prototypes. In: Workshop on RFID Security 2008, Budapest, July 9-11 (2008)
13. Hutter, M., Mangard, S., Feldhofer, M.: Power and EM attacks on passive RFID devices. In: Paillier, P., Verbauwhede, I. (eds.) CHES 2007. LNCS, vol. 4727, pp. 320–333. Springer, Heidelberg (2007)
14. Brier, E., Clavier, C., Olivier, F.: Correlation power analysis with a leakage model. In: Joye, M., Quisquater, J.-J. (eds.) CHES 2004. LNCS, vol. 3156, pp. 16–29. Springer, Heidelberg (2004)
15. Hutter, M., Medwed, M., Hein, D., Wolkerstorfer, J.: Attacking ECDSA-Enabled RFID Devices. In: Abdalla, M., Pointcheval, D., Fouque, P.-A., Vergnaud, D. (eds.) ACNS 2009. LNCS, vol. 5536, p. 534. Springer, Heidelberg (2009)
16. DPA Contest 2008/2009, http://www.dpacontest.org/
17. Le, T.H., Clédière, J., Canovas, C., Robisson, B., Servière, C., Lacoume, J.-L.: A proposition for correlation power analysis enhancement, pp. 174–186 (2006)
18. Le, T.H., Canovas, C., Clédière, J.: An overview of side channel analysis attacks, 33-43 (2008), 1368319

Secure Delegation of Elliptic-Curve Pairing*

Benoît Chevallier-Mames[1], Jean-Sébastien Coron[2], Noel McCullagh[3],
David Naccache[4], and Michael Scott[3]

[1] benoit.chevalliermames@gemplus.com
[2] Université du Luxembourg
6, rue Richard Coudenhove-Kalergi
L-1359 Luxembourg, Luxembourg
jean-sebastien.coron@uni.lu
[3] School of Computing, Dublin City University
Glasnevin, Dublin 9, Ireland
{noel.mccullagh,mike}@computing.dcu.ie
[4] École normale supérieure
Département d'informatique, Groupe de cryptographie
45, rue d'Ulm, F-75230 Paris CEDEX 05, France
david.naccache@ens.fr

Abstract. In this paper we describe a simple protocol for secure delegation of the elliptic-curve pairing. A computationally limited device (typically a smart-card) will delegate the computation of the pairing $e(A, B)$ to a more powerful device (for example a PC), in such a way that 1) the powerful device learns nothing about the points A and B, and 2) the limited device is able to detect when the powerful device is cheating.

Keywords: Elliptic-curve pairing, secure delegation protocol, Boneh-Franklin IBE.

1 Introduction

Since the discovery of the first practical identity-based cryptosystem based on the elliptic-curve pairing [1], pairing-based cryptography has become a very active research area. Many pairing-based protocols have been proposed with novel and attractive properties, for example for key-exchange [6] and digital signatures [3].

The increasing popularity of pairing-based cryptosystems and their foreseeable deployment in computationally constrained devices such as smart-cards and dongles spurred recent research in the implementation of pairing (e.g. [8]). Unfortunately, although pairing is a cubic-time operation, pairing implementation attempts in limited devices such as smart-cards reveal that the embedded code may be slow, resource-consuming and tricky to program.

---

* Work done while authors Chevallier-Mames, Coron and Naccache were with Gemplus (now Gemalto). Authors McCullagh and Scott are also affiliated to NoreTech.

D. Gollmann, J.-L. Lanet, J. Iguchi-Cartigny (Eds.): CARDIS 2010, LNCS 6035, pp. 24–35, 2010.
© IFIP International Federation for Information Processing 2010

Given that several PC-based pairing libraries exist, it seems natural to find-out whether a smart-card could interact with such packages to privately compute the elliptic-curve pairing. Note that beyond preserving operands from preying eyes, the card must also ascertain that bogus libraries don't mislead it into generating wrong results.

In this paper, we propose a simple protocol for secure delegation of elliptic-curve pairing. A computationally limited device (for example a smart-card) will delegate the computation of the elliptic-curve pairing $e(A, B)$ to a more powerful device (for example a PC), in such a way that 1) the powerful device learns nothing about the points A and B, and 2) the limited device is able to detect when the powerful device is cheating. The limited device will restrict itself to simple curve or field operations. We also describe some efficient variants of our protocol if one of the points A and B or both are already publicly known, or when the point A can be considered as constant, as it is the case for the Boneh-Franklin identity-based encryption scheme [1].

2   Preliminaries

2.1   Bilinear Map

Our protocol for secure pairing delegation is actually more general than just elliptic-curve pairing : as most pairing-based cryptosystems, it works for any bilinear map. Therefore, we briefly review the basic facts about bilinear maps. We follow the notations in [2]. We refer the reader to [7] for an extensive background on elliptic-curve pairing.

1. $\mathcal{G}_1$ and $\mathcal{G}_2$ are two (additive) cyclic groups of prime order p;
2. G_1 is a generator of $\mathcal{G}_1$ and G_2 is a generator of $\mathcal{G}_2$;
3. ψ is a computable isomorphism from $\mathcal{G}_1$ to $\mathcal{G}_2$ with $\psi(G_1) = G_2$,
4. e is a computable bilinear map $e : \mathcal{G}_1 \times \mathcal{G}_2 \to \mathcal{G}_T$;
5. $\mathcal{G}_T$ is a multiplicative cyclic group of order p.

A bilinear map is a map $e : \mathcal{G}_1 \times \mathcal{G}_2 \to \mathcal{G}_T$ with the following properties :

1. Bilinear: for all $U \in \mathcal{G}_1, V \in \mathcal{G}_2$ and $a, b \in \mathbb{Z}$, $e(a \cdot U, b \cdot V) = e(U, V)^{a \cdot b}$
2. Non-degenerate: $e(G_1, G_2) \neq 1$

Note that the previous conditions imply that $e(G_1, G_2)$ is a generator of $\mathcal{G}_T$.

2.2   Computational Indistinguishability

We recall the notion of computational indistinguishability [5], which will be used in the definition of secure pairing delegation. Two distribution ensemble $X = \{X_n\}_{n \in \mathbb{N}}$ and $Y = \{Y_n\}_{n \in \mathbb{N}}$ are said to be computationally indistinguishable and denoted $X \stackrel{c}{\equiv} Y$ if for every (probabilistic) polynomial-time algorithm A, and every $c > 0$, there exists an integer N such that for all $n > N$

$$|\Pr[A(X_n) = 1] - \Pr[A(Y_n) = 1]| < \frac{1}{n^c}$$

3 Secure Pairing Delegation

In this section, we formalize the security notions for secure pairing delega-tion. Our setting is the following : a computationally limited device, called the card and denoted C, will delegate the computation of the pairing $e(A, B)$ to a more powerful device, called the terminal and denoted T. Both devices C and T are actually probabilistic polynomial-time Turing machines. We denote by $\text{View}_T(A, B)$ the terminal's view when interacting with C with points A, B. The terminal's view includes the randomness used by the terminal, and the data received from the card.

The security notions could be formalized in the general framework of secure multiparty computation (for standard definitions, see for example [4]). However, we observe that our setting is much simpler than for general secure multiparty computation : the terminal has no secret and outputs nothing; moreover only the terminal can be malicious. Therefore, we adapt the general notions for secure multiparty computation to our restricted setting. We obtain that a protocol for pairing delegation is secure if it satisfies the three following security notions :

Completeness: after completion of the protocol with an honest terminal, the card obtains $e(A, B)$, except with negligible probability.

Secrecy: a (possibly cheating) terminal should not learn any information about the points A and B. More formally, for any malicious terminal T, there exists a simulator S such that for any A, B, the output of S is computationally indistin-guishable from the terminal's view :

$$S \overset{c}{\equiv} \text{View}_T(A, B)$$

Note that the simulator S is not given A, B as input.

Correctness: The card should be able to detect a cheating terminal, except with negligible probability. More formally, for any cheating terminal T and for any A, B, the card outputs either $\bot$ or $e(A, B)$, except with negligible probability.

4 Our Protocol

In order to delegate the pairing computation, one could think of the follow-ing protocol. On input A, B, the card could generate random x, y and ask the terminal to compute the pairing :

$$\alpha = e(x \cdot A, y \cdot B)$$

The card would then recover $e(A, B)$ by simply computing :

$$e(A, B) = \alpha^{(x \cdot y)^{-1}}$$

However, it is easy to see that this is not a secure pairing delegation protocol. Namely, although the terminal learns nothing about A, B, the card cannot detect a cheating terminal. Namely, if the terminal outputs α^r for some r instead of α, the card will obtain $e(A, B)^r$ instead of $e(A, B)$, and will not be able to detect the cheating terminal. In the following, we describe a secure pairing delegation protocol, such that if the terminal is cheating, then the card outputs either the correct $e(A, B)$ or nothing with overwhelming probability.

4.1   Description

The card and the terminal are given as input a description of the groups $\mathcal{G}_1$, $\mathcal{G}_2$ and $\mathcal{G}_T$, and a description of the bilinear map $e : \mathcal{G}_1 \times \mathcal{G}_2 \to \mathcal{G}_T$. The card and the terminal receive the generators G_1 and G_2; we also assume that the card receives $e(G_1, G_2)$. The card is given as input the points A and B and must eventually output $e(A, B)$. Recall that $\mathcal{G}_1$, $\mathcal{G}_2$ and $\mathcal{G}_T$ are additive groups of order p.

1. The card generates a random $g_1 \in \mathbb{Z}_p$ and a random $g_2 \in \mathbb{Z}_p$, and queries the three following pairings to the terminal :

$$\alpha_1 = e(A + g_1.G_1, G_2), \quad \alpha_2 = e(G_1, B + g_2.G_2)$$

$$\alpha_3 = e(A + g_1.G_1, B + g_2.G_2)$$

2. The card checks that $\alpha_1, \alpha_2, \alpha_3 \in \mathcal{G}_T$, by checking that $(\alpha_i)^p = 1$ for $i = 1, 2, 3$. Otherwise, the card outputs $\perp$ and halts.

3. The card computes a purported value for $e(A, B)$:

$$e_{AB} = \alpha_1^{-g_2} \cdot \alpha_2^{-g_1} \cdot \alpha_3 \cdot e(G_1, G_2)^{g_1 g_2} \tag{1}$$

4. The card generates four random values $a_1, r_1, a_2, r_2 \in \mathbb{Z}_p$ and queries the pairing :

$$\alpha_4 = e(a_1.A + r_1.G_1, a_2.B + r_2.G_2)$$

5. The card computes :

$$\alpha_4' = (e_{AB})^{a_1 a_2} \cdot (\alpha_1)^{a_1 r_2} \cdot (\alpha_2)^{a_2 r_1} \cdot e(G_1, G_2)^{r_1 r_2 - a_1 g_1 r_2 - a_2 g_2 r_1} \tag{2}$$

and checks that $\alpha_4' = \alpha_4$. In this case, the card outputs e_{AB}; otherwise it outputs $\perp$.

4.2   Security Proof

The following theorem shows that our protocol is secure :

Theorem 1. *The previous protocol is a secure pairing delegation protocol.*

Proof. The completeness property is easily established. We obtain from the bilinear property :

$$e(A + g_1.G_1, B + g_2.G_2) = e(A, B) \cdot e(A, G_2)^{g_2} \cdot e(G_1, B)^{g_1} \cdot e(G_1, G_2)^{g_1 g_2}$$

Then, for an honest terminal, we have :

$$\alpha_1 = e(A + g_1.G_1, G_2) = e(A, G_2) \cdot e(G_1, G_2)^{g_1} \tag{3}$$
$$\alpha_2 = e(G_1, B + g_2.G_2) = e(G_1, B) \cdot e(G_1, G_2)^{g_2} \tag{4}$$
$$\alpha_3 = e(A + g_1.G_1, B + g_2.G_2) \tag{5}$$

Combining the four previous equations, we obtain :

$$\alpha_3 = e(A, B) \cdot (\alpha_1)^{g_2} \cdot (\alpha_2)^{g_1} \cdot e(G_1, G_2)^{-g_1 g_2}$$

which, using (1), shows that the card computes the correct $e_{AB} = e(A, B)$. Moreover, using :

$$\alpha_4 = e(a_1.A + r_1.G_1, a_2.B + r_2.G_2)$$
$$= e(A, B)^{a_1 a_2} \cdot e(A, G_2)^{a_1 r_2} \cdot e(G_1, B)^{r_1 a_2} \cdot e(G_1, G_2)^{r_1 r_2}$$

we obtain from equations (3) and (4) :

$$\alpha_4 = (e_{AB})^{a_1 a_2} \cdot (\alpha_1)^{a_1 r_2} \cdot (\alpha_2)^{r_1 a_2} e(G_1, G_2)^{r_1 r_2 - a_1 g_1 r_2 - a_2 g_2 r_1}$$

which, using (2), gives $\alpha_4 = \alpha_4'$ and shows that the card eventually outputs the correct $e_{AB} = e(A, B)$.

The secrecy property follows from the fact that the terminal receives only random, independently distributed points in the groups $\mathcal{G}_1$ and $\mathcal{G}_2$. Therefore, the simulator $\mathcal{S}$ simply consists in running the terminal $\mathcal{T}$ with randomly generated points. The simulator's output and the terminal's view when interacting with $\mathcal{C}$ are then identically distributed.

The correctness property is established as follows : we show that if the value e_{AB} computed by the card at step 3 is not equal to $e(A, B)$, then the element α_4' computed by the card at step 5 has a nearly uniform distribution in $\mathcal{G}_T$, independent from the terminal's view. Then, the probability that $\alpha_4 = \alpha_4'$ at step 5 will be roughly $1/p$. Therefore, the card will output $\perp$, except with negligible probability.

We let $U = a_1.A + r_1.G_1$ and $V = a_2.B + r_2.G_2$. Moreover, we let $a, b, u, v \in \mathbf{Z}_p$ be such that $A = a.G_1$, $B = b.G_2$, $U = u.G_1$, $V = v.G_2$, which gives :

$$u = a_1 \cdot a + r_1 \tag{6}$$
$$v = a_2 \cdot b + r_2 \tag{7}$$

The card checks that $\alpha_1, \alpha_2, \alpha_3 \in \mathcal{G}_T$. Therefore, we must have $e_{AB} \in \mathcal{G}_T$, and since $e(G_1, G_2)$ is a generator of $\mathcal{G}_T$, we can let $\beta_1, \beta_2, \beta_3 \in \mathbf{Z}_p$ be such that :

$$\alpha_1 = e(A, G_2) \cdot e(G_1, G_2)^{g_1 + \beta_1} \tag{8}$$
$$\alpha_2 = e(G_1, B) \cdot e(G_1, G_2)^{g_2 + \beta_2} \tag{9}$$
$$e_{AB} = e(A, B) \cdot e(G_1, G_2)^{\beta_3} \tag{10}$$

Therefore, the value e_{AB} is correct iff $\beta_3 = 0$.

From the previous observation, we also have $\alpha'_4 \in \mathcal{G}_T$. Therefore, we can assume that $\alpha_4 \in \mathcal{G}_T$, since otherwise $\alpha'_4 \neq \alpha_4$ and the card outputs $\perp$. Then we can let $\beta_4, \beta'_4 \in \mathbb{Z}_p$ be such that :

$$\alpha_4 = e(U, V) \cdot e(G_1, G_2)^{\beta_4} \tag{11}$$

$$\alpha'_4 = e(U, V) \cdot e(G_1, G_2)^{\beta'_4} \tag{12}$$

Therefore, the card outputs e_{AB} iff $\beta_4 = \beta'_4$.

In the following, we assume that $u \neq 0$ and $v \neq 0$. Since (u, v) is uniformly distributed in $\mathbb{Z}_p$, this happens with probability $(1 - 1/p)^2 \geq 1 - 2/p$.

We show that if $\beta_3 \neq 0$, then β'_4 has a nearly uniform distribution in $\mathbb{Z}_p$, independent from the terminal's view, and therefore $\beta_4 = \beta'_4$ happens with negligible probability.

From equations (2), (8), (9), (10) and (12), we obtain :

$$\beta'_4 = a_1 a_2 \beta_3 + a_1 r_2 \beta_1 + a_2 r_1 \beta_2 \tag{13}$$

The terminal's view includes the points $A + g_1.G_1$, $B + g_2.G_2$, U and V and the group elements $\alpha_1, \alpha_2, \alpha_3$ and α_4. Therefore, the terminal's view is entirely determined by $(\beta_1, \beta_2, \beta_3, \beta_4, u, v, r)$, where r is the randomness used by the terminal. Moreover, given $(\beta_1, \beta_2, \beta_3, \beta_4, u, v, r)$, the element (a_1, a_2) is uniformly distributed over $\mathbb{Z}_p^2$.

From equations (6), (7) and (13), we obtain :

$$\beta'_4 = a_1 a_2 (\beta_3 - b\beta_1 - a\beta_2) + a_1(v\beta_1) + a_2(u\beta_2)$$

Lemma 1. *Let p be a prime integer and let $a, b, c, d \in \mathbb{Z}$ such that $(a, b, c) \neq (0, 0, 0)$. Then the number of solutions $(x, y) \in \mathbb{Z}_p^2$ to the polynomial equation $a \cdot xy + b \cdot x + c \cdot y + d = 0$ mod p is at most $2p - 1$.*

Proof. The proof is straightforward and is therefore omitted.

Since $u, v \neq 0$, then $\beta_3 \neq 0$ implies $(\beta_3 - b\beta_1 - a\beta_2, v\beta_1, u\beta_2) \neq (0, 0, 0)$. Then using the previous lemma, for any $\gamma \in \mathbb{Z}_p$, the probability over $(a_1, a_2) \in \mathbb{Z}_p^2$ that $\beta'_4 = \gamma$ is such that :

$$\Pr[\beta'_4 = \gamma] \leq \frac{2p - 1}{p^2} \leq \frac{2}{p}$$

Therefore, if $\beta_3 \neq 0$, the probability that $\beta'_4 = \beta_4$ is at most $2/p$.

Since we have that $u = 0$ or $v = 0$ with probability at most $2/p$, we conclude that if $e_{AB} \neq e(A, B)$, then the card outputs $\perp$, except with probability at most $4/p$. $\qquad\square$

Note that the security of the protocol is not based on any computational assumption; namely the protocol achieves unconditional security.

4.3   Efficiency

Our protocol requires a total of 4 scalar multiplications in $\mathcal{G}_1$ and $\mathcal{G}_2$, and a total of 10 exponentiations in $\mathcal{G}_T$. Our protocol is actually a one-round protocol since the four pairing queries can be performed in the same round.

5   Efficient Variants with Public A or B

In this section, we describe more efficient variants of our protocol, when one of the points A and B or both are already publicly known.

For example, when decrypting with Boneh and Franklin's identity-based encryption scheme [1], the point A is the user's private key, and the point B is some part of the ciphertext. Therefore, the point B is already publicly known and does not need to be protected. Similarly, when encrypting with Boneh and Franklin's scheme, the point A is the recipient's identity, and the point B is the trusted party's public-key. Therefore, both points A and B are already publicly known and don't need to be protected.

When the point B is publicly known, the definition of the secrecy property is modified by simply giving B to the simulator. When both points A and B are publicly known, the secrecy property is not necessary anymore.

5.1   Secure Pairing Delegation with Public B

The protocol is the same as the protocol described in the previous section, except that we can take $g_2 = 0$ since the point B does not need to be protected.

1. The card generates a random $g_1 \in \mathbb{Z}_p$ and queries the three following pairings to the terminal :

$$\alpha_1 = e(A + g_1.G_1, G_2), \quad \alpha_2 = e(G_1, B), \quad \alpha_3 = e(A + g_1.G_1, B)$$

2. The card checks that $\alpha_1, \alpha_2, \alpha_3 \in \mathcal{G}_T$, by checking that $(\alpha_i)^p = 1$ for $i = 1, 2, 3$. Otherwise, the card outputs $\perp$ and halts.

3. The card computes a purported value for $e(A, B)$:

$$e_{AB} = (\alpha_2)^{-g_1} \cdot \alpha_3 \tag{14}$$

4. The card generates four random values $a_1, r_1, a_2, r_2 \in \mathbb{Z}_p$ and queries the pairing :

$$\alpha_4 = e(a_1.A + r_1.G_1, a_2.B + r_2.G_2)$$

5. The card computes :

$$\alpha_4' = (e_{AB})^{a_1 a_2} \cdot (\alpha_1)^{a_1 r_2} \cdot (\alpha_2)^{a_2 r_1} \cdot e(G_1, G_2)^{r_1 r_2 - a_1 g_1 r_2} \tag{15}$$

and checks that $\alpha_4' = \alpha_4$. In this case, the card outputs e_{AB}; otherwise it outputs $\perp$.

The protocol is more efficient than the protocol of Section 4 since only 3 scalar multiplications in $\mathcal{G}_1$ and $\mathcal{G}_2$, and 8 exponentiations in $\mathcal{G}_T$ are required.

Theorem 2. *The previous protocol with public B is a secure pairing delegation protocol.*

Proof. The proof is similar to the proof of theorem 1 and is therefore omitted.

5.2   Secure Pairing Delegation with Public A and B

The protocol is similar to the previous protocol except that we can also take $g_1 = 0$ since A does not need to be protected.

1. The card queries the three following pairings to the terminal :
$$\alpha_1 = e(A, G_2), \quad \alpha_2 = e(G_1, B), \quad \alpha_3 = e(A, B)$$

2. The card checks that $\alpha_1, \alpha_2, \alpha_3 \in \mathcal{G}_T$, by checking that $(\alpha_i)^p = 1$ for $i = 1, 2, 3$. Otherwise, the card outputs $\perp$ and halts.

3. The card computes a purported value for $e(A, B)$:
$$e_{AB} = \alpha_3$$

4. The card generates four random values $a_1, r_1, a_2, r_2 \in \mathbb{Z}_p$ and queries the pairing :
$$\alpha_4 = e(a_1.A + r_1.G_1, a_2.B + r_2.G_2)$$

5. The card computes :
$$\alpha_4' = (e_{AB})^{a_1 a_2} \cdot (\alpha_1)^{a_1 r_2} \cdot (\alpha_2)^{a_2 r_1} \cdot e(G_1, G_2)^{r_1 r_2}$$

and checks that $\alpha_4' = \alpha_4$. In this case, the card outputs e_{AB}; otherwise it outputs $\perp$.

The protocol is more efficient than the protocol of Section 4 since only 2 scalar multiplications in $\mathcal{G}_1$ and $\mathcal{G}_2$, and 7 exponentiations in $\mathcal{G}_T$ are required.

Theorem 3. *The previous protocol with public A and B is a secure pairing delegation protocol.*

Proof. The proof is similar to the proof of theorem 1 and is therefore omitted.

6   Efficient Variant for Constant Point

In this section, we provide two efficient variants of the previous protocol, when the point A can be considered as constant. In the first protocol, both points A and B are public, whereas in the second protocol, A is private whereas B is public.

Those two variants are particularly useful for Boneh and Franklin's identity-based encryption scheme [1]. Namely, when encrypting with Boneh and Franklin's IBE, the point B is the trusted server public-key, and the point A is the receiver's identity-based public-key. Therefore, B can be considered as constant, and both A and B are public. This corresponds to the first protocol (with constant B instead of constant A, but the protocol modification is straightforward).

Moreover, when decrypting with Boneh and Franklin's IBE, the point A is the user's private key, and the point B is some part of the ciphertext. Therefore, A can be considered as constant and private, whereas B can be considered as public. This corresponds to the second protocol.

6.1   Efficient Variant for Constant A and Public A, B

As in the previous protocol, the card and the terminal are given as input a description of the groups $\mathcal{G}_1$, $\mathcal{G}_2$ and $\mathcal{G}_T$, and a description of the bilinear map $e : \mathcal{G}_1 \times \mathcal{G}_2 \to \mathcal{G}_T$. Moreover, the card receives $e(A, Q)$ for some random $Q \in \mathcal{G}_2$. The point Q and $e(A, Q)$ are kept private by the card. The card is given as input the point B and must eventually output $e(A, B)$.

1. The card generates a random $r \in \mathbb{Z}_p$ and queries the following pairings to the terminal :
$$\alpha_1 = e(A, B), \quad \alpha_2 = e(A, r \cdot B + Q)$$

2. The card checks that
$$(\alpha_1)^r \cdot e(A, Q) = \alpha_2 \tag{16}$$

and that $(\alpha_1)^p = 1$. In this case, it outputs α_1, otherwise it outputs $\perp$.

The protocol is more efficient than the protocol of section 5.2 since it requires only one scalar multiplication and 2 exponentiations in $\mathcal{G}_T$.

Theorem 4. *The previous protocol with constant public A and public B is a secure pairing delegation protocol.*

Proof. The completeness property is straightforward to establish. The protocol's correctness is showed as follows :
Let b be such $B = b \cdot G_2$. Let q be such that $Q = q \cdot G_2$. Let

$$u = r \cdot b + q \mod p$$

which gives $r \cdot B + Q = u \cdot G_2$. We have that the terminal's view is entirely determined by (b, u) and by the randomness used by $\mathcal{T}$. Since r and q are randomly generated in $\mathbb{Z}_p$, we obtain that the distribution of r is independent from the terminal's view. Let β_1, β_2 be such that :

$$\alpha_1 = e(A, B) \cdot e(A, G_2)^{\beta_1}$$
$$\alpha_2 = e(A, r \cdot B + Q) \cdot e(A, G_2)^{\beta_2}$$

We have that β_1, β_2 are a function of the terminal's view, and that $\alpha_1 = e(A, B)$ if $\beta_1 = 0$. Moreover, we obtain from (16) that the card outputs α_1 iff :

$$r \cdot \beta_1 = \beta_2 \mod p \qquad (17)$$

Assume now that $\beta_1 \neq 0$. Then since β_1 and β_2 are a function of the terminal's view, and the distribution of r is independent from the terminal's view, equality (17) holds with probability at most $1/p$. Therefore, for any cheating terminal, the card outputs either $\perp$ or the correct $e(A, B)$, except with probability at most $1/p$. □

6.2   Efficient Variant for Constant Private A and for Public B

As in the previous protocol, the card and the terminal are given as input a description of the groups $\mathcal{G}_1$, $\mathcal{G}_2$ and $\mathcal{G}_T$, and a description of the bilinear map $e : \mathcal{G}_1 \times \mathcal{G}_2 \rightarrow \mathcal{G}_T$. Moreover, the card receives $e(A, Q)$ for some random $Q \in \mathcal{G}_2$. The points A, Q and the value $e(A, Q)$ are kept private by the card. The card is given as input the point B and must eventually output $e(A, B)$.

1. The card generates random $x, y, z \in \mathbb{Z}_p$ and queries the following pairings to the terminal :

$$\alpha_1 = e(x \cdot A, B), \quad \alpha_2 = e(y \cdot A, z \cdot (B + Q))$$

2. The card computes :

$$e_{AB} = (\alpha_1)^{x^{-1}}, \quad \alpha_3 = (\alpha_2)^{(yz)^{-1}}$$

3. The card checks that

$$e_{AB} \cdot e(A, Q) = \alpha_3 \qquad (18)$$

and that $(e_{AB})^p = 1$. In this case, it outputs e_{AB}; otherwise it outputs $\perp$.

The protocol is more efficient than the protocol of section 5.1 as it requires only 3 scalar multiplications and 3 exponentiations in $\mathcal{G}_T$.

Theorem 5. *The previous protocol with constant private A and public B is a secure pairing delegation protocol.*

Proof. The protocol's completeness is easily established. The protocol's secrecy follows from the fact that the terminal receives only randomly distributed points. The protocol's correctness is established as follows :
    Let b be such $B = b \cdot G_2$. Let q be such that $Q = q \cdot G_2$. Let

$$u = z \cdot (b + q) \mod p$$

which gives $z \cdot (B + Q) = u \cdot G_2$. The terminal's view is then entirely determined by $(b, u, x \cdot A, y \cdot A)$ and by the randomness used by $\mathcal{T}$. Since z and q are randomly generated in $\mathbb{Z}_p$, we obtain that the distribution of z is independent from the terminal's view.

Let β_1, β_2 be such that :

$$\alpha_1 = e(x \cdot A, B)^{1+\beta_1}$$
$$\alpha_2 = e(y \cdot A, z \cdot (B + Q))^{1+\beta_2}$$

We have that β_1 and β_2 are a function of the terminal's view. Moreover, we obtain :

$$e_{AB} = e(A, B)^{1+\beta_1}$$
$$\alpha_3 = e(A, B + Q)^{1+\beta_2}$$

Therefore, $e_{AB} = e(A, B)$ iff $\beta_1 = 0$. Moreover, we obtain from (18) that the card outputs e_{AB} if :

$$e(A, B + Q)^{\beta_1} = e(A, B)^{\beta_2}$$

which gives :

$$b \cdot \beta_1 = (b + q) \cdot \beta_2 \mod p \tag{19}$$

Then since b, β_1, β_2 are a function of the terminal's view, and the distribution of q is uniform in $\mathbb{Z}_p$, independent of the terminal's view, we obtain that if $\beta_1 \neq 0$, the equality (19) holds with probability at most $1/p$. Therefore, for any cheating terminal, the card outputs either $\perp$ or the correct $e(A, B)$, except with probability $1/p$. $\qquad\square$

7   Conclusion

In this paper we have described a simple protocol for secure delegation of elliptic-curve pairing. Our protocol allows a computationally limited device (for example a smart-card) to delegate the computation of the pairing $e(A, B)$ to a more powerful device (for example a PC), in such a way that 1) the powerful device learns nothing about the points A and B, and 2) the limited device is able to detect when the powerful device is cheating. We have also described more efficient variants of our protocol when one of the points or both are already publicly known, and when one of the points can be considered as constant.

We observe that our protocols achieve unconditional security. An interesting research direction would be to further optimize the protocols by trading-off unconditional security against computational security. A second interesting question consists in bounding the number of protocol rounds (passes) necessary to delegate pairing in diverse contexts.

References

1. Boneh, D., Franklin, M.: Identity based encryption from the Weil pairing. SIAM J. of Computing 32(3), 586–615 (2003); Extended abstract In: Kilian, J. (ed.) CRYPTO 2001. LNCS, vol. 2139, pp. 213–229. Springer, Heidelberg (2001)
2. Boneh, D., Shacham, H., Lynn, B.: Short signatures from the Weil pairing. In: Boyd, C. (ed.) ASIACRYPT 2001. LNCS, vol. 2248, pp. 514–532. Springer, Heidelberg (2001)

3. Boneh, D., Boyen, X.: Short Signatures Without Random Oracles. In: Cachin, C., Camenisch, J.L. (eds.) EUROCRYPT 2004. LNCS, vol. 3027, pp. 56–73. Springer, Heidelberg (2004)
4. Canetti, R.: Security and Composition of Multiparty Cryptographic Protocols. Journal of Cryptology 13, 143–202 (2000)
5. Goldwasser, S., Micali, S.: Probabilistic Encryption. JCSS 28(2), 270–299 (1984); Previous version in STOC 2002 (2002)
6. Joux, A.: A one round protocol for tripartite Diffie-Hellman. In: Bosma, W. (ed.) ANTS 2000. LNCS, vol. 1838, pp. 385–394. Springer, Heidelberg (2000)
7. Menezes, A.: Elliptic Curve Public Key Cryptosystems. Kluwer Academic Publishers, Dordrecht (1993)
8. Scott, M., Barreto, P.: Compressed Pairings. In: Franklin, M. (ed.) CRYPTO 2004. LNCS, vol. 3152, pp. 140–156. Springer, Heidelberg (2004)

Side-Channel Leakage across Borders

Jörn-Marc Schmidt, Thomas Plos, Mario Kirschbaum, Michael Hutter,
Marcel Medwed, and Christoph Herbst

Institute for Applied Information Processing and Communications (IAIK)
Graz University of Technology, Inffeldgasse 16a, 8010 Graz, Austria
{joern-marc.schmidt,thomas.plos,mario.kirschbaum,michael.hutter,
marcel.medwed,christoph.herbst}@iaik.tugraz.at

Abstract. More and more embedded devices store sensitive information that is protected by means of cryptography. The confidentiality of
this data is threatened by information leakage via side channels like the
power consumption or the electromagnetic radiation. In this paper, we
show that the side-channel leakage in the power consumption is not limited to the power-supply lines and that any input/output (I/O) pin can
comprise secret information. The amount of leakage depends on the design and on the state of the I/O pin. All devices that we examined leaked
secret information through their I/O pins. This implies that any I/O pin
that is accessible for an adversary could be a security hole. Moreover, we
demonstrate that the leakage is neither prevented by transmitter/receiver
circuits as they are used in serial interfaces, nor by a galvanic isolation of
a chip and its output signals via optocouplers. An adversary that is able
to manipulate, for example, the pins of a PC's I/O port, can attack any
device that is connected to this port without being detected from outside.

Keywords: Power Analysis, I/O Pin, Microcontroller, Optocoupler,
Serial Interface.

1 Introduction

Security-related devices are an integral part of our everyday life. Typically, it is
rather difficult to verify whether a device reaches a certain security level or not.
Insufficient security protection remains often unnoticed until a successful attack
is found. The security level is basically determined by two factors: the choice of
the cryptographic algorithm (including the protocol), and the way the algorithm
is implemented.

Even if a cryptographic algorithm is mathematically secure, its implementation in hardware might not be. About one decade ago, Kocher *et al.* published a
ground-breaking paper about differential power analysis (DPA) attacks [1]. They
showed that analyzing the power consumption of a cryptographic device can reveal secret information that is stored in it, e.g. an encryption key. Since that
time, many research groups have gradually improved power-analysis attacks and
performed them on a variety of devices, like smart cards [2], field-programmable
gate arrays (FPGAs) [3], and radio-frequency identification (RFID) devices [4].

D. Gollmann, J.-L. Lanet, J. Iguchi-Cartigny (Eds.): CARDIS 2010, LNCS 6035, pp. 36–48, 2010.
© IFIP International Federation for Information Processing 2010

Power-analysis attacks are a very powerful technique that even works in presence of strong noise. In a first step, an adversary generates key hypotheses, which contain all possible values for a small part of the secret key (e.g. one byte). Intermediate values of the attacked algorithm are calculated from the key hypotheses and a set of different input values. Based on the intermediate values, the adversary estimates the power consumption of the device by means of an appropriate power model. During the second step, the power consumption of the device is measured and recorded (leading to the so-called power traces) while it computes the intermediate values. In the third and last step, the power-consumption estimations for each key hypothesis are compared with the measured power traces by means of statistical methods. If the adversary uses an appropriate power model, the analysis leads to the correct key. The adversary has successfully revealed a part of the secret key. This procedure is repeated for the remaining parts. Experience shows that in case of unprotected cryptographic devices, some hundred up to a few thousand input values and corresponding power traces are sufficient to distinctly reveal the whole secret key [5].

Most of the published side-channel attacks measure the power consumption of the target device via a resistor in one of the power-supply lines. Other methods measure, for example, the electromagnetic radiation during the computation of the cryptographic algorithm [6,7]. In order to prevent the leakage of sensitive information via the power-supply lines, countermeasures are integrated into cryptographic devices. Various countermeasure approaches have been presented in the past, for example, by using special logic styles [8,9,10], by inserting filters [11], or by decoupling the power consumption with switched capacitors [12,13].

It was first mentioned by Shamir [12] that side-channel information can also leak through the input/output (I/O) pins of a device. Oren et al. [14] presented practical results about analyzing the power consumption of a PC via its universal serial bus (USB) port. In [15], Plos pointed out the problem of side channel leakage via I/O pins of RFID tags. However, there is no work so far that investigates the effectiveness of side-channel attacks via I/O pins in detail and that compares them with the results from classical attacks in the power-supply lines.

In this paper, we discuss the possibilities to measure the voltage variations at I/O pins. We show that power-analysis attacks are feasible in the same way by using the I/O pins. This presents an alternative attack method whenever a direct measurement in the power-supply lines is not possible. We evaluated the voltage variations at the I/O pins of five devices for different pin-configurations. For each device, we found at least one configuration that leaked information at the I/O pins. The standard microcontrollers, for example, leaked information in any configuration. In addition, we measured a device with capacitors as filters in the power-supply lines, which reduced the leakage in the ground line, but not at the I/O pins. This demonstrates that protecting only the power-supply lines is not sufficient and that additional precautions should be taken to prevent I/O pin leakage. For embedded systems with more than one device integrated onto a board, measuring the voltage variations at an I/O pin can be an improvement compared to measuring the power consumption of the whole system. We show that information leakage also occurs if the I/O pin is not directly measured, but after passing a signal amplifier. We demonstrate this by successfully performing a DPA attack on a serial interface that uses a receiver/transmitter module. Hence, an adversary can perform attacks without being noticed by the owner of the device, e.g. by manipulating the serial interface of a PC to which the device is connected to. Moreover, we demonstrate that even a galvanic isolation via optocouplers does not totally suppress the information leaking at the I/O pin.

The remaining paper is organized as follows. After giving a brief introduction into I/O pins in Section 2, we present our measurement setup in Section 3. The results of the measurements are given in Section 4. Afterwards, Section 5 discusses some practical scenarios that arise from the presented attacks, including (among others) a DPA measurement on the clock signal as well as DPA measurements of an I/O pin that is separated by an optocoupler. Finally, conclusions are drawn in Section 6.

2   I/O Pins

I/O pins are the interface between an integrated circuit and the outside world. They are used to transfer data and control signals. Depending on their design, I/O pins can act in one direction only or they can support both directions: input and output.

Especially input pins require a protection mechanism to prevent damage of the inner circuits caused by an overvoltage. This mechanism is called electrostatic discharge (ESD) protection and typically consists of two diodes that drain off the overvoltage to the positive supply voltage (VDD) or to ground (GND). In addition, a resistor is inserted to limit the current flowing over the diodes. Figure 1 shows an I/O pin that comprises such an ESD-protection circuit.

In contrast to input pins, output pins have a low-resistance connection to VDD or GND. Thus, a dedicated ESD-protection is not necessary for them. Since output pins have to drive logic signals off-chip, a circuit that is able to provide enough current is required. These circuits are often implemented as parallel transistors of increasing width and length [16].

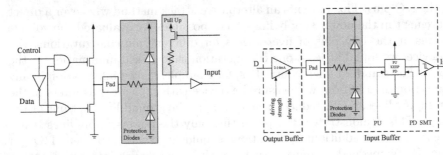

Fig. 1. Schematic of a standard I/O pin. The control signal can switch the pin to tri-state.

Fig. 2. Schematic of a programmable output and a programmable input buffer of the ASIC prototype chip

Pins that can either be configured as input or as output, provide a so-called *tri-state*. This state allows to define the value of the pin externally, i.e. the pin acts as input. Thereby, the output transistors are disabled and the pin is in a high-impedance state. Such an I/O pin is depicted in Figure 1. The schematic features also a pull-up resistor, which holds the input pin in a high state whenever it is not driven externally. This prevents the pin from being in a random or undefined state. Other constructions provide pull-down resistors to put a pin into a low state if no external signal is present.

Figure 2 shows a programmable output and a programmable input buffer of the application-specific integrated circuit (ASIC) prototype chip that we used for some of our measurements. The ASIC input buffer contains ESD protection structures similar to the one described above. The input buffer can be programmed to work as pull up, as pull down, or as keeper[1]. Additionally, the input buffer can be programmed to work as a Schmitt trigger to switch the input value only if a clearly different signal is applied. Also the output buffer can be programmed to some degree. The driving strength can vary between 2 mA and 16 mA, and the slew rate of the output buffer can be either set to *slow* or to *fast*. On our prototype chip, the input buffers are programmed as pull down with Schmitt-trigger functionality disabled. The output buffers are configured to have a driving strength of 2 mA with the slew rate set to *fast*.

3   Measurement Setup

For a general characterization of the I/O pin leakage of the devices, we compare the leakage in the GND supply line to the information that leaves the device via the I/O pins in different configurations. We test five devices, an Atmel AT-Mega163 8-bit microcontroller on a smart card, an 8-bit 8051 microcontroller AT89S8253 from Atmel, a 32-bit ARM7 microcontroller LPC2148 from NXP, a Virtex-II Pro XC2VP7 FPGA, and an ASIC chip. Each of them contains an implementation of the Advanced Encryption Standard (AES) that uses a key length of 128 bits. None of these implementations include side-channel countermeasures.

For each measurement, we perform a Differential Power Analysis (DPA) attack. The goal of our DPA attacks on the AES implementations is to reveal the secret key. During the last years, several approaches for DPA attacks on AES implementations have been proposed ([17,18,19]). Our DPA attacks are based on the Hamming distance of two intermediate byte values. The target of the attack is the result of the SubBytes transformation in the first round of the AES algorithm. We use the Pearson correlation coefficient for matching our power estimations with the measurements.

Our measurement setup mainly consists of a PC, an oscilloscope, measurement probes, and the device under test. A Matlab script running on the PC controls the whole measurement. It sends the plaintexts to the device via a serial interface

---

[1] The input value does not change when the signal is disconnected from the pin if the buffer is programmed as keeper.

and reads the power traces from the oscilloscope that measures the voltage on the I/O pin and the voltage drop across a resistor in the ground line of the device.

A classical measurement in the GND line is performed in parallel to the measurement at the I/O pin. The power measurement delivers a basis for comparison with the results from I/O pin measurements. For each device, the pin configurations output high, output low, and input (with $10\,\text{k}\Omega$ pull-down resistor) are measured. Each measurement uses the same fixed AES key and the same input plaintexts.

Since no side-channel countermeasures are included in our implementations, a DPA attack was possible with some hundred to a few thousand traces. Our measurements show that the same attacks are possible when measuring the I/O pins instead of the power-supply lines.

4   Practical Results

This section shows the practical outcomes of our measurements. We describe the special properties of all five devices, present the analysis results, and discuss them.

4.1   Atmel ATMega163 8-Bit Microcontroller on a Smart Card

In the first experiment, we measured a programmable smart card with an integrated 8-bit microcontroller. The microcontroller is an ATMega163 from Atmel, which has a reduced instruction set (RISC) architecture. The ATMega163 comprises various features, including internal EEPROM, a serial interface, a

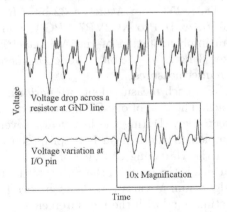

Fig. 3. Measurement setup for the Atmel ATMega163 smart card. One probe measures the trigger signal, the other probe measures the voltage variation of a fix programmed I/O pin.

Fig. 4. Comparison between the power consumption measured in the GND line and the voltage variations at an I/O pin of the AT89S8253. The I/O pin was set to logic low for the measurement.

serial peripheral interface, and an analog comparator. A self-made smart-card reader, which is depicted in Figure 3, was used to establish the communication between the PC and the smart card. Since the smart card only provides an 8-pin connector, the number of pins of the microcontroller that are accessible is strongly limited. However, there is one unused I/O pin that we measured in our experiments.

We conducted four DPA attacks on the smart card and compared them with respect to the maximum achievable correlation. The first attack measured the power consumption of the smart card in the GND line of the power supply. The remaining three attacks targeted the voltage variations at the unused I/O pin with different configurations: pin defined as output and logic high, pin defined as output and logic low, and pin defined as input (tri-state).

All attacks were successful. The reference measurement in the GND supply line led to a maximum correlation of 0.57. The voltage variations at the I/O pin defined as output delivered similar values: 0.64 for logic high and 0.56 for logic low. Defining the I/O pin as input reduced the maximum correlation to about 0.11.

4.2   Virtex-II Pro FPGA XC2VP7

For testing the leakage at an I/O pin of an FPGA, we targeted a Xilinx XC2VP7 of a SASEBO board[2]. Our AES implementation for the FPGA includes one extra pin for the measurements, which varied between input and output. A measurement in the GND line resulted in a correlation of 0.06, setting the output pin to low reduced the correlation to 0.03. A correlation of 0.01 was achieved for the pin configured as input. For a pin that was set to high, no correlation was measured by using up to 300 000 power traces.

In order to characterize further details of the leakage, we added area constrains to the implementation that forced the place and route utilities to concentrate on one half of the chip and leave the second half unprogrammed. In addition, two wires were routed through the device to an output pin, one straight through the programmed logic, and one through the *empty* part. The measurements revealed no difference between the information leakage of the two pins.

4.3   ARM 32-Bit RISC Processor

The LPC2148 from NXP is an ARM7TDMI-S based microcontroller with a 32-bit architecture. Our device under test features a wide range of peripherals like USB, analog-to-digital converters, and several bus standards. None of those peripherals was turned off during the measurements. Thus, the noise level was comparable to an unprotected real-world application.

Our development board gave access to the I/O pins of the microcontroller. The measurement at the I/O pins was threefold: output pin set to one, output

---

[2] The control FPGA of the SASEBO board was programmed to forward the serial interface.

pin set to zero, and input pin pulled down to GND. For the correct AES key, the power measurements in the GND line achieved a correlation of 0.56. The traces acquired at the high output pin still yielded a correlation of 0.44. The voltages at the low output pin and at the input pin correlated with 0.15 and 0.12, respectively.

4.4   Atmel 8051 Microcontroller

The data-dependent I/O leakage of an 8051 8-bit microcontroller was investigated on an AT89S8253 from Atmel. The microcontroller is shipped with 32 programmable I/O pins that can be accessed by four 8-bit bi-directional ports. One port provides eight open-drain pins, which can be configured to logic low (actively sinking current) or to a high impedance state. The pins of the three remaining ports can be configured as sink or source input/output that are equipped with internal pull-up resistors.

We performed four attacks. First, we measured the power consumption in the GND line of the prototyping board and obtained a correlation of 0.59 for the correct key hypothesis. Next, we performed attacks on 20 different I/O pins, which where configured to logic low. All attacks were successful and led to nearly the same correlation of 0.56. This demonstrates that the leakage does not depend on the measured I/O pin (the standard deviation of the correlation was 0.01). A comparison between two power traces, one measured at the GND line and one at the I/O pin configured to output logic low is given in Figure 4. After that experiment, we performed an attack on a pin that was configured to logic high. The attack was successful with a correlation of 0.30. Our last attack on this device targeted the open-drain port, which was configured as a high-impedance output. The attack was also successful and led to a correlation of 0.22.

4.5   180 nm CMOS ASIC Prototype Chip

The ASIC prototype chip for testing the leakage of I/O pins was produced in a 180 nm CMOS process technology from UMC [20] and uses the standard cell library from Faraday [21]. The chip contains an AES crypto module with a size of $0.1\,mm^2$, which equals approximately 10 770 GEs.

First, a DPA attack based on the power consumption measured in the GND line of the prototype chip was performed. The result of this attack served as a reference for the other DPA attacks that targeted the voltage variations at I/O pins. The other DPA attacks were performed on an output pin with logic level low, on an output pin with logic level high, and on an input pin with logic level low (programmed as pull-down, see Section 2).

All attacks on the AES crypto module on the ASIC prototype chip were successful. The reference attack based on the power measurement in the GND line led to a maximum correlation of 0.0119. The other DPA attacks led to quite similar results: 0.0124 for the low output pin, 0.011 for the high output pin, and 0.0121 for the low input pin.

Table 1. Summary of the Results

Device	Corr. in GND	Correlation (Percentage of GND)		
		Output High	Output Low	Input
ATMega163 (Smart Card)	0.57	0.64 (112%)	0.56 (98%)	0.11 (19%)
LPC2148 (ARM7)	0.56	0.44 (79%)	0.15 (27%)	0.12 (21%)
AT89S8253 (8051)	0.59	0.30 (54%)	0.56 (95%)	0.22 (37%)
XC2VP7 (FPGA)	0.06		0.03 (50%)	0.01 (17%)
ASIC Prototype (180 nm)	0.0119	0.011(92%)	0.0124(104%)	0.0121(101%)

4.6 Summary of the Practical Results

Table 1 summarizes the results of our DPA attacks on the five different devices. It can clearly be seen that DPA attacks based on voltage variations at I/O pins can successfully be mounted on many devices even if the VDD line or GND line are not directly accessible. Furthermore, regardless of the configuration of the I/O pin, a successful DPA attack is possible. The fact that conventional DPA attacks can easily be performed by measuring the voltage variations at I/O pins opens new possibilities for adversaries to attack cryptographic devices, even if the accessibility of the target is limited. Some practical scenarios demonstrating new attack variants are discussed in the following section.

5   Practical Scenarios

In order to transfer our results into a more practical context, we performed additional experiments, which demonstrate the relevance of our research. Since the AT89S8253 shows the strongest information leakage of all tested devices, we focus on this device in the following experiments. Considering the results presented in the previous section, it is very likely that the following scenarios work with the other devices alike.

5.1   Signal Filter

Throughout this paper, our experiments assumed that the power-supply lines of the device under test are not accessible for an adversary and hence a direct measurement of the consumed power is not possible. This can be the case, for example, if a filter suppresses the leakage in the power supply lines. We used a cascade of capacitors as filter to reduce the data-dependent signal. Although our filter significantly reduced the data dependency in the GND line, we were not able to eliminate it totally. However, our approach did not influence the leakage in the I/O pins. The experiment demonstrates that the information leakage via the I/O pins does not depend on the information leakage in the power-supply lines.

5.2   Clock Supply

A special case of an I/O pin is the clock interface. While capacitors can filter the power-supply lines to prevent information leakage, this approach is not applicable in the same simple way to the clock supply. We tried two different scenarios. First, an on-board crystal oscillator generated the clock signal. For the measurement, we concentrated on the positive part of the signal and cut the negative part off to get a better measurement resolution. Our attack was successful with a correlation of 0.4, which is about two third of the correlation in the GND line, as depicted in Figure 5 and Figure 6. Second, an external signal generator provided the signal. We achieved a correlation of 0.5. Hence, whenever the clock signal is accessible, it is a potential threat to the security of the device.

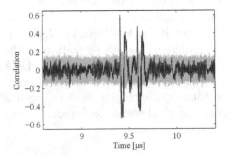
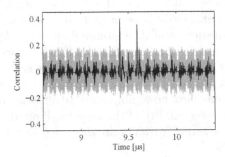

Fig. 5. Correlation plot of AT89S8253 measured with a passive probe in the GND line of the power supply. The measurement serves as reference.

Fig. 6. Correlation plot of AT89S8253 measured with a passive probe at the clock interface, supplied with an on-board crystal oscillator

5.3   Serial Interface

A very common way to transfer data between devices is a serial port. The results from the previous section showed that I/O pins leak information. This includes the pins of the serial interface. However, in an embedded system, the device is often supplied by a lower voltage than the one required for the serial connection (+/- 12 V). Hence, a signal amplifier converts the logical signals from the device to the voltage range required for the serial connection. An adversary may only have access to those signals, not to I/O pins directly. Fortunately for an adversary, the information is not suppressed by the amplifier. We measured the receive (RX) and transmission (TX) line of a signal converter (MAX232) directly on the board and achieved a correlation of 0.1 in the TX line and in the RX line, compared to a correlation of 0.6 for a direct measurement in the GND line. A correlation plot for the TX line is given in Figure 7. Using a 1 m cable that is connected to a computer and measuring at the input port of the PC reduced the correlation to 0.05. Hence, an adversary that is able to modify the serial port of a computer can successfully attack devices without the device owners' knowledge who connects the device to a PC.

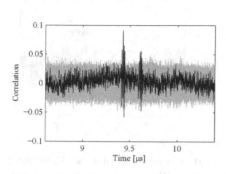

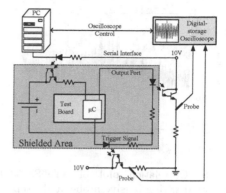

Fig. 7. Correlation plot of AT89S8253 measured with a passive probe at the serial interface on the transmission line after the signal converter (MAX232) directly on the test board.

Fig. 8. Measurement setup with galvanically isolated circuits. The measurement signal, the trigger, as well as the transmission line of the serial interface are transferred via optocouplers.

5.4 Device and Measurement Circuit Separated via Optocoupler

A common idea when talking about information leakage via power lines is to separate the circuit in which the computation takes place from the *outside world*. In order to transfer information between the device and the outside world, it is possible to use optocouplers. These small devices consist of a light-emitting diode and a phototransistor. Thus, they allow data transfer without an electric connection. We performed two different measurements. In the first one, only the trigger signal and the signal of the I/O pin were separated via optocouplers. In the second experiment, the two circuits were galvanically isolated.

In the setup for the first measurement, one optocoupler provides the trigger signal, another one was connected to a high output pin. The influence of the pin on the second circuit was measured via an oscilloscope. We could successfully perform a DPA and achieved a correlation of 0.02. The corresponding correlation plot is given in Figure 9.

However, this measurement setup still has a common ground connection since the PC is connected to the oscilloscope and to the device. Thus, the measurement circuit and the target circuit are not galvanically isolated. In order to achieve a galvanic isolation, the device was powered by a battery and the transmission line of the serial connection was established via an optocoupler[3] in the setup for our second measurement. The whole measurement circuit was put into a shielding box to suppress possible coupling between the measurement circuit and the target circuit. Figure 8 sketches the measurement setup. Even with the galvanic isolation, we achieved a correlation of 0.01. Figure 10 shows the corresponding plot.

---

[3] The setup did not use the RX line of the serial interface.

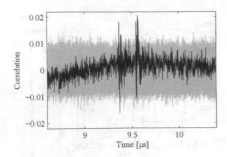
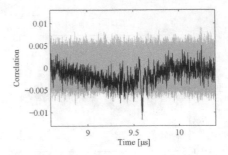

Fig. 9. Correlation plot of AT89S8253 measured with a passive probe at the separated circuit with common ground

Fig. 10. Correlation plot of AT89S8253 measured with a passive probe at the galvanically isolated circuit

5.5 Summery of Practical Scenarios

Table 2 summarizes the results of the practical scenarios provided in this section. In addition to the achieved correlation, the table provides the estimated number of traces required to succeed with an attack. The numbers were calculated with the rule of thumb from [5]: $n = 3 + 8 \frac{z_{1-\alpha}^2}{ln^2 \frac{1+\rho}{1-\rho}}$, with n the number of required traces, ρ the correlation coefficient for the correct hypothesis, and α the confidence. For $\alpha = 0.0001$ we get a value $z_{0.9999} = 3.719$.

Table 2. Summary of the Results of the Practical Scenarios

Scenario	Correlation	Required Samples
Reference in GND	0.6	61
Clock with Signal Generator	0.5	95
Clock with Crystal Oscillator	0.4	158
Serial Interface (RX and TX)	0.1	2 751
Serial Interface at a Distance of 1 m	0.05	11 050
Optocouplers with Common Ground	0.02	69 140
Galvanic Isolation via Optocouplers	0.01	276 604

6 Conclusion

In this paper we demonstrate that side-channel information not only leaks via the power supply lines but also via I/O pins. We performed DPA attacks on five different devices that have integrated a hardware or a software implementation of the AES-128. Our investigations show that DPA attacks can be mounted even if the access to the examined device is severely limited. For example, if the power supply lines are not at an adversary's disposal, or if the adversary wants to attack a device that consists of several chips but has only access to the chip of interest by some sort of interface. Moreover, our results make clear that even in the presence of filtering techniques, signal converters, or optocouplers, successful DPA attacks are possible.

Acknowledgement

The work described in this paper has been supported through Austrian Government funded project *PowerTrust* established under the Trust in IT Systems program FIT-IT.

The authors want to thank Akashi Satoh (National Institute of Advanced Industrial Science and Technology, Japan) and designers of SASEBO for the board we used for the FPGA measurements.

The information in this document reflects only the authors' views, is provided as is and no guarantee or warranty is given that the information is fit for any particular purpose. The user thereof uses the information at its sole risk and liability.

References

1. Kocher, P.C., Jaffe, J., Jun, B.: Differential Power Analysis. In: Wiener, M. (ed.) CRYPTO 1999. LNCS, vol. 1666, pp. 388–397. Springer, Heidelberg (1999)
2. Messerges, T.S., Dabbish, E.A., Sloan, R.H.: Investigations of Power Analysis Attacks on Smartcards. In: USENIX Workshop on Smartcard Technology (Smartcard 1999), May 1999, pp. 151–162 (1999)
3. Örs, S.B., Oswald, E., Preneel, B.: Power-Analysis Attacks on FPGAs – First Experimental Results. In: Walter, C.D., Koç, Ç.K., Paar, C. (eds.) CHES 2003. LNCS, vol. 2779, pp. 35–50. Springer, Heidelberg (2003)
4. Hutter, M., Mangard, S., Feldhofer, M.: Power and EM Attacks on Passive 13.56 MHz RFID Devices. In: Paillier, P., Verbauwhede, I. (eds.) CHES 2007. LNCS, vol. 4727, pp. 320–333. Springer, Heidelberg (2007)
5. Mangard, S., Oswald, E., Popp, T.: Power Analysis Attacks – Revealing the Secrets of Smart Cards. Springer, Heidelberg (2007), ISBN 978-0-387-30857-9
6. Agrawal, D., Archambeault, B., Rao, J.R., Rohatgi, P.: The EM Side-channel(s). In: Kaliski Jr, B.S., Koç, Ç.K., Paar, C. (eds.) CHES 2002. LNCS, vol. 2523, pp. 29–45. Springer, Heidelberg (2003)
7. Gandolfi, K., Mourtel, C., Olivier, F.: Electromagnetic Analysis: Concrete Results. In: Koç, Ç.K., Naccache, D., Paar, C. (eds.) CHES 2001. LNCS, vol. 2162, pp. 251–261. Springer, Heidelberg (2001)
8. Tiri, K., Akmal, M., Verbauwhede, I.: A Dynamic and Differential CMOS Logic with Signal Independent Power Consumption to Withstand Differential Power Analysis on Smart Cards. In: Proceedings of 28th European Solid-State Circuits Conference - ESSCIRC 2002, Florence, Italy, September 24-26, pp. 403–406. IEEE, Los Alamitos (2002)
9. Tiri, K., Verbauwhede, I.: A Logic Level Design Methodology for a Secure DPA Resistant ASIC or FPGA Implementation. In: 2004 Design, Automation and Test in Europe Conference and Exposition (DATE 2004), Paris, France, February 16-20, vol. 1, pp. 246–251. IEEE Computer Society, Los Alamitos (2004)
10. Popp, T., Mangard, S.: Masked Dual-Rail Pre-Charge Logic: DPA-Resistance without Routing Constraints. In: Rao, J.R., Sunar, B. (eds.) CHES 2005. LNCS, vol. 3659, pp. 172–186. Springer, Heidelberg (2005)
11. Coron, J.S., Kocher, P.C., Naccache, D.: Statistics and Secret Leakage. In: Frankel, Y. (ed.) FC 2000. LNCS, vol. 1962, pp. 157–173. Springer, Heidelberg (2001)

12. Shamir, A.: Protecting Smart Cards from Passive Power Analysis with Detached Power Supplies. In: Paar, C., Koç, Ç.K. (eds.) CHES 2000. LNCS, vol. 1965, pp. 71–77. Springer, Heidelberg (2000)
13. Corsonello, P., Perri, S., Margala, M.: A New Charge-Pump Based Countermeasure Against Differential Power Analysis. In: Proceedings of the 6th International Conference on ASIC (ASICON 2005), vol. 1, pp. 66–69. IEEE, Los Alamitos (2005)
14. Oren, Y., Shamir, A.: How not to protect pcs from power analysis. Rump Session, Crypto 2006 (August 2006),
    http://iss.oy.ne.ro/HowNotToProtectPCsFromPowerAnalysis.pdf
15. Plos, T.: Evaluation of the Detached Power Supply as Side-Channel Analysis Countermeasure for Passive UHF RFID Tags. In: Fischlin, M. (ed.) RSA Conference 2009. LNCS, vol. 5473, pp. 444–458. Springer, Heidelberg (2009)
16. Weste, N.H.E., Eshraghian, K.: Principles of CMOS VLSI Design - A Systems Perspective, 2nd edn. VLSI Systems Series. Addison-Wesley, Reading (1993) (reprinted with corrections October 1994), ISBN 0-201-53376-6
17. Brier, E., Clavier, C., Olivier, F.: Correlation Power Analysis with a Leakage Model. In: Joye, M., Quisquater, J.-J. (eds.) CHES 2004. LNCS, vol. 3156, pp. 16–29. Springer, Heidelberg (2004)
18. Örs, S.B., Gürkaynak, F.K., Oswald, E., Preneel, B.: Power-Analysis Attack on an ASIC AES Implementation. In: Proceedings of the International Conference on Information Technology: Coding and Computing (ITCC 2004), Las Vegas, Nevada, USA, April 5-7, vol. 2, pp. 546–552. IEEE Computer Society, Los Alamitos (2004)
19. Schramm, K., Leander, G., Felke, P., Paar, C.: A Collision-Attack on AES: Combining Side Channel- and Differential-Attack. In: Joye, M., Quisquater, J.-J. (eds.) CHES 2004. LNCS, vol. 3156, pp. 163–175. Springer, Heidelberg (2004)
20. United Microelectronics Corporation: The United Microelectronics Corporation Website, http://www.umc.com/
21. Faraday Technology Corporation: Faraday FSA0A_C 0.18 μm ASIC Standard Cell Library (2004), http://www.faraday-tech.com.
22. Mangard, S., Aigner, M., Dominikus, S.: A Highly Regular and Scalable AES Hardware Architecture. IEEE Transactions on Computers 52(4), 483–491 (2003)
23. Wolkerstorfer, J., Oswald, E., Lamberger, M.: An ASIC implementation of the AES SBoxes. In: Preneel, B. (ed.) CT-RSA 2002. LNCS, vol. 2271, pp. 67–78. Springer, Heidelberg (2002)

Designing a Side Channel Resistant Random Number Generator

Suresh N. Chari[1], Vincenzo V. Diluoffo[2], Paul A. Karger[1], Elaine R. Palmer[1], Tal Rabin[1], Josyula R. Rao[1], Pankaj Rohotgi[1,*], Helmut Scherzer[3,**], Michael Steiner[1], and David C. Toll[1]

[1] IBM Corporation, Thomas J. Watson Research Center
P.O. Box 704, Yorktown Heights, NY 10598, USA
{schari,diluoffo,erpalmer,talr,jrrao,msteiner,toll,pkarger}@us.ibm.com,
pankaj.rohatgi@cryptography.com
[2] IBM Corporation, Systems and Technology Group
150 Kettletown Rd., Southbury, CT 06488, USA
[3] IBM Deutschland GmbH, Secure Systems and Smart Cards
Schönaicher Str. 220, D-71032 Böblingen, Germany
helmut.scherzer@gi-de.com

Abstract. This paper describes the design of the random number generator (RNG) in the Caernarvon high assurance smart card operating system. Since it is used in the generation of cryptographic keys and other sensitive materials, the RNG has a number of stringent security requirements that the random bits must be of *good* quality i.e. the bits must not be predictable or biased. To this end, a number of standards such as the German AIS 31 mandate that true random bits be *continuously* tested before use in sensitive applications such as key generation. A key issue in implementing this standard is that such testing before use in key generation greatly increases the attack surface for *side-channel* attacks. For example, template attacks which can extract information about the random bits from even a *single* run provided we use the same bits at *many* different points in the computation. Because of these potential risks, the Caernarvon operating system uses pseudo random number generators which are initially seeded by *externally* generated high quality random bits, and then perturbed by bits from the true random number generator. We describe a PRNG design which yields high quality random bits while also ensuring that it is not susceptible to *side-channel* attacks and provide an informal argument about its effectiveness.

1 Introduction

This paper describes the design of a side-channel resistant random number generator for the Caernarvon [31] high-assurance smart card operating system project.

---

* Now with Cryptography Research, 575 Market Street, 11th Floor, San Francisco, CA 94105, USA.
** Now with Giesecke & Devrient GmbH, Postfach 80 07 29, D-81607, München, Germany.

D. Gollmann, J.-L. Lanet, J. Iguchi-Cartigny (Eds.): CARDIS 2010, LNCS 6035, pp. 49–64, 2010.
© IFIP International Federation for Information Processing 2010

The Caernarvon OS is intended to test if it is possible to build very high levels of assurance into smart card operating systems - it is to be evaluated at Common Criteria EAL7 under the German evaluation scheme. The choices we have evaluated and the features of our design would also be applicable to a number of other high security environments. In particular, practical considerations such as resistance to side-channel attacks and minimizing the wear on persistent memory which have guided our design will be relevant in many different applications.

High assurance systems such as Caernarvon require high quality random bits to support a multitude of uses. In Caernarvon the use cases include:

- **Key Generation.** Random sources are typically used to generate keys for symmetric ciphers such as DES and AES. Frequently, they are also used to generate keying material in algorithms such as Diffie-Hellman key exchange. Occasionally they are used to generate asymmetric cryptographic keys such as RSA keys.
- **Random nonce and other parameter generation.** Smart card systems use RNGs to generate nonces and randomness used in cryptographic protocols.
- **Blinding.** Commonly used countermeasures to defeat timing attacks use random numbers to blind data and keys.
- **Masking.** Increasingly, random numbers are used to mask operands to protect against side-channel attacks such as SPA/DPA[20], EM analysis[1], etc.

The security and effectiveness of the implementation of cryptographic algorithms and functions crucially rely on the random numbers used in the above operations: they should be of "good" quality and should be kept secret. Random numbers that are predictable or biased may open the crypto algorithms (or their keys) to attack. Equally, it is of little use to generate keys for cryptographic algorithms if random numbers used to generate these keys leak to the outside world.

Smart cards and other systems typically contain a *true* random number generator (TRNG), *i.e.* a physical source of entropy. These are implemented by circuits which generate random numbers and whose physical properties are chosen to produce high quality random bits which could pass all the standard tests for random sequences. However, the use of true RNGs is not without potential problems. For example, it has been observed that hardware random number generators may "age", *i.e.* the quality of the random numbers degrades over time. Also, small devices, such as smart cards, can sometimes be vulnerable to differential fault attacks [5, 4] against the the hardware RNG itself, such that it generates predictable numbers or even always generates the same number.

Given the potential for such problems, a number of standards place stringent requirements on the use and testing of random numbers from a hardware RNG. For Common Criteria evaluations under the German scheme, these requirements are specified in AIS 31 [15] which requires that the RNG be tested on system start up, (*i.e.* on every activation of the smart card), and also that the used random numbers are continuously tested. The tests specified in AIS 31 are those defined in FIPS 140-2 [27]. These testing requirements, of course, have significant impact on performance and usability. Performing FIPS 140-2 tests on card activation takes a significant amount of time, which would be noticeable by any user of the card. Further, performing such tests would be very difficult while still meeting the stringent timing constraints imposed on smart card startup by the ISO 7816-3 standard [16]. Continuous RNG tests, executed as the smart card performs crypto operations, also exacerbate performance problems.

Such testing of random bits can also adversely affect the security of the implementation: Side-channel attacks such as SPA/DPA [20], EMF [1], template attacks [7], and other "TEMPEST" attacks [30] are capable of extracting useful information from even a single operation of a device. While it is difficult to extract significant information from *just* reading the TRNG output, the leakage is amplified if the *same* sensitive value is used at many different places in the computation. Template attacks work by building a "database" of signatures of the side channel for each possible value of some sensitive byte or bits; the likelihood of building a good distinguishing signature increases direcly in proportion to the number of places the same value is used or manipulated. If we run a series of tests on the output of the TRNG before other uses, then we manipulate the output bits of the TRNG without modification at many different places. This increases the attack surface of side-channel attacks!

We even proposed testing the TRNG output with one set of bits, confirming that the TRNG is operating correctly, and then immediately generating a new set of random bits from the TRNG to use without testing. However, our evaluation laboratory concluded that this proposal would not comply with the AIS 31 requirements. Thus, we concluded that it was unrealistic to use a TRNG directly for a high-assurance system that must comply with AIS 31 and also resist side-channel attacks.

Instead, we adopted a compelling alternative: pseudo random number generators (PRNGs) which generate a sequence of random bits starting from an initial (random) seed. There are many secure methods to construct PRNGs: for example the algorithms specified in FIPS 186-2 [11]. Our design generates good quality random bits compliant to relevant standards while simultaneously ensuring that the PRNG cannot be attacked using side-channels. Our PRNG is based on a random seed generated *off-line* using a fully tested source of true random bits. This seed is stored in persistent memory and feeds a component PRNG whose output is the seed for a second component PRNG whose output is used for card operations. The first PRNG is run for each activation of the smart card and its state is fed back to memory. Thus, we minimize the number of updates to persistent memory which is crucial due to the limited number of write cycles for EEPROM/Flash. We use the TRNG to perturb the values of the seeds to protect against any possible compromise of the stored seeds. Since this perturbation of the seeds does not constitute direct use of TRNG output for cryptographic purposes, AIS 31 does not apply, but AIS 20 [14] does. We argue that this construction results in a good quality stream of random bits and justify the security of our construction and its resistance to side channel attacks. The construction of our PRNG is similar to that of Petit, et. al. [22] who also design a similar PRNG with the goal of resistance to side channel attacks. We note here that our construction [8] precedes theirs.

This paper is organized as follows: Section 2 describes Caernarvon and provides relevant background on hardware RNGs and standards which govern their testing. Sections 3 and 3.1 describe the construction of our PRNG, and Section 4 argues that the quality of random numbers produced by the PRNG is good. We discuss the security of our construction and specifically the resistance to side-channel attacks in Section 5, and Section 6 describes related work.

2 Background

2.1 Caernarvon Operating System

The Caernarvon operating system was designed to be evaluated under the Common Criteria [10] at EAL7, the highest defined level of assurance, under the German evaluation scheme. It demonstrates that high assurance for smart cards is technically feasible and commercially viable. Historically, smart card processors have not supported hardware protection features necessary to separate the OS from the applications, and one application from another [18]. The assurance in the Caernarvon OS is based on exploiting the first smart card processors to offer such hardware protection features.

The Caernarvon OS implements a formally specified, mandatory security policy [23] providing multi–level security, suitable for both government agencies and commercial users. The mandatory security policy requires effective authentication of its users independent of applications, for which the Caernarvon OS contains a privacy-preserving, two–way authentication protocol [24] integrated with the policy. The Caernarvon OS also includes a strong cryptographic library that has been separately certified under the Common Criteria at EAL5+ for use with other systems. While the initial platform for the operating system was smart cards, the design could also be used in other embedded devices, such as USB tokens, PDAs, cell phones, etc.

2.2 Hardware Random Number Generators

Smart cards and other similar systems typically feature true random number generators (TRNG) built from physical sources of noise. There has been considerable amount of work on harnessing such physical sources to produce good quality unbiased random output (see, for example, [2, 21, 13]).

Since they are built from physical sources, the output of TRNGs may include biases. Thus, before use in sensitive applications, the output needs to be tested to ensure quality. A good description of an potential evaluation methodology for TRNGs is described by Schindler, et. al.[25]. This and other standards offer testing guidelines but do not endorse or exclude any TRNG design principles.

It should be noted that, as of July 2009, as stated on page 1 of FIPS 140-2, Annex C [6], "There are no FIPS Approved non-deterministic random number generators." FIPS-140-2 refers to hardware or TRNGs as *non-deterministic*.

2.3   Testing Requirement Standards

The following are some of the standards for testing of RNGs before using the output in cryptographic and other sensitive applications.

The AIS 31 RNG Testing Requirements. Killman and Schindler [19] proposed tests for RNGs to ensure that evaluated systems do not suffer from failure models of hardware RNGs. This was later implemented in an Application Note and Interpretation of the Scheme(AIS 31) [15] and recommends that the output of hardware RNGs be testing carefully prior to use with start-up and continuous tests. While such testing will certainly result in better quality, we feel that the recommendations do not take into account the potential for side channel attacks on the implementation of such testing. Section 2.4 discusses some of these attacks and how they can be applied to RNG testing phases. It is our belief that the AIS 31 mandated testing can significantly increase the attack surface for side channel attacks. This issue was first discussed by Karger [17].

Because AIS 31 does not consider this increased potential for side-channel attacks due to testing, Common Criteria Guidance Documents for several evaluated smart card chips[1] require that cryptographic use of the random numbers generated by a true RNG be subject to the tests of FIPS 140-2 [27, Section 4.9.1], thereby requiring the increased attack surface.

We note that the latest protection profile for smart card chips [26] does discuss the risks of the inherent leakage. However, an update to AIS 31 is still needed, because the potential risks are not limited only to smart cards.

FIPS Tests. FIPS-140, the definitive US standard for cryptographic devices, did include a number of test on the output of RNGs which have been dropped since 2002. The draft of the upcoming FIPS 140-3 [28] includes a number of tests for *pseudo* random number generators (PRNGs). FIPS 140-3 mandates the following tests for PRNGs (Random bit generator(RBG) in their terminology):

- Deterministic components of a Random Bit Generator (RBG) shall be subject to the Cryptographic Algorithm Test in Section 4.9.1 (of FIPS 140-3).
- Data output from the RBG shall pass the Continuous RBG Test as specified in Section 4.9.2 (of FIPS 140-3).

The cryptographic algorithm test requires that the algorithms used in the PRNG be tested before they are used. The continuous test is that each generated random number be saved so that the next one generated compared with the previous one. The standard further specifies that if an entropy source (a hardware RNG) is used, then the minimum entropy test must be performed on each output of the source. We note that the same performance and security issues are applicable to these tests. For instance, it will be difficult to perform the cryptographic algorithm test at start-up while still meeting the maximum latency requirements of ISO 7816-3 [16]. As argued earlier, any testing performed on random bits can increase the attack surface for side channel attacks.

---

[1] Guidance documents are defined in the Common Criteria [9] assurance component AGD_USR.1. Citations can not be provided due to non-disclosure requirements.

2.4　Side Channel Attacks

High assurance systems must be built to resist attacks which exploit information such as power consumption [20], EM emanations [1], template attacks [7], TEMPEST attacks [30] and other such by-products of the implementation of sensitive operations that are capable of extracting useful information during the computation. Here we only highlight how these attacks affect our design choices for the RNG.

Simple Power Attacks (SPA) and its EM equivalent (SEMA) target leakages that occur in a single execution of the device, *e.g.* through conditional execution of code depending on a sensitive value. While these are very powerful they are easy to protect against, and most implementations guard against such obvious leakage. These attacks also target other leakages that can occur in a single step, *e.g.* in some hardware reading a byte from EEPROM leaks the Hamming weight of the byte that is read.

Differential Power and EM attacks (DPA/DEMA) exploit statistical biases that occur in side channels due to manipulation of sensitive values. The attacks work by first amplifying these biases by running the device with multiple different inputs. For these attacks to be successful, the same sensitive values must be manipulated in all different runs of the device.

Template attacks extract useful information from a single sample of the side channel from the device. These work by building signatures of the side channel for each possible value of some sensitive byte (or a few bits) using a test device. Given a single run of the device under test they attempt to identify using statistical techniques the most likely value of the sensitive byte. Key to the success of these attacks is building the right set of signatures. The likelihood of building better signatures increases with the number of places in the computation that the *same* byte is manipulated. For instance, if random bits sampled from an RNG are subject to a number of tests where the same bits are being manipulated, then the likelihood of building good signatures increases.

2.5　Constraints of Persistent Memory

Smart cards use EEPROM and/or Flash as persistent memory since they have no access to off-chip memory. The PRNG in the Caernarvon system is designed to use persistent memory across runs of the card.

Write operations to EEPROM or Flash memory are slow, usually in the 1 to 6 millisecond range each, depending on the technology generation. Further, the write block size for EEPROM is limited, for example, to 128 bytes. Thus writing any significant amount of data to a file is likely to take multiple write operations, plus additional writes to update the control block information. Furthermore, EEPROM and Flash memories have a limited number of write cycles before they start to fail, for example between 100,000 and 500,000 for EEPROM, and only 10,000 for Flash.

Our PRNG described below will store PRNG state in persistent storage but do this once per run of the card. The Caernarvon operating system includes extensive techniques to mitigate these problems for more general applications.

3   RNG Design Overview

The design criteria for the PRNG are the following:

- **Quality.** The random bits produced in each run of the smart card should be unpredictable. Further, the random bits in any run should be unpredictable, even knowing the bits in any other run.
- **Security.** The random number generator should be resistant to side-channel attacks such as SPA/DPA [20], EM Analysis [1] and Template Attacks [7].
- **Effectiveness.** The RNG should make effective use of persistent storage minimizing updates to such storage.

Given these requirements the design follows quite naturally: First, quality necessitates a seed sampled from a high entropy source, but obtaining this from an on-chip source would require testing the bits. As noted, this can increase the surface for side channel attacks, thus lowering the effective entropy of the on-chip source. Thus our PRNG is seeded by random bits which are stored in EEP-ROM which can, of course, be generated offline securely and comprehensively tested. The FIPS 140-2 standard [27] does not impose requirements or tests on this external source of entropy. However, the draft for FIPS 140-3 requires that the claimed minimum entropy of the source be provided to the cryptographic module which is then required to verify that the claimed value is sufficient for intended applications. This is currently not part of our design, but we note that the device can't directly test the source entropy. The best one could do is check for plausible error conditions, such as strings of all constants, etc.

The PRNG in the Caernarvon operating system is shown in Fig. 1. It consists of two component PRNGs cascaded: the first is called the Lifetime PRNG or the LPRNG and the second is called the Activation PRNG or APRNG. LPRNG is seeded by random bits which are stored in persistent memory. Each invocation of either component can be *optionally* seeded with additional random bits from an on-chip source of randomness. We stress that the strength of the random bits generated by the composite PRNG *primarily* depends on the quality of the external seed LSEED. For instance, if this seed is revealed due to a compromise of the off-chip process then this can compromise the PRNG. Adding on-chip randomness can ensure that the output of the PRNG is not a deterministic function of LSEED. While the PRNG doesn't depend on this on-chip source for its strength, a pedantic reading of the standards may require us to test this input. Template and other side channel attacks can significantly reduce the effective entropy of the on-chip source. Adding this to the seed obtained from the external source can not *decrease* the strength of the PRNG. Further, while complying with standards, one could argue that since the claimed strength is only dependent on LSEED, we may not need to test this additional optional input. AIS 31 [19] recognizes this type of use as functionality class P1 which does not require such extensive testing.

Each invocation changes the internal state of the PRNG which is used in the next invocation. For the LPRNG, this is stored back in EEPROM as the seed for the next run as shown. The output of the first invocation of the LRPNG

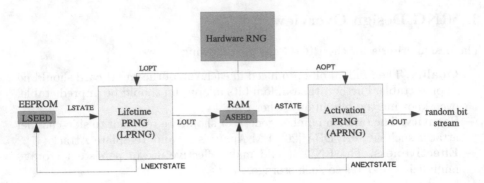

Fig. 1. Functional Outline of Caernarvon PRNG

is the seed for the APRNG whose output is used whenever random bits are required in this run of the smart card. In the Caernarvon OS, we choose as PRNG implementations schemes recommended by FIPS 186-2 [11]. The analysis of our random number generator does not depend on the choice of the PRNG block chosen from amongst those recommended in Annex C of the FIPS 140-2 standard [6]. We have chosen the algorithm for generating random values from the Appendix 3.2 of the Digital Signature Algorithm standard [11] with the method described in Appendix 3.4 using the DES algorithm to implement the $G()$ function. We note here that the recommendations given by NIST [3] are more recent and should be the choice for an updated design.

3.1   Detailed Description of the PRNG

This section briefly describes the construction of the two PRNGs and documents the choices made from relevant standards.

LPRNG is seeded by a 160 bit value LSEED from EEPROM. The value t chosen as 67452301 EFCDAB89 98BADCFE 10325476 C3D2E1F0 is used in the "compress" function at each invocation. The pseudo-code for the update function of LPRNG is

```
Inputs:
    - LSTATE: content of LSEED, stored in persistent storage; initially
      generated from an external source of entropy and installed in the
      chip at initialization.
    - LOPT: optional input from Hardware RNG (corresponding to input
      labelled ''optional user-input'' in FIPS 186-2).

Update:
a. LSTATE = (LSTATE + LOPT)
b. LOUT = G(t, LSTATE)
c. LNEXTSTATE = (LSTATE + 1 + LOUT)

Output:
    - LOUT: used as new seed ASEED by APRNG.
    - LSTATENEXT: new state used to replace previous LSEED
```

This sequence is executed exactly once during an activation of the card. The initial value of LSTATE is obtained from persistent storage LSEED. To potentially add more entropy, we chose to add randomness from an on-chip source via LOPT. Testing the bits LOPT will, of course, reduce the effective entropy of the source due to side channel attacks. As we have noted before, the strength of our PRNG rests solely on the strength of LSEED and hence we argue that this may be enough to address the requirements of the standards even without testing LOPT.

The output of LPRNG, i.e. LOUT = G(t, LSTATE), is used to seed the APRNG. The updated state LNEXTSTATE is written back to persistent storage. Our implementation ensures that until this state is successfully updated in persistent storage, APRNG will not be activated. This ensures that if random bits are used anywhere in this activation of the card, then the value of LSEED will indeed be different in future activations. This prevents the attack where the card is disabled before the write back to EEPROM is completed resulting in the same sequence of random bits across different activations.

The "compress" function G() will be based on the DES algorithm, specified in Section 3.4 of FIPS 186-2, chosen because of on-chip DES hardware. The properties of our RNG would be the same for compress functions built from other algorithms. For new designs, a better choice would be the HMAC-SHA1 based construction of deterministic RBGs given by [3].

The APRNG uses LOUT, the output from the LRPNG, as its seed. It is constructed similar to LPRNG with optional additional input from on-chip random sources. Its pseudo-code is:

```
Inputs:
   - ASTATE: content of ASEED, on activation the output of the LPRNG.
   - AOPT: optional input chosen from source of randomness This is done
     at most once. Further invocations will NOT have any additional input.

Update:
a. ASTATE = (ASTATE + AOPT)
b. AOUT = G(t, ASTATE)
c. ANEXTSTATE = (ASTATE + 1 + AOUT)

Output:
   - AOUT: randomness returned to caller of APRNG.
   - ASTATENEXT: new state used to replace previous ASEED.
```

This generates 160 bits of randomness for each invocation and updates the internal state of APRNG.

The Caernarvon random number generation process described above realizes the requirements we had earlier listed. First, cryptographic keys and other sensitive values are generated from the output of a PRNG. Thus, we do not need to test the quality before use which may result in exposure through side channel attacks. However, the quality of the random bits is still high since the seed used by the PRNG is sampled from an high entropy source off-line. The strength of our PRNG rests (almost) exclusively on the strength of the off-line process for generating LSEED. We note that even if testing of optional input from on-chip random sources results in reduced levels of entropy due to side channel attacks, it is still sufficient when combined with LSEED. The analysis will show that the quality is maintained across different activations of the card. Further we note that the update to the seed in LPRNG is done only once per activation of the card, and thus we make effective use of persistent storage.

4   Cryptographic Analysis

This section justifies the cryptographic strength of the PRNG construction. First, we argue generically that the chaining construction of the PRNG is secure assuming we start with a secure individual PRNG construction. This and the assumption that the PRNG schemes recommended by the FIPS 186-2 standard are secure yield a proof of security of our chaining construction. We also argue that our PRNG is a class $K4$ DRNG according to the AIS 20 [14] standard.

In following lemma we state that our construction as shown in Figure 1 is a special instance (with $n = 2$) of a general class of secure PRNGs composed by chaining a primitive PRNG n times:

Lemma 1. *Let $r_{\text{chain}(n)}$ be a PRNG formed by chaining n primitive PRNGs r_{prim}. If there is a distinguisher which can distinguish the output of $r_{\text{chain}(n)}$ from a uniformly distributed random string of equal length then there is also a distinguisher distinguishing the output of r_{prim} from a random string.*

Proof. Without loss of generality, assume that r_{prim} has a seed length of l, each inner PRNG r_{prim}^i reseeds its child m times before getting reseeded itself and we output externally lm^n bytes, i.e., each r_{prim}^i expands a seed to length lm. When reseeding a particular PRNG r_{prim}^i we talk of a new *instance* of that PRNG.

For this case, you can visualize $r_{\text{chain}(n)}$ as a m-ary tree of depth n where the ith level corresponds to the instances of the ith PRNG r_{prim}^i and the jth child of a node corresponds to the jth chunk of l bytes returned by the corresponding instance of the PRNG. The concatenation of the leaf nodes is the output produced by $r_{\text{chain}(n)}$.

The lemma follows from an inductive hybrid argument. The hybrids at depth n are $r_{\text{chain}(n)}$, $r_{\text{chain}(n)}$ with each of the m sub-trees of depth $n - 1$ recomputed from a fresh random seed (instead of the seed derived from the parent), and for progressive hybrids we replace the sub-trees in increasing order of index with a sub-tree where all nodes are freshly sampled random elements.

The distribution induced by the extreme hybrids correspond to the distribution of $r_{\text{chain}(n)}$ and of a random distribution, respectively. It is also easy to see that neighboring hybrids either differ by (a) a single value which is either a random lm string or a single expansion of r_{prim} from a random and independent seed or (b) a sub-tree which correspond to an (independent) $n - 1$ PRNG $r_{\text{chain}(n-1)}$ or a random tree. Hence, we can reduce a distinguisher of any pair of hybrids in a distinguisher of either r_{prim} or $r_{\text{chain}(n-1)}$ from random data. The latter in turn can be reduced recursively into hybrids until we arrive in hybrids differing all only in a r_{prim} distinguishing problem. As there are only a polynomial number of hybrids, any non-negligible advantage in distinguishing $r_{chain(n)}$ from a random string can be converted into a non-negligible distinguisher of r_{prim} from a random string. □

Thus if we are given a secure PRNG primitive and the seed to the PRNG chain is chosen uniformly at random then our construction is cryptographically secure. Thus under the assumption that the FIPS 186-2 PRNG is secure and assuming proper secret and random seed generation at smart card personalization time, our overall realization is cryptographically secure as well. (Note that to our knowledge there is no published security proof (in a strong cryptographic sense) for the FIPS-186-2 PRNG. However, sound design principles, a number of easy to made security arguments and empirical evidence give us a reasonable assurance of its security.)

Informally, note that in the construction of the PRNG, on each invocation we add the output of the PRNG back to its internal state. Thus the PRNG is *forward secure i.e.* given the internal state after k invocations we can not infer the random outputs from prior invocations of the PRNG. Thus, the PRNG design fulfills the requirements of a $K4$ DRNG according to the AIS-20 standard. More precisely, the fulfillment of the individual criteria is as follows:

- $K1$ **DRNG:** This is a simple requirement which requires that we identify an integer value c such that every sequence of c outputs of the PRNG is distinct. By our assumption, the output of the core PRNG primitive *i.e.* the FIPS 186-2 generator is indistinguishable from random so it trivially satisfies this requirement ignoring the eventual cycling of the 160 bit output.
- $K2$ **DRNG:** Specifically, we are asked to characterize the statistical properties of the RNG such as the monobit test, poker test and tests on runs. We note that the FIPS 186-2 generators and hence our construction will satisfy all these criteria.
- $K3$ **DRNG:** This level requires us to assert that the entropy of the PRNG is at least 80. We note here that our PRNG operates on 160 bit seeds which are chosen off-line from a high entropy source which is carefully tested. Thus our PRNG achieves this level.
- $K4$ **DRNG:** For this level, we are required to argue that the PRNG is *forward-secure* as describe above. As argued, our PRNG meets this criterion.

FIPS 186-2 does not impose any requirements on the user input, i.e. it does not need to be random or secret to guarantee pseudo-randomness of the output stream or the security of the algorithm. Thus, replacing the user input with the output of the HW/RNG does not affect the security of the implementation, even if the HW/RNG malfunctions. On the other hand, if the HW/RNG is functioning properly then the output of LPRNG is truly random, and the output of APRNG is pseudo-random. This shows that there is no requirement to test the statistical properties of the bits of the HW/RNG, as they do not affect the security of the cryptographic aspects of the system. Yet, when it is functioning properly we gain entropy.

5   Attacks and Defenses

A key criterion for our design was resistance to side-channel attacks against the functioning of the PRNG. We have considered the following attacks.

- Simple Power Analysis/Simple EM Analysis (SPA/SEMA).
- Differential Power Analysis/Differential EM Analysis (DPA/DEMA)
- Template attacks using Power or EM or both.

Our design and implementation has been guided by techniques which are effective in the mitigation of these attacks. In particular, the following techniques which minimize and practically eliminate the threat posed by these attacks.

Technique 1. The strength of our PRNG relies on the entropy of the external seed supplied to the card. Using off-chip sources greatly reduces the attack surface for template attacks as discussed below. Our PRNG is *only* claimed to be as strong as this external seed. The addition of the input from an on-chip source does not affect this claim.

Technique 2. The execution sequence of all PRNG code is independent of its internal state.

Technique 3. As defined, both the component PRNGs can be optionally provided additional seeding material from on-chip sources. Due to the testing requirements this can only be counted on to provide a marginal additional source of entropy. However, even this amount can add to the strength of the PRNG. While it is certainly not feasible to base the entire PRNG on sampling from the on-chip source due to the low effective entropy, adding this optional input can be beneficial.

Technique 4. The implementation utilizes the hardware RNG to implement random masking/share based computation of the PRNG specification. While side channel attacks will only result in lowered entropy we argue below that this is sufficient to protect against statistical side-channel attacks.

As discussed below these techniques provide adequate countermeasures against side-channel attacks. The Caernarvon Persistent Storage Management code provides a CRC check on bits being stored. This will be disabled due to potential leakage of information.

5.1   Simple Power Analysis (SPA)

Simple power/EM analysis attacks target leakage that occurs in a single activation of the card such as through conditional execution depending on sensitive state OR high leakage on any given step of the computation. Our implementation is careful to ensure that the PRNG code execution sequence is independent of state (Technique 2). Thus SPA/SEMA attacks are limited to leakage at individual steps such as reading of bytes from EEPROM in the case of LPRNG. Masking steps in the computation, even when sampled from the hardware RNG, can also reduce the information that is revealed during the computation.

5.2 Differential Power Analysis (DPA)

Classical DPA is not a problem with LPRNG/APRNG since an attacker cannot invoke the update function of any PRNG many times with the same secret state. The state gets modified at each invocation of the update function and this constantly evolving secret state is a good defense against DPA style attacks; the attacker gets only one sample to attack any secret state. Note that in our implementation we actually add random masks with the bits sampled from an on-chip source. As we have discussed before, we can only count on this being a low entropy source. However, even with this source of bits, masking can further prevent DPA. We reiterate that the main defense is that DPA is not easy to mount since the keys change at every invocation.

5.3 Template Attacks

Template attacks can be used to classify the single signal received during the operation of the LPRNG/APRNG on a given unknown state. The efficacy of this attack relies on having a large enough "signature" or "template" of computation manipulating the *same* sensitive value. The attacker can build offline a series of templates for this signature corresponding to different values of this sensitive input and use them to identify the specific value on a given activation of the card.

The main defense against template attacks is the use of an off-chip source to generate LSEED. This can be directly used in the computation of the PRNG and thus we can be certain that building templates this will be difficult. This is because of the properties of the PRNG there is rapid diffusion and LSEED will not be manipulated unmodified at too many points. We do allow for the optional input sampled from the on-chip RNG. With full conformance to the standards, there is a good chance that template attacks can substantially reduce the effective entropy. Note, however, that the PRNG is still secure since LSEED is not tested. The masking of the computation using Technique 4 above will also make it difficult to build effective templates even though it is sampled from a source with low effective entropy.

Resistance to side channel attacks can be best argued with a description of the implementation, since there are many implementation details relevant to the argument. Further, to convincingly argue against side channel attacks we have to formalize the precise attack models along the lines of Petit *et. al.*[22]. We have not built such a model for our system.

6   Additional Related Work

Several recent designs for hardware random number generators have appeared, including Dole's [12] that describes networked computers generating and sharing entropy in proportion to the need for random numbers, Walsh and Beisterfeldt's [33] that generates high-quality random numbers by sampling the output of a Voltage Controlled Oscillator (VCO) at a frequency much lower than the frequency of the oscillator output, and Sprunk's [29] which uses a TRNG to drive a PRNG. Tsoi, Leung and Leong [32] show compact FPGA implementations of both a TRNG and a PRNG, but they do not connect them together. Furthermore, none of these designs address the possibility of side channel attacks or the issues of EEPROM memory wear.

7 Conclusions

We have seen that generation of cryptographically strong random numbers is actually quite difficult. While many of the standards concerning the testing of random numbers generated by hardware or true random number generators (TRNG) quite properly worry about hardware failures, they do not adequately cover the possibility of side channel attacks during RNG testing. We have shown a novel combination of a TRNG with a PRNG that alleviates both the testing concerns and the side-channel concerns that also limits the possibility of EEPROM or Flash memories being worn out from re-writing seed values too frequently. While our examples have all focused on cryptographic algorithms, such as DES, SHA-1, DSA, and RSA, the principles equally well apply to newer algorithms, such as elliptic curves, AES, and SHA-256, etc.

We must recommend that both the NIST FIPS 140 standard and the German AIS 31 guideline be updated to reflect these kinds of issues, so that future developers can more easily construct random number-based systems that are truly secure against both hardware failures and side-channel attacks.

References

[1] Agrawal, D., Archambeault, B., Rao, J.R., Rohatgi, P.: The EM side-channel(s). In: Kaliski Jr., B.S., Koç, Ç.K., Paar, C. (eds.) CHES 2002. LNCS, vol. 2523, pp. 29–45. Springer, Heidelberg (2003)
[2] Bagini, V., Bucci, M.: A design of reliable true random number generator for cryptographic applications. In: Koç, Ç.K., Paar, C. (eds.) CHES 1999. LNCS, vol. 1717, pp. 204–218. Springer, Heidelberg (1999)
[3] Barker, E., Kelsey, J.: Recommendation for random number generation using deterministic random bit generators (revised). NIST SP800-90, National Institute of Standards and Technology, Gaithersburg, MD (March 2007), http://csrc.nist.gov/publications/nistpubs/800-90/SP800-90revised_March2007.pdf
[4] Biham, E., Shamir, A.: Differential fault analysis of secret key cryptosystems. In: Kaliski Jr., B.S. (ed.) CRYPTO 1997. LNCS, vol. 1294, pp. 513–525. Springer, Heidelberg (1997)
[5] Boneh, D., DeMillo, R.A., Lipton, R.J.: On the importance of checking cryptographic protocols for faults. In: Fumy, W. (ed.) EUROCRYPT 1997. LNCS, vol. 1233, pp. 37–51. Springer, Heidelberg (1997)
[6] Campbell, J., Easter, R.J.: Annex c: Approved random number generators for FIPS PUB 140-2, security requirements for cryptographic modules. FIPS PUB 140-2, Annex C, National Institute of Standards and Technology, Gaithersburg, MD (Draft of July 31, 2009), http://csrc.nist.gov/publications/fips/fips140-2/fips1402annexc.pdf

[7] Chari, S., Rao, J.R., Rohatgi, P.: Template attacks. In: Kaliski Jr., B.S., Koç, Ç.K., Paar, C. (eds.) CHES 2002. LNCS, vol. 2523, pp. 13–28. Springer, Heidelberg (2003)

[8] Chari, S.N., Diluoffo, V.V., Karger, P.A., Palmer, E.R., Rabin, T., Rao, J.R., Rohatgi, P., Scherzer, H., Steiner, M., Toll, D.C.: Method, apparatus and system for resistence to side channel attacks on random number generators. United States Patent No. 7496616 (Filed November 12, 2004, Issued February 24, 2009)

[9] Common Criteria for Information Technology Security Evaluation, Part 3: Security assurance requirements. Version 2.3 CCMB2005-08-003 (August 2005), http://www.commoncriteriaportal.org/public/files/ccpart3v2.3.pdf

[10] Common Criteria for Information Technology Security Evaluation, Parts 1, 2, and 3. Version 2.3 CCMB2005-08-001, CCMB2005-08-002, and CCMB2005-08-003 (August 2005), http://www.commoncriteriaportal.org/thecc.html

[11] Digital signature standard. FIPS PUB 186-2, with Change Notice 1, 5 October 2001, National Institute of Standards and Technology, Gaithersburg, MD (January 2000),
http://csrc.nist.gov/publications/fips/archive/
fips186-2/fips186-2.pdf

[12] Dole, B.: Distributed state random number generator and method for utilizing same. United States Patent No. US6628786B1, September 30 (2003)

[13] Epstein, M., Hars, L., Krasinski, R., Rosner, M., Zheng, H.: Design and implementation of a true random number generator based on digital circuit artifacts. In: Walter, C.D., Koç, Ç.K., Paar, C. (eds.) CHES 2003. LNCS, vol. 2779, pp. 152–165. Springer, Heidelberg (2003)

[14] Functionality classes and evaluation methodology for deterministic random number generators. AIS 20, Version 1, Bundesamt für Sicherheit in der Informationstechnik (BSI), Bonn, Germany, December 2 (1999),
http://www.bsi.bund.de/zertifiz/zert/interpr/ais20e.pdf

[15] Functionality classes and evaluation methodology for physical random number generators. AIS 31, Version 1, Bundesamt für Sicherheit in der Informationstechnik (BSI), Bonn, Germany, September 25 (2001),
http://www.bsi.bund.de/zertifiz/zert/interpr/ais31e.pdf

[16] ISO 7816-3, Identification cards - Integrated circuit(s) with contacts - Part 3: Electronic signals and transmission protocols, Second edition. ISO Standard 7816-3, International Standards Organization (December 1997)

[17] Karger, P.A.: The importance of high-assurance security in pervasive computing. In: Hutter, D., Müller, G., Stephan, W., Ullmann, M. (eds.) Security in Pervasive Computing. LNCS, vol. 2802, p. 9. Springer, Heidelberg (2004),
http://web.archive.org/web/20040524183841/,
http://www.dfki.de/spc2003/karger.pdf

[18] Karger, P.A., Toll, D.C., McIntosh, S.K.: Processor requirements for a high security smart card operating system. In: Proc. 8th e-Smart Conference. Eurosmart, Sophia Antipolis, France, September 19-21 (2007), Available as IBM Research Division Report RC 24219 (W0703-091),
http://domino.watson.ibm.com/library/CyberDig.nsf/Home

[19] Killman, W., Schindler, W.: A proposal for: Functionality classes and evaluation methodology for true (physical) random number generators. Tech. rep., T-Systems debis Systemhaus Information Security Services and Bundesamt für Sicherheit in der Informationstechnik (BSI), Bonn, Germany (September 25, 2001), http://www.bsi.bund.de/zertifiz/zert/interpr/trngk31e.pdf

[20] Kocher, P., Jaffe, J., Jun, B.: Differential Power Analysis: Leaking Secrets. In: Wiener, M. (ed.) CRYPTO 1999. LNCS, vol. 1666, pp. 143–161. Springer, Heidelberg (1999)

[21] Maher, D.P., Rance, R.J.: Random number generators founded on signal and information theory. In: Koç, Ç.K., Paar, C. (eds.) CHES 1999. LNCS, vol. 1717, pp. 219–230. Springer, Heidelberg (1999)

[22] Petit, C., Standaert, F.X., Pereira, O., Malkin, T., Yung, M.: A block cipher based pseudo random number generator secure against side-channel key recovery. In: ASIACCS 2008, Tokyo, Japan, March 18–20, pp. 56–65 (2008)

[23] Schellhorn, G., Reif, W., Schairer, A., Karger, P., Austel, V., Toll, D.: Verification of a formal security model for multiapplicative smart cards. In: Cuppens, F., Deswarte, Y., Gollmann, D., Waidner, M. (eds.) ESORICS 2000. LNCS, vol. 1895, pp. 17–36. Springer, Heidelberg (2000)

[24] Scherzer, H., Canetti, R., Karger, P.A., Krawczyk, H., Rabin, T., Toll, D.C.: Authenticating Mandatory Access Controls and Preserving Privacy for a High-Assurance Smart Card. In: Snekkenes, E., Gollmann, D. (eds.) ESORICS 2003. LNCS, vol. 2808, pp. 181–200. Springer, Heidelberg (2003)

[25] Schindler, W., Killmann, W.: Evaluation criteria for true (physical) random number generators used in cryptographic applications. In: Kaliski Jr., B.S., Koç, Ç.K., Paar, C. (eds.) CHES 2002. LNCS, vol. 2523, pp. 431–449. Springer, Heidelberg (2003)

[26] Security IC platform protection profile. Tech. Rep. BSI-PP-0035, developed by Atmel, Infineon Technologies AG, NXP Semiconductors, Renesas Technology Europe, and STMicroelectronics, registered and certified by Bundesamt für Sicherheit in der Informationstechnik (BSI), Bonn, Germany, June 15 (2007), http://www.commoncriteriaportal.org/files/ppfiles/pp0035b.pdf

[27] Security requirements for cryptographic modules. FIPS PUB 140-2, Change Notice 2, National Institute of Standards and Technology, Gaithersburg, MD, December 3 (2002), http://csrc.nist.gov/publications/fips/fips140-2/fips1402.pdf

[28] Draft - security requirements for cryptographic modules. FIPS PUB 140-3, National Institute of Standards and Technology, Gaithersburg, MD, April 6 (2007), http://csrc.nist.gov/publications/fips/fips140-3/fips1403Draft.pdf

[29] Sprunk, E.J.: Robust random number generator. United States Patent No. US6253223B1, June 26 (2001)

[30] Tempest fundamentals (u). Declassified in 2000 under Freedom of Information Act NACSIM 5000, National Security Agency, Ft. George G. Meade, MD, February 1 (1982), http://cryptome.org/nacsim-5000.zip

[31] Toll, D.C., Karger, P.A., Palmer, E.R., McIntosh, S.K., Weber, S.: The caernarvon secure embedded operating system. Operating Systems Review 42(1), 32–39 (2008)

[32] Tsoi, K.H., Leung, K.H., Leong, P.H.W.: Compact FPGA-based true and pseudo random number generators. In: 11th Annual IEEE Symp. on Field-Programmable Custom Computing Machines, Napa, CA, April 9–11 (2003)

[33] Walsh, J.J., Biesterfeldt, R.P.: Method and apparatus for generating random numbers. United States Patent No. US6480072B1, November 12 (2002)

Simple Power Analysis on Exponentiation Revisited

Jean-Christophe Courrège[1], Benoit Feix[2], and Mylène Roussellet[2]

[1] CEACI-THALES
18 Avenue Edouard BELIN
31401 Toulouse, France
Jean-Christophe.courrege@thalesgroup.fr
[2] INSIDE CONTACTLESS
41 Parc Club du Golf
13856 Aix-en-Provence, Cedex 3, France
{bfeix,mroussellet}@insidefr.com

Abstract. Power Analysis has been studied since 1998 when P. Kocher *et al.* presented the first attack. From the initial Simple Power Analysis more complex techniques have been designed and studied during the previous decade such as Differential and Correlation Power Analysis. In this paper we revisit Simple Power Analysis which is at the heart of side channel techniques. We aim at showing its true efficiency when studied rigorously. Based on existing Chosen Message attacks we explain in this paper how particular message values can reveal the secret exponent manipulated during a modular exponentiation with a single power consumption curve. We detail the different ways to achieve this and then show that some blinded exponentiations can still be threatened by Simple Power Analysis depending on the implementation. Finally we will give advice on countermeasures to prevent such enhanced Simple Power Analysis techniques.

Keywords: Public key cryptography, long integer arithmetic, modular exponentiation, power analysis.

1 Introduction

The appearance of public key cryptography [DH76] and of the RSA cryptosystem [RSA78] was the beginning of modern cryptography. The use of these schemes, and especially RSA, has become very popular and more and more systems have based their security on it. Thus, in order to implement these systems efficiently, various modular multiplication algorithms have been designed to be embedded in constrained hardware resources devices such as Trusted Platform Modules (TPM) and smart cards.

Another consideration has become a key point for developers is the tamper resistance topic. For years smart cards had been considered as tamper resistant devices until Kocher *et al.* introduced in 1996 the Timing Attacks [Koc96] and few years later the Power Analysis Attacks [KJJ99]. Their techniques, named

D. Gollmann, J.-L. Lanet, J. Iguchi-Cartigny (Eds.): CARDIS 2010, LNCS 6035, pp. 65–79, 2010.

Simple Power Analysis (SPA) and Differential Power Analysis (DPA), threaten any naive cryptographic algorithm implementation. As electronic devices are composed of thousands of logical gates that switch differently depending on the executed operations, the power consumption depends on the executed instructions and the manipulated data. Thus by analyzing the power consumption of the device on an oscilloscope it is possible to observe its behavior and then to deduce from this power curve the secret data manipulated.

From the initial SPA and DPA of Kocher *et al.* many studies were presented to introduce new attack techniques on different popular cryptographic schemes and to improve the power curve processing in order to recover secrets with fewer curves than the classical DPA. Others presented some countermeasures to these attacks. In this paper we focus on SPA and show it is more powerful than what can be inferred from reading current side channel papers. To illustrate our paper and assertions some practical results are presented on some secure implementations.

The paper is organized as follows. First we recall in sections 2 and 3 the fundamentals notations and techniques on which our work is based. Section 2 gives an overview of long integer arithmetic for public key embedded implementations. Section 3 describes the Side Channel Analysis techniques related to this paper. We present in Section 4 some chosen message SPA techniques and explain the reasons of observed power leakages. We also explain how these power leakages can be exploited to mount enhanced SPA on non-chosen or blinded message exponentiations. In Section 5 we analyze the efficiency of the classical countermeasures and give some advice on their use for preventing enhanced SPA. We conclude our research in Section 7.

2   Embedded Implementations of Exponentiation

We recall here the mathematical principles and the arithmetic algorithms that are used to implement public key algorithms in embedded devices.

2.1   Long Integer Multiplication

In this paper we use the following notation: $x = (x_{k-1} \dots x_1 x_0)_b$ corresponds to integer x decomposition in base b, i.e. the x decomposition in t-bit words with $b = 2^t$ and $k = \lceil log_b(x) \rceil$.

Algorithm 2.1 presents to the classical long integer multiplication algorithm used to compute $x \times y$.

2.2   Long Integer Modular Multiplication

Chip manufacturers usually embed arithmetic coprocessors to compute modular multiplications $x \times y \mod n$ for long integers x, y and n. In this paper we choose to illustrate our analysis on the Barrett and the Montgomery [Mon85] reductions. But other techniques exist such as the interleaved multiplication-reduction with Knuth, Sedlack or Quisquater methods [Dhe98]. Our analysis can also be adapted to these methods.

Algorithm 2.1 Long Integer Multiplication

INPUT: $x = (x_{k-1}x_{k-2}\ldots x_1x_0)_b, y = (y_{k-1}y_{k-2}\ldots y_1y_0)_b$
OUTPUT: $\mathsf{LIM}(x,y) = x \times y$

Step 1. for i from 0 to $2k - 1$ **do** $w_i = 0$
Step 2. for i from 0 to $k - 1$ **do**
$\quad c \leftarrow 0$
$\quad$ for j from 0 to $k - 1$ **do**
$\quad\quad (uv)_b \leftarrow w_{i+j} + x_j \times y_i + c$
$\quad\quad w_{i+j} \leftarrow v$ and $c \leftarrow u$
$\quad w_{i+k} \leftarrow v$
Step 3. Return(w)

Multiplication with Barrett Reduction. Here a modular multiplication $x \times y \bmod n$ is the combination of a long integer multiplication $\mathsf{LIM}(x,y)$ followed by a Barrett reduction by the modulus value n. We use the notation $\mathsf{BarrettRed}(a,n)$ for this reduction, thus $\mathsf{BarrettRed}(\mathsf{LIM}(a,m),n)$ corresponds to the computation of $a \times m \bmod n$. We do not detail the Barrett reduction algorithm here, for more details the reader can refer to [MOV96] or [ACD+06].

Montgomery Modular Multiplication. Given a modulus n and two integers x and y, of size v in base b, with $\gcd(n,b) = 1$ and $r = b^{\lceil log_b(n)\rceil}$, MontMul algorithm computes:

$$\mathsf{MontMul}(x, y, n) = x \times y \times r^{-1} \bmod n$$

Refer to papers [Mon85] and [KAK96] for details of MontMul implementation.

We denote by $\mathsf{ModMul}(x,y,n)$ the operation $x \times y \bmod n$, it can be done using Barrett or Montgomery processing.
Then the Square and Multiply algorithm used for an exponentiation becomes:

Algorithm 2.2 Exponentiation

INPUT: integers m and n with $m < n$, k-bit exponent $d = (d_{k-1}d_{k-2}\ldots d_1d_0)_2$
OUTPUT: $\mathsf{Exp}(m,d,n) = m^d \bmod n$

Step 1. $a = 1$
Step 2. Process ModMul precomputations
Step 3. for i from $k - 1$ to 0 **do**
$\quad a = \mathsf{ModMul}(a,a,n)$
$\quad$ if $d_i = 1$ **then** $a = \mathsf{ModMul}(a,m,n)$
Step 4. Return(a)

2.3 The RSA Cryptosystem

Let p and q be two secret prime integers and $n = p \times q$ be the public modulus used in the RSA cryptosystem. Let e be the public exponent and d the corresponding private exponent such that $e \cdot d = 1 \mod \phi(n)$ where $\phi(n) = (p-1)(q-1)$. Signing with RSA a message m consists of computing the value $s = m^d \mod n$. Signature s is then verified by checking that $s^e \mod n$ is equal to m.

3   Simple Power Analysis

Power Analysis has been studied for years since it was introduced by Kocher, Jaffe and Jun in [KJJ99]. Many attacks on the most frequently used cryptosystems (DES, AES, RSA, ECC ...) have been published and improvements on power analysis techniques have been done during the last decade. For example Correlation Power Analysis publication from Brier, Clavier and Olivier [BCO04] requires far fewer curves for recovering the key than the original DPA. More recently many studies have been published to improve the Side Channel methodology [GBTP08], [SGV08], [PR09].

The initial publication [KJJ99] on SPA showed how to recover the secret exponent during a modular exponentiation from a single power consumption curve. Impressive results are obtained when the squaring and the multiplying operations have different recognizable and sizeable patterns. If so the bits of the secret exponent can directly be *read* on the power curve of a classical Square and Multiply algorithm. Indeed two consecutives squares on the curve imply the exponent bit is 0 while when a squaring is followed by a multiplication the exponent bit is 1.

This SPA corresponds to the power leakage related to differences in the executed code. The leakage is caused by the fact that the executed code is different for a squaring than for a multiplication. An efficient countermeasure against this SPA is the Side-Channel Atomicity introduced by Chevalier-Mames, Ciet and Joye [CCJ04]. In their implementation the code executed during the whole exponentiation loop is the same for a squaring and a multiplication step. Consequently, it is no more possible to distinguish which operation is performed. Their method improves resistance to classical SPA without adding supplementary multiplications contrary to the Square and Multiply Always algorithm.

Yen *et al.* introduced in [YLMH05] a new type of SPA attack based on the use of particular message values. It defeats previous countermeasures considered as resistant against SPA. In their paper Yen *et al.* use as an input message $m = n - 1$ for modular exponentiation. The only two values involved during the exponentiation $m^d \mod n$ are 1 and $n-1$. The Hamming weights of these data are so different by simply observing the power trace, it is very easy to determine the moments when 1 is involved in a multiplication. Only three different operation cases can be processed during the exponentiation: 1×1, $1 \times n-1$ or $n-1 \times n-1$ with three different and recognizable signal patterns. It is then simple to deduce the sequence of squarings and multiplications and to recover the secret exponent.

Other attacks named Doubling and Collision attacks have been presented in [FV03] and [YLMH05] but they need at least two executions of an exponentiation with the same exponent to mount the attack. However in this paper we choose to only consider attacks recovering the secret from a single power consumption curve and thus counterfeiting the exponent blinding countermeasure. Therefore we do not consider Doubling and Collision attacks here.

4 Enhanced Simple Power Analysis on Exponentiation

In Yen *et al.* attack and the other techniques introduced in this paper, SPA does not aim at distinguishing differences in code execution but rather to detect when specific data are manipulated through their specific power signature. Indeed power signatures during an operation $(x \times y)$ or $(x \times y \mod n)$ will depend on values x and y. If x and/or y have very particular Hamming weights then it will lead to a very characteristic power trace for the multiplication. We present here many values which can generate a recognizable pattern and thus lead to the exponent being recovered from a single power trace.

We illustrate our analysis on the ModMul operation using the Barrett reduction and especially during the computation of LIM(x,y). The same analysis can be done in other kind of modular multiplication methods, for instance in the modular Montgomery multiplication method MontMul(x,y).

4.1 Origin of Power Leakage

The power leakage appears during the operation $x_i \times y_j$ of the long integer multiplication LIM(x,y). Any operation $x_i \times y_j$ has a power consumption related to the number of bit flips of the bit lines manipulated. When one of the operands is null or has very few bits set, for instance is equal to 0, or 2^i with i in $0 \ldots t-1$, the t-bit multiplication has a lower power consumption than the average one. We can then distinguish in a long integer multiplication when such a value is manipulated.

If the value of the multiplicand m contains one (or more) of the t-bit word(s) set to 0 or 2^i with i in $0 \ldots t-1$, during an atomic exponentiation loop we can recognize each time this value m is manipulated, i.e. each time the exponent bit is 1.

The condition for this SPA to succeed is that one (or more) of the t-bit word(s) of x or y is set to 0 (or in some cases it could be also to 2^i with i in $0 \ldots t-1$). We consider here that the leakage appears only for zero values.

We can then quantify the power consumed by the device for computing $x_i \times y_j$. We denote by $C(x_i, y_j)$ this power consumption . As illustrated in Table 1 we can distinguish three categories depending on whether x_i and y_j values are 0 or not.

When $x_i = 0$ and $y_j = 0$ the device only manipulates zero bits. Thus the amount of power consumed by the multiplication is *Low*, we denote it as C_{Low}. A multiplication with non zero values ($x_i \neq 0$ and $y_j \neq 0$) yields a higher power consumption: we consider this as *High* and denote it as C_{High}. Finally when $x_i \neq 0$ and $y_j = 0$ the amount of power consumed by a multiplication is considered as *Medium*: we denote it as C_{Medium}.

Table 1. Power Signal quantity for $x_i \times y_j$

x_i	y_j	$C(x_i, y_j)$
$x_i \neq 0$	$y_j \neq 0$	C_{High}
$x_i \neq 0$	$y_j = 0$	C_{Medium}
$x_i = 0$	$y_j = 0$	C_{Low}

In the operation $\mathsf{LIM}(x,y)$ we can graphically estimate the power curve by $C_{LIM(x,y)} = \sum_{i=0}^{k-1} \sum_{j=0}^{k-1} C(x_i, y_j) \cdot T(k,i,j)$ with $C(x_i, y_j)$ being the power consumption of the device for computing $x_i \times y_j$ and T a function which represents the number of cycles executed for a set (k,i,j). This corresponds to the schematic power curve of Figure 1.

A graphical estimation of power consumption expected depending on whether we have C_{High}, C_{Medium} or C_{Low} is given in Figure 2.

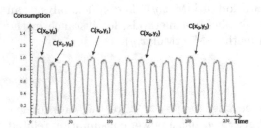

Fig. 1. $C_{LIM(x,y)}$: power curve representation of operation $\mathsf{LIM}(x,y)$ with $k = 4$

Fig. 2. Three cases of estimated power curves for $C(x_i, y_j)$

When an operation $x_i \times y_j$ leads to $C(x_i, y_j)$ being C_{Low} or C_{Medium} we can identify this operation in the curve. This explains why the SPA introduced by Yen *et al.* allows the secret exponent recovering with a single curve for a well chosen message. Indeed when comparing the three possible operations occurring in an exponentiation with the input chosen message $m = n - 1$ we obtain for $k = 3$ the Table 2. In this table we observe that $C_{LIM(x,y)}$ has different recognizable patterns for each long integer multiplication.

Table 2. The three possible power traces for $\mathsf{LIM}(x,y)$ in Yen *et al.*'s attack for $k = 3$

$x \times y$	x in base b	y in base b	$C_{LIM(x,y)}$
$(n-1) \times (n-1)$	$a = (a_2, a_1, a_0)_b$	$a = (a_2, a_1, a_0)_b$	$C_H\|C_H\|C_H\|C_H\|C_H\|C_H\|C_H\|C_H\|C_H$
$1 \times (n-1)$	$a = (0,0,1)_b$	$m = (m_2, m_1, m_0)_b$	$C_H\|C_M\|C_M\|C_H\|C_M\|C_M\|C_H\|C_M\|C_M$
1×1	$a = (0,0,1)_b$	$a = (0,0,1)_b$	$C_H\|C_M\|C_M\|C_M\|C_L\|C_L\|C_M\|C_L\|C_L$

More Chosen Messages. From this analysis we can enumerate other chosen messages leading to successful SPA on atomic exponentiations such as messages with one or many t-bit word equal to 0 or 2^i with i in $0 \ldots t-1$. Messages with a globally low Hamming weight can also lead to a medium or low power consumption and allow to recover the secret exponent in a single power curve.

4.2 Experiments and Practical Results

We experimented this attack on many different multipliers processors to confirm our theoretical analysis. In this section we present some results we obtained on two different devices.

First Device. We implemented a Montgomery Modular exponentiation on a 32×32-bit multiplier, in this case we have t equal to 32. We chose as input messages for exponentiations the following values with $k = 4$: $m_1 = (\alpha, \alpha, 0, 0)$, $m_2 = (\alpha, 0, 0, 0)$ where α is 32-bit random value.

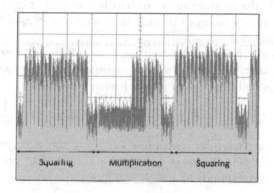

Fig. 3. Part of exponentiation power curves with messages m_1 and m_2 and $k = 4$, zoom on $\mathsf{LIM}(m_1,a)$ (black) and $\mathsf{LIM}(m_2,a)$ (grey)

Figure 3 represents a part of the measured exponentiation curves of these two messages. The black curve corresponds to the exponentiation with message m_1 and grey curve with m_2. The multiplication is clearly identifiable by a lower power consumption compared to the squaring. Message m_2 takes one more 32-bit word equal to 0 than m_1. This results in Figure 3 in a low power consumption longer for grey curve than for black curve during the multiplication.

In this case we also observed that C_{Medium} is close to C_{High} but the two can be distinguished.

Second Device. We designed an 8×64-bit hardware multiplier with the associated long integer exponentiation. In the multiplication $x \times y$ the operand x is manipulated by 64-bit words when the operand y is taken by 8-bit words.

The message is placed in the second operand y for the multiplications during the exponentiation.

We chose several messages containing one or more zero 8-bit words and executed the corresponding long integer exponentiations. We then simulated the power consumption of the synthesized multiplier we have designed. By analyzing these power curves we can observe that a zero byte y_j in operand y produces a lower power consumption curve in the cycles where y_j is manipulated. We are then able to recover the whole secret exponent in an exponentiation when a zero byte is present in the message value.

We have explained here the potential power leakages related to multiplication and exponentiation computations and confirmed our analysis with some practical results. In the next paragraph we study the probability of leakage depending on the multiplier and modulus bit lengths.

4.3   Leakage Probability

In this paragraph letters p and q design probabilities.

Probability of leakage during a multiplication. Let x_i be a t-bit word, and p be the probability for x_i to be null, then we have $P(x_i = 0) = \frac{1}{2^t} = p$ and $P(x_i \neq 0) = 1 - p$.

If Y is the event {None of the t-bit word is null in a k-word integer} with $P(Y) = (1 - p)^k$, then we have $\overline{Y}$ which corresponds to the event {at least one of the t-bit words is null in a k-word integer} with probability:

$$q = P(\overline{Y}) = 1 - P(Y) = 1 - (1 - p)^k = 1 - (1 - \frac{1}{2^t})^k$$

During a long integer modular multiplication $x \times y$ the leakage appears only if at least one of the k t-bit words of x or/and y is null. The probability for this leakage to appear corresponds to $1 - (1 - p)^{2k}$.

Probability of leakage during an exponentiation. During an exponentiation we focus on the probability of having a leakage in a t-bit multiplication $x \times y$ when only y takes part in the leakage and not x (or the opposite). Indeed during an exponentiation $m^d \mod n$ the message m is used during each multiplication at step 3 of Algorithm 2.2, when $d_i = 1$. Thus if the value m contains a t-bit word m_i leading to leakage in the operations $m_i \times a_j$ and/or $m_i \times a$ then each multiplication by m_i and thus by m could be identified and the secret exponent d can be recovered from a single power curve.

In this case the probability of having one or many of the t-bit words of m leading to a signing pattern is:

$$q = 1 - (1 - p)^k = 1 - (1 - \frac{1}{2^t})^k$$

This is also the probability of having an SPA leaking curve for a single execution of the exponentiation.

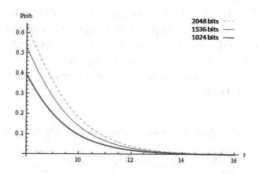

Fig. 4. Probability of having a message with a signing pattern depending of multiplier size (t) and modulus size (1024, 1536, 2048)

In the case of an 8-bit multiplier Figure 4 shows that the probability of having a message with a signing pattern is about 0.394 for a 1024-bit modulus, 0.528 for a 1536-bit modulus and 0.633 for a 2048-bit modulus. When the multiplier is greater than 16 bits this probability decreases for all modulus sizes.

It also obvious that bigger the key length is and smaller the multiplier size (t) is, the higher the probability of recovering the secret exponent d in a single curve is.

Using Poisson law as an approximation of binomial law we have the property that with $1/q$ exponentiation power curves the probability for recovering the secret exponent is $(1 - \frac{1}{exp(1)})$. Thus the probability P_{leak} of recovering the secret exponent using one of the h/q acquired curves is approximated by $P_{leak} = P(h/q) = 1 - (\frac{1}{exp(1)})^h$.

Figures 5 and 6 show how many curves would be needed to have, with a probability close to 1, a message leading to a signing pattern which can be used for our SPA attack. With an 8-bit multiplier (Figure 5), a very few messages (5 to 10) are necessary to obtain an exploitable leakage with high probability.

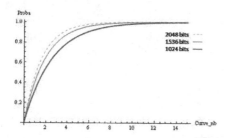

Fig. 5. Probability P_{leak} for an 8-bit multiplier depending on the number of curves acquired and modulus size (1024, 1536, 2048)

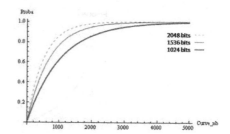

Fig. 6. Probability P_{leak} for a 16-bit multiplier depending on the number of curves acquired and modulus size (1024, 1536, 2048)

For a 16-bit multiplier (Figure 6) between 3000 and 5000 curves are needed for
a success probability close to 1. But for a multiplier size greater than 16 the
number of curves needed for recovering the secret exponent makes the attack
not practical; example is given for $t = 32$ in Appendix A.

The bigger the multiplier, the greater the number of collected curves needed.
Examples are given in Table 3.

Table 3. Number of messages needed to have $P_{leak} \geq 0.99$

Modulus	Multiplier size		
size	8	16	32
1024	12	4720	$\approx 2^{29}$
1536	9	3150	$\approx 2^{29}$
2048	8	2360	$\approx 2^{28}$

4.4 Enhanced Simple Power Analysis on Blinded Exponentiations

In this section we consider that the exponentiation is secured using message and
exponent blinding.

Exponent Blinding. This common countermeasure consists in randomizing
the secret exponent d by $d^\star = d + r_1 \cdot n \mod \phi(n)$ with r_1 being a random value.
However here the exponent blinding has no effect on our analysis since a single
curve is used to recover the private exponent and recovering $d^\star$ is equivalent to
recovering d.

Randomized Chosen Message. Now we consider that the message is randomized additively by the classical countermeasure: $m^* = m + r_1 \cdot n \mod r_2 \cdot n$,
with r_1 and r_2 being two l-bit random values. In this case we have m^* equal
to $m + u \cdot n$ with u being a l-bit value equal to $r_1 \mod r_2$. In this case an attack could consist of choosing a message $m^\star$ being 1 or 2^i, guessing a random

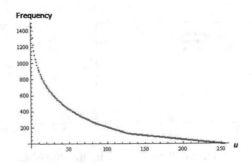

Fig. 7. Distribution of u for $l = 8$

value u_{guess}, computing message m from guessed randomized message $m^\star$, i.e. $m = m^\star - u_{guess} \cdot n$, and executing at least 2^l exponentiations with input message m. One of the 2^l exponentiation power curves should present leakages and should allow the secret exponent to be recovered with SPA.

However if r_1 and r_2 are effectively chosen in a pure random way we observe that this attack could be done faster. Indeed if we analyze the distribution of values $u = r_1 \bmod r_2$ we observe that values do not appear with same probability and that the more frequent are the smallest ones. The most frequent one being $u = 0$. It is illustrated in Figure 7 for $l = 8$. While less pronouced the same phenomenon can also be observed for bigger l values. The best attack method in this case would consist of choosing $u_{guess} = 0$ (or 1 or 2) and executing the exponentiation many times until a leaking power curve is obtained.

Unknown Message. When analyzing the leakage probabilities of Section 4.3 it appears that the number of curves needed to recover the secret exponent for a fixed multiplier size only depends on the modulus length, even if the message is unknown to the attacker. For instance for a 1024-bit modulus and a 16-bit multiplier by collecting 5000 power consumption curves of exponentiations done with unknown different messages the probability of recovering the secret exponent is close to 1.

Synthesis. As the additive randomization of the message does not significantly increase message length, the amount of messages needed does not increase either. Thus if the attacker can choose input messages of the blinded exponentiation, he will choose the attack which requires less effort comparing number of chosen message acquisitions needed (when guessing the random) with the number of curves to collect to have $P_{leak} = 1$.

5   Countermeasures and Recommendations

5.1   Balancing the Power Consumption

The attack presented in this paper is based on the fact that manipulating zero t-bit values results in low power consumption cycles. Thus a method to prevent this attack would consist in using balanced power consumption technology such as dual rail technique. In this case the manipulation of a value with a low Hamming weight (for instance 0) will no longer have a different power consumption than the one due to the manipulation of other values.

5.2   Random Choice for Blinding

As we showed previously the values $r_1 \bmod r_2$ are not uniformly distributed when r_1 and r_2 are random. A better solution consists of choosing a fixed value for r_2 and a random value for r_1. From our analysis the best choice for r_2 is

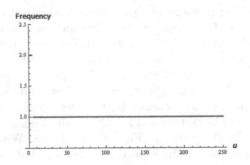

Fig. 8. Distribution of u for $l = 8$ and $r_2 = 251$

to take the biggest l-bit prime number. In that case r_2 will never divide r_1, thus u cannot be null and u values are uniformly distributed as it is showed in Figure 8.

Another consideration is that the random length choice is also directly related to the multiplier size. In section 4.4 we have seen that while the number of possible random values u is smaller than the number of messages to test given by the leakage probability analysis, it is easier to test all random values u. Regarding this statistical properties we showed that when the multiplier is small (8 or 16 bits) the quantity of curves needed for a successful Simple Power Analysis is reasonable.

Thus by combining a multiplier with a size of at least equal to 32 bits, with big random number r_1 (longer than 32 or 64 bits) and the biggest prime integer r_2, the feasibility of the attack explained in this paper is significantly reduced.

6   Remarks on RSA CRT and ECC

We presented our analysis on exponentiation computations. It corresponds directly to straightforward implementations of RSA signature and decryption algorithms as they simply consist of an exponentiation with the secret exponent. In case of RSA CRT the analysis is a little bit different since the input message is reduced modulo p and q before the exponentiations. Even if data manipulated into the multiplications are twice shorter than the modulus n, similar analysis can be conducted on reduced messages. However the countermeasure which consists in fixing the random value r_2, must not be used in RSA CRT implementations as it would not be protected against the correlation analysis on the CRT recombination presented in [AFV07].

ECC are also concerned. The analysis depends on the kind of coordinates and algorithm chosen for the scalar multiplication, anyway implementations using small multipliers and/or small random numbers for coordinates randomization [Cor99] have to be avoided.

7   Conclusion

In this paper we have explained the origin of the power leakages during multiplications and presented other ways to mount Simple Power Analysis attacks. Indeed by observing differences in data power signatures instead of differences in code execution, using some well chosen messages allows the whole secret exponent of RSA cryptosystem to be recovered from a single curve. Moreover we have shown that some improvements in SPA attacks lead to the recovery of the secret exponent on secured exponentiations using blinding countermeasures and with non chosen messages. We analyzed the blinding countermeasures and gave advice to developers to protect their implementations against this enhanced SPA. Judicious choice and large random numbers in blinding countermeasures combined with large size multipliers, especially greater than 32 bits, are recommended for SPA resistance.

Acknowledgments

The authors would like to thank Christophe Clavier for the fruitful discussions we had and the improvements he suggested to us. Thanks also to Sean Commercial and Vincent Verneuil for their valuable comments and advice on this manuscript.

References

[ACD+06]   Avanzi, R.-M., Cohen, H., Doche, C., Frey, G., Lange, T., Nguyen, K., Verkauteren, F.: Handbook of Elliptic and Hyperelliptic Curve Cryptography (2006)

[AFV07]   Amiel, F., Feix, B , Villegas, K.. Power Analysis for Secret Recovering and Reverse Engineering of Public Key Algorithms. In: Adams, C., Miri, A., Wiener, M. (eds.) SAC 2007. LNCS, vol. 4876, pp. 110–125. Springer, Heidelberg (2007)

[BCO04]   Brier, E., Clavier, C., Olivier, F.: Correlation Power Analysis with a Leakage Model. In: Joye, M., Quisquater, J.-J. (eds.) CHES 2004. LNCS, vol. 3156, pp. 16–29. Springer, Heidelberg (2004)

[CCJ04]   Chevallier-Mames, B., Ciet, M., Joye, M.: Low-cost Solutions for Preventing Simple Side-Channel Analysis: side-channel atomicity. IEEE Transactions on Computers 53(6), 760–768 (2004)

[Cor99]   Coron, J.-S.: Resistance against differential power analysis for elliptic curve cryptosystems. In: Koç, Ç.K., Paar, C. (eds.) CHES 1999. LNCS, vol. 1717, pp. 292–302. Springer, Heidelberg (1999)

[DH76]   Diffie, W., Hellman, M.E.: New Directions in cryptography. IEEE Transactions on Information Theory 22(6), 644–654 (1976)

[Dhe98]   Dhem, J.-F.: Design of an efficient public-key cryptographic library for RISC-based smart cards. PhD thesis, Université catholique de Louvain, Louvain (1998)

[FV03]   Fouque, P.-A., Valette, F.: The Doubling Attack - why upwards is better than downwards. In: Walter, C.D., Koç, Ç.K., Paar, C. (eds.) CHES 2003. LNCS, vol. 2779, pp. 269–280. Springer, Heidelberg (2003)

[GBTP08]   Gierlichs, B., Batina, L., Tuyls, P., Preneel, B.: Mutual Information Analysis. In: Oswald, E., Rohatgi, P. (eds.) CHES 2008. LNCS, vol. 5154, pp. 426–442. Springer, Heidelberg (2008)

[KAK96]   Koç, Ç.K., Acar, T., Kaliski, B.-S.: Analysing and comparing Montgomery multiplication algorithms. IEEE Micro 16(3), 26–33 (1996)

[KJJ99]   Kocher, P.C., Jaffe, J., Jun, B.: Differential Power Analysis. In: Wiener, M. (ed.) CRYPTO 1999. LNCS, vol. 1666, pp. 388–397. Springer, Heidelberg (1999)

[Koc96]   Kocher, P.C.: Timing attacks on implementations of Diffie-Hellman, RSA, DSS, and other systems. In: Koblitz, N. (ed.) CRYPTO 1996. LNCS, vol. 1109, pp. 104–113. Springer, Heidelberg (1996)

[Mon85]   Montgomery, P.L.: Modular multiplication without trial division. Mathematics of Computation 44(170), 519–521 (1985)

[MOV96]   Menezes, A., van Oorschot, P.C., Vanstone, S.A.: Handbook of Applied Cryptography. CRC Press, Boca Raton (1996)

[PR09]   Prouff, E., Rivain, M.: Theoretical and practical aspects of mutual information based side channel analysis. In: Abdalla, M., Pointcheval, D., Fouque, P.-A., Vergnaud, D. (eds.) ACNS 2009. LNCS, vol. 5536, pp. 499–518. Springer, Heidelberg (2009)

[RSA78]   Rivest, R.L., Shamir, A., Adleman, L.: A method for obtaining digital signatures and public-key cryptosystems. Communications of the ACM 21, 120–126 (1978)

[SGV08]   Standaert, F.-X., Gierlichs, B., Verbauwhede, I.: Partition vs. comparison side-channel distinguishers: An empirical evaluation of statistical tests for univariate side-channel attacks against two unprotected cmos devices. In: Lee, P.J., Cheon, J.H. (eds.) ICISC 2008. LNCS, vol. 5461, pp. 253–267. Springer, Heidelberg (2009)

[YLMH05]   Yen, S.-M., Lien, W.-C., Moon, S., Ha, J.: Power Analysis by Exploiting Chosen Message and Internal Collisions - Vulnerability of Checking Mechanism for RSA-decryption. In: Dawson, E., Vaudenay, S. (eds.) Mycrypt 2005. LNCS, vol. 3715, pp. 183–195. Springer, Heidelberg (2005)

A   Leakage Probability for t Up to 32

The following figures give the probability of leakage for a 32-bit multiplier and the leakage probability increasement regarding the number of exponentiation executions.

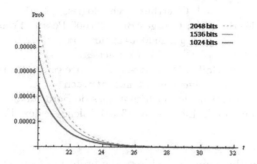

Fig. 9. Probability of having a message with a signing pattern for 32-bit multiplier depending on modulus size (1024, 1536, 2048)

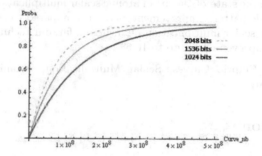

Fig. 10. Probability P_{leak} for a 32-bit multiplier depending on the number of curves acquired and modulus size (1024, 1536, 2048)

Atomicity Improvement for Elliptic Curve Scalar Multiplication

Christophe Giraud[1] and Vincent Verneuil[2,3,⋆]

[1] Oberthur Technologies,
4, allée du doyen Georges Brus, 33 600 Pessac, France
`c.giraud@oberthur.com`
[2] Inside Contactless,
41, parc du Golf, 13 856 Aix-en-Provence cedex 3, France
`vverneuil@insidefr.com`
[3] Institut de Mathématiques de Bordeaux,
351, cours de la Libération, 33 405 Talence cedex, France

Abstract. In this paper we address the problem of protecting elliptic curve scalar multiplication implementations against side-channel analysis by using the atomicity principle. First of all we reexamine classical assumptions made by scalar multiplication designers and we point out that some of them are not relevant in the context of embedded devices. We then describe the state-of-the-art of atomic scalar multiplication and propose an atomic pattern improvement method. Compared to the most efficient atomic scalar multiplication published so far, our technique shows an average improvement of up to 10.6%.

Keywords: Elliptic Curves, Scalar Multiplication, Atomicity, Side-Channel Analysis.

1 Introduction

1.1 Preamble

We consider the problem of performing scalar multiplication on elliptic curves over $\mathbb{F}_p$ in the context of embedded devices such as smart cards. In this context, efficiency and side-channel resistance are of utmost importance. Concerning the achievement of the first requirement, numerous studies dealing with scalar multiplication efficiency have given rise to efficient algorithms including sliding-window and signed representation based methods [19].

Regarding the second requirement, side-channel attacks exploit the fact that physical leakages of a device (timing, power consumption, electromagnetic radiation, etc) depend on the operations performed and on the variables manipulated. These attacks can be divided into two groups: the *Simple Side-Channel Analysis* (SSCA) [25] which tries to observe a difference of behavior depending on the value of the secret key by using a single measurement, and the *Differential Side-Channel Analysis* (DSCA) [26] which exploits data value leakages by

---

⋆ A part of this work has been done while at Oberthur Technologies.

D. Gollmann, J.-L. Lanet, J. Iguchi-Cartigny (Eds.): CARDIS 2010, LNCS 6035, pp. 80–101, 2010.

performing statistical treatment over several hundreds of measurements to retrieve information on the secret key. Since 1996, many proposals have been made to protect scalar multiplication against these attacks [12, 23, 7]. Amongst them, *atomicity* introduced by Chevallier-Mames et al. in [9] is one of the most interesting methods to counteract SSCA. This countermeasure has been widely studied and Longa recently proposed an improvement for some scalar multiplication algorithms [27].

In this paper we present a new atomicity implementation for scalar multiplication, and we detail the atomicity improvement method we employed. This method can be applied to minimize atomicity implementation cost for sensitive algorithms with no security loss. In particular our method allows the implementation of atomic scalar multiplication in embedded devices in a more efficient way than any of the previous methods.

The rest of this paper is organized as follows. We finish this introduction by describing the scalar multiplication context which we are interested in and by mentioning an important observation on the cost of field additions. In Section 2 we recall some basics about Elliptic Curves Cryptography. In particular we present an efficient scalar multiplication algorithm introduced by Joye in 2008 [21]. Then we recall in Section 3 the principle of atomicity and we draw up a comparative chart of the efficiency of atomic scalar multiplication algorithms before this work. In Section 4, we propose an improvement of the original atomicity principle. In particular, we show that our method, applied to Joye's scalar multiplication, allows a substantial gain of time compared to the original atomicity principle. Finally, Section 5 concludes this paper.

1.2   Context of the Study

We restrict the context of this paper to practical applications on embedded devices which yields the constraint of using standardized curves over $\mathbb{F}_p$[1]. As far as we know, NIST curves [17] and Brainpool curves [14,15] cover almost all curves currently used in the industry. We thus exclude from our scope Montgomery curves [32], Hessian curves [20], and Edwards curves[2] [16] which do not cover NIST neither Brainpool curves.

Considering that embedded devices – in particular smart cards – have very constrained resources (i.e. RAM and CPU), methods requiring heavy scalar treatment are discarded as well. In particular it is impossible to store scalar precomputations for some protocols such as ECDSA [1] where the scalar is randomly generated before each scalar multiplication. Most of the recent advances in this

---

[1] The curves over $\mathbb{F}_p$ are generally recommended for practical applications [33, 34].

[2] An elliptic curve over $\mathbb{F}_p$ is expressible in Edwards form only if it has a point of order 4 [6] and is expressible in twisted Edwards form only if it has three points of order 2 [4]. Since NIST and Brainpool curves have a cofactor of 1 there is not such equivalence. Nevertheless, for each of these curves, it is possible to find an extension field $\mathbb{F}_{p^q}$ over which the curve has a point of order 4 and is thus birationally equivalent to an Edwards curve. However the cost of a scalar multiplication over $\mathbb{F}_{p^q}$ is prohibitive in the context of embedded devices.

field cannot thus be taken into account: Double Base Number System [13, 31], multibase representation [28], Euclidean addition chains and Zeckendorf representation [30].

1.3   On the Cost of Field Additions

In the literature, the cost of additions and subtractions over $\mathbb{F}_p$ is generally neglected compared to the cost of field multiplication. While this assumption is relevant in theory, we found out that these operations were not as insignificant as predicted for embedded devices. Smart cards for example have crypto-coprocessors in order to perform multi-precision arithmetic. These devices generally offer the following operations: addition, subtraction, multiplication, modular multiplication and sometimes modular squaring. Modular addition (respectively subtraction) must therefore be carried out by one classical addition (resp. subtraction) and one conditional subtraction (resp. addition) which should always be performed – i.e. the effective operation or a dummy one – for SSCA immunity. Moreover every operation carried out by the coprocessor requires a constant extra software processing δ to configure the coprocessor. As a result, the cost of field additions/subtractions is not negligible compared to field multiplications. Fig. 1 is an electromagnetic radiation measurement during the execution on a smart card of a 192-bit modular multiplication followed by a modular addition. Large amplitude blocks represent the 32-bit crypto-coprocessor activity while those with smaller amplitude are only CPU processing. In this case the time ratio between modular multiplication and modular addition is approximately 0.3.

From experiments on different smart cards provided with an arithmetic coprocessor, we estimated the average cost of modular additions/subtractions

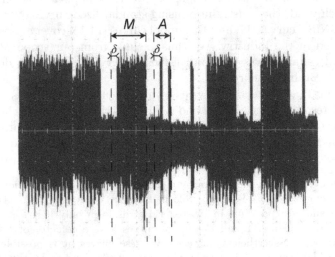

Fig. 1. Comparison between modular multiplication (M) and modular addition (A) timings

Table 1. Measured A/M ratio on smart cards with crypto-coprocessor for NIST and Brainpool ECC bit lengths

Bit length	160	192	224	256	320	384	512	521
A/M		0.36	0.30	0.25	0.22	0.16	0.13	0.09	0.09

compared to modular multiplications. Our results are presented in Table 1 where A and M denote the cost of a field addition/subtraction and the cost of a field multiplication respectively. We observe that the average value of A/M for considered bit lengths is about 0.2.

Another useful field operation is negation in $\mathbb{F}_p$, i.e. the map $x \to -x$, which can be carried out by one non-modular subtraction $p - x$. The cost N of this operation is therefore half the cost of modular addition/subtraction and thus we fix $N/M = 0.5\,A/M$.

In the following sections we also consider the cost S of field squaring. The cost of a squaring compared to a multiplication depends on the functionalities of the corresponding crypto-coprocessor. When a dedicated squaring is available a commonly accepted value for S/M is 0.8 [8, 18] which is also corroborated by our experiments. Otherwise squarings must be carried out as multiplications and the ratio S/M is thus 1.

2 Elliptic Curves

In this section we recall some generalities about elliptic curves, and useful point representations. Then we present two efficient scalar multiplication algorithms.

Cryptology makes use of elliptic curves over binary fields $\mathbb{F}_{2^n}$ and large characteristic prime fields $\mathbb{F}_p$. In this study we focus on the latter case and hence assume $p > 3$.

2.1 Group Law over $\mathbb{F}_p$

An elliptic curve $\mathcal{E}$ over $\mathbb{F}_p$, $p > 3$ can be defined as an algebraic curve of affine Weierstraß equation:

$$\mathcal{E} : y^2 = x^3 + ax + b \tag{1}$$

where $a, b \in \mathbb{F}_p$ and $4a^3 + 27b^2 \not\equiv 0 \pmod{p}$.

The set of points of $\mathcal{E}$ – i.e. the pairs $(x, y) \in \mathbb{F}_p{}^2$ satisfying (1) –, plus an extra point $\mathcal{O}$ called *point at infinity* form an abelian group where $\mathcal{O}$ is the neutral element. In the following, we present the corresponding law depending on the selected point representation.

Affine Coordinates. Under the group law a point $P = (x_1, y_1)$ lying on the elliptic curve $\mathcal{E}$ admits an opposite $-P = (x_1, -y_1)$.

The sum of $P = (x_1, y_1)$ and $Q = (x_2, y_2)$, with $P, Q \neq \mathcal{O}$ and $P \neq \pm Q$, is the point $P + Q = (x_3, y_3)$ such that:

$$\begin{cases} x_3 = ((y_2 - y_1)/(x_2 - x_1))^2 - x_1 - x_2 \\ y_3 = (x_1 - x_3)(y_2 - y_1)/(x_2 - x_1) - y_1 \end{cases} \tag{2}$$

The double of the point $P = (x_1, y_1)$, with $P \neq \mathcal{O}$ and $y_1 \neq 0$, is the point $2P = (x_2, y_2)$ as defined below, or $\mathcal{O}$ if $y_1 = 0$.

$$\begin{cases} x_2 = ((3x_1{}^2 + a)/(2y_1))^2 - 2x_1 \\ y_2 = (x_1 - x_2)(3x_1{}^2 + a)/(2y_1) - y_1 \end{cases} \tag{3}$$

Each point addition or point doubling requires an inversion in $\mathbb{F}_p$. This operation can be very time consuming and leads developers on embedded devices to use other kinds of representations with which point operations involve no field inversion. In the following part of this section, we detail two of them.

Jacobian Projective Coordinates. By denoting $x = X/Z^2$ and $y = Y/Z^3$, $Z \neq 0$, we obtain the Jacobian projective Weierstraß equation of the elliptic curve $\mathcal{E}$:

$$Y^2 = X^3 + aXZ^4 + bZ^6 \ , \tag{4}$$

where $a, b \in \mathbb{F}_p$ and $4a^3 + 27b^2 \neq 0$. Each point $P = (x, y)$ can be represented by its Jacobian projective coordinates $(q^2x : q^3y : q)$ with $q \in \mathbb{F}_p$. Conversely, every point $P = (X : Y : Z)$ different from $\mathcal{O}$ can be represented in affine coordinates by $(x, y) = (X/Z^2, Y/Z^3)$.

The opposite of a point $(X : Y : Z)$ is $(X : -Y : Z)$ and the point at infinity $\mathcal{O}$ is denoted by the unique point with $Z = 0$, $\mathcal{O} = (1 : 1 : 0)$.

The sum of $P = (X_1 : Y_1 : Z_1)$ and $Q = (X_2 : Y_2 : Z_2)$, with $P, Q \neq \mathcal{O}$ and $P \neq \pm Q$, is the point $P + Q = (X_3 : Y_3 : Z_3)$ such that:

$$\begin{cases} X_3 = F^2 - E^3 - 2AE^2 \\ Y_3 = F(AE^2 - X_3) - CE^3 \\ Z_3 = Z_1Z_2E \end{cases} \quad \text{with} \quad \begin{aligned} A &= X_1Z_2{}^2 \\ B &= X_2Z_1{}^2 \\ C &= Y_1Z_2{}^3 \\ D &= Y_2Z_1{}^3 \\ E &= B - A \\ F &= D - C \end{aligned} \tag{5}$$

If P is given in affine coordinates – i.e. $Z_1 = 1$ – it is possible to save up one field squaring and four multiplications in (5). Such a case is referred to as *mixed affine-Jacobian addition*. On the other hand if P has to be added several times, storing $Z_1{}^2$ and $Z_1{}^3$ saves one squaring and one multiplication in all following additions involving P. This latter case is referred to as *readdition*.

The double of the point $P = (X_1 : Y_1 : Z_1)$ is the point $2P = (X_2 : Y_2 : Z_2)$ such that:

$$\begin{cases} X_2 = C^2 - 2B \\ Y_2 = C(B - X_2) - 2A^2 \\ Z_2 = 2Y_1Z_1 \end{cases} \quad \text{with} \quad \begin{aligned} A &= 2Y_1{}^2 \\ B &= 2AX_1 \\ C &= 3X_1{}^2 + aZ_1{}^4 \end{aligned} \tag{6}$$

When curve parameter a is -3, doubling can be carried out taking $C = 3 \left(X_1 + Z_1{}^2\right)\left(X_1 - Z_1{}^2\right)$ which saves two squarings in (6). We denote this operation by *fast doubling*.

Adding up field operations yields $12M + 4S + 7A$ for general addition, $11M + 3S + 7A$ for readdition, $8M + 3S + 7A$ for mixed addition, $4M + 6S + 11A$ for general doubling formula and $4M + 4S + 12A$ for fast doubling.

Modified Jacobian Projective Coordinates. This representation, introduced in [11], is derived from the Jacobian projective representation to which a fourth coordinate is added for computation convenience. In this representation, a point on the curve $\mathcal{E}$ is thus represented by $(X : Y : Z : aZ^4)$, where $(X : Y : Z)$ stands for the Jacobian representation.

Modified Jacobian projective coordinates provide a particularly efficient doubling formula. Indeed, the double of a point $P = (X_1 : Y_1 : Z_1 : W_1)$ is given by $2P = (X_2 : Y_2 : Z_2 : W_2)$ such that:

$$\begin{cases} X_2 = A^2 - 2C \\ Y_2 = A\,(C - X_2) - D \\ Z_2 = 2Y_1 Z_1 \\ W_2 = 2DW_1 \end{cases} \text{with} \quad \begin{array}{l} A = 3X_1{}^2 + W_1 \\ B = 2Y_1{}^2 \\ C = 2BX_1 \\ D = 2B^2 \end{array} \tag{7}$$

Doubling hence requires only $4M + 4S + 12A$ for all a values. On the other hand, addition is less efficient compared to Jacobian projective representation: by applying formula (5), we need to compute the fourth coordinate which is required in point doubling, adding an overhead of $1M + 2S$ [21].

On S–M Trade-Offs. Addition and doubling formulas presented above are voluntarily not state-of-the-art, see [5]. Indeed, recent advances have provided Jacobian formulas where some field multiplications have been traded for faster field squarings [27, Sec. 4.1]. These advances have been achieved by using the so-called *S–M trade-off* principle which is based on the fact that computing ab when a^2 and b^2 are known can be done as $2ab = (a + b)^2 - a^2 - b^2$. This allows a squaring to replace a multiplication since the additional factor 2 can be handled by considering the representative of the Jacobian coordinates equivalence class $(X : Y : Z) = (2^2X . 2^3Y : 2Z)$.

Nevertheless such trade-offs not only replace field multiplications by field squarings but also add field additions. In the previous example at least 3 extra additions have to be performed, thus taking $S/M = 0.8$ implies that the trade-off is profitable only if $A/M < 0.067$ which is never the case with devices considered using standardized curves as seen in Section 1.3. These new formulas are thus not relevant in the context of embedded devices.

2.2 Scalar Multiplication

Generalities. The operation consisting in calculating the multiple of a point $k \cdot P = P + P + \cdots + P$ (k times) is called *scalar multiplication* and the integer k is thus referred to as the *scalar*.

Scalar multiplication is used in ECDSA signature [1] and ECDH key agreement [2] protocols. Implementing such protocols on embedded devices requires particular care from both the efficiency and the security points of view. Indeed scalar multiplication turns out to be the most time consuming part of the aforementioned protocols, and since it uses secret values as scalars, side-channel analysis endangers the security of those protocols.

Most of the scalar multiplication algorithms published so far are derived from the traditional *double and add* algorithm. This algorithm can scan the binary representation of the scalar in both directions which leads to the *left-to-right* and *right-to-left* variants. The former is generally preferred over the latter since it saves one point in memory.

Moreover since computing the opposite of a point P on an elliptic curve is virtually free, the most efficient methods for scalar multiplication use signed digit representations such as the Non-Adjacent Form (NAF) [3]. Under the NAF representation, an n-bit scalar has an average Hamming weight of $n/3$ which implies that one point doubling is performed every bit of scalar and one point addition is performed every three bits.

In the two next subsections, we present a left-to-right and a right-to-left NAF scalar multiplication algorithms.

Left To Right Binary NAF Scalar Multiplication. Alg. 1 presents the classical NAF scalar multiplication algorithm.

Algorithm 1. Left-to-right binary NAF scalar multiplication [19]

INPUTS : $P = (X_1 : Y_1 : Z_1) \in \mathcal{E}(\mathbb{F}_p)$, $k = (k_{l-1} \ldots k_1 k_0)_{\text{NAF}}$
OUTPUT : $k \cdot P$

---

1. $(X_2 : Y_2 : Z_2) \leftarrow (X_1 : Y_1 : Z_1)$
2. $i \leftarrow l - 2$
3. **while** $i \geq 0$ **do**
   $(X_2 : Y_2 : Z_2) \leftarrow 2 \cdot (X_2 : Y_2 : Z_2)$
   if $k_i = 1$ **then**
       $(X_2 : Y_2 : Z_2) \leftarrow (X_2 : Y_2 : Z_2) + (X_1 : Y_1 : Z_1)$
   if $k_i = -1$ **then**
       $(X_2 : Y_2 : Z_2) \leftarrow (X_2 : Y_2 : Z_2) - (X_1 : Y_1 : Z_1)$
   $i \leftarrow i - 1$
4. **return** $(X_2 : Y_2 : Z_2)$

Point doubling can be done in Alg. 1 using general Jacobian doubling formula or fast doubling formula. Since NIST curves fulfill $a = -3$ and each Brainpool curve is provided with an isomorphism to a curve with $a = -3$, we thus assume that fast doubling is always possible. Point addition can be performed using mixed addition formula if input points are given in affine coordinates or by using readdition formula otherwise.

It is possible to reduce the number of point additions by using window techniques[3] which need the precomputation of some first odd multiples of the point P. Table 2 recalls the number of point additions per bit of scalar when having from 0 (simple NAF) to 4 precomputed points. More than 4 points allows even better results but seems not practical in the context of constrained memory.

---

[3] By *window techniques* we mean the sliding window NAF and the Window NAF_w algorithms, see [19] for more details.

Table 2. Average number of point additions per bit of scalar using window NAF algorithms

Nb. of precomp. points	0	1	2	3	4
Precomputed points	–	$3P$	$3P, 5P$	$3P, 5P, 7P$	$3P, \ldots, 9P$
Point additions / bit	$1/3 \approx 0.33$	$1/4 = 0.25$	$2/9 \approx 0.22$	$1/5 = 0.20$	$4/21 \approx 0.19$

Right To Left Binary NAF Mixed Coordinates Multiplication. We recall here a very efficient algorithm performing right-to-left NAF scalar multiplication. Indeed this algorithm uses the fast modified Jacobian doubling formula which works for all curves – i.e. for all a – without needing the slow modified Jacobian addition.

This is achieved by reusing the idea of *mixed coordinates* scalar multiplication (i.e. two coordinate systems are used simultaneously) introduced by Cohen, Ono and Miyaji in [11]. The aim of this approach is to make the best use of two coordinates systems by processing some operations with one system and others with the second. Joye proposed in [21] to perform additions by using Jacobian coordinates, doublings – referred to as $*$ – by using modified Jacobian coordinates, and to compute the NAF representation of the scalar on-the-fly, cf. Alg. 2[4].

In the same way as their left-to-right counterpart benefits from precomputed points, right-to-left algorithms can be enhanced using window techniques if extra memory is available [35, 22]. In this case precomputations are replaced by postcomputations the cost of which is negligible for the considered window sizes and bit lengths.

Algorithm 2. Right-to-left binary NAF mixed coordinates multiplication [21]

INPUTS : $P = (X_1 : Y_1 : Z_1) \in \mathcal{C}(\mathbb{F}_p)$, k
OUTPUT : $k \cdot P$

---

1. $(X_2 : Y_2 : Z_2) \leftarrow (1 : 1 : 0)$
2. $(R_1 : R_2 : R_3 : R_4) \leftarrow (X_1 : Y_1 : Z_1 : aZ_1{}^4)$
3. **while** $k > 1$ **do**
       if $k \equiv 1 \mod 2$ **then**
           $u \leftarrow 2 - (k \mod 4)$
           $k \leftarrow k - u$
           if $u = 1$ **then**
               $(X_2 : Y_2 : Z_2) \leftarrow (X_2 : Y_2 : Z_2) + (R_1 : R_2 : R_3)$
           else
               $(X_2 : Y_2 : Z_2) \leftarrow (X_2 : Y_2 : Z_2) + (R_1 : -R_2 : R_3)$
       $k \leftarrow k/2$
       $(R_1 : R_2 : R_3 : R_4) \leftarrow 2 * (R_1 : R_2 : R_3 : R_4)$
4. $(X_2 : Y_2 : Z_2) \leftarrow (X_2 : Y_2 : Z_2) + (R_1 : R_2 : R_3)$
5. **return** $(X_2 : Y_2 : Z_2)$

---

[4] In Alg. 2, Jacobian addition is assumed to handle the special cases $P = \pm Q$, $P = \mathcal{O}$, $Q = \mathcal{O}$ as discussed in [21].

In [21] the author suggests protecting Alg. 2 against SSCA by using the so-called atomicity principle. We recall in the next section the principle of this SSCA countermeasure.

3   Atomicity

In this section we recall the principle of atomicity and its application to scalar multiplication. Other countermeasures exist in order to thwart SSCA such as regular algorithms [12, 24, 22] and unified formulas [7, 16]. However regular algorithms require costly extra curve operations, and unified formulas for Weierstrass curves over $\mathbb{F}_p$ – only known in the affine and homogeneous coordinate systems, see [7] – are also very costly. Therefore atomicity turns out to be more efficient in the context of embedded devices. It is thus natural to compare the efficiency of the two scalar multiplication methods presented in Section 2.2 protected by atomicity.

We recall in the following how atomicity is generally implemented on elliptic curves cryptography, for a complete atomicity principle description see [9].

3.1   State-of-the-Art

The atomicity principle has been introduced in [10]. This countermeasure consists in rewriting all the operations carried out through an algorithm into a sequence of identical *atomic patterns*. The purpose of this method is to defeat SSCA since an attacker has nothing to learn from an uniform succession of identical patterns.

In the case of scalar multiplications, a succession of point doublings and point additions is performed. Each of these operations being composed of field operations, the execution of a scalar multiplication can be seen as a succession of field operations. The atomicity consists here in rewriting the succession of field operations into a sequence of identical atomic patterns. The atomic pattern (1) proposed in [9] is composed of the following field operations: a multiplication, two additions and a negation. R_i's denote the crypto-coprocessor registers.

$$(1) \quad \begin{bmatrix} R_1 \leftarrow R_2 \cdot R_3 \\ R_4 \leftarrow R_5 + R_6 \\ R_7 \leftarrow -R_8 \\ R_9 \leftarrow R_{10} + R_{11} \end{bmatrix}$$

This choice relies on the observation that during the execution of point additions and point doublings, no more than two additions and one negation are required between two multiplications. Atomicity consists then of writing point addition and point doubling as sequences of this pattern – as many as there are field multiplications (including squarings).

Therefore this countermeasure induces two kinds of costs:

- Field squarings have to be performed as field multiplications. Then this approach is costly on embedded devices with dedicated hardware offering modular squaring operation, i.e. when $S/M < 1$.

– Dummy additions and negations are added. Their cost is generally negligible from a theoretical point of view but, as shown in Section 1.3, the cost of such operations must be taken into account in the context of embedded devices.

To reduce these costs, Longa proposed in his PhD thesis [27, Chap. 5] the two following atomic patterns in the context of Jacobian coordinates:

$$
(2)
\begin{bmatrix}
R_1 & \leftarrow R_2 \cdot R_3 \\
R_4 & \leftarrow -R_5 \\
R_6 & \leftarrow R_7 + R_8 \\
R_9 & \leftarrow R_{10} \cdot R_{11} \\
R_{12} & \leftarrow -R_{13} \\
R_{14} & \leftarrow R_{15} + R_{16} \\
R_{17} & \leftarrow R_{18} + R_{19}
\end{bmatrix}
\qquad
(3)
\begin{bmatrix}
R_1 & \leftarrow R_2{}^2 \\
R_3 & \leftarrow -R_4 \\
R_5 & \leftarrow R_6 + R_7 \\
R_8 & \leftarrow R_9 \cdot R_{10} \\
R_{11} & \leftarrow -R_{12} \\
R_{13} & \leftarrow R_{14} + R_{15} \\
R_{16} & \leftarrow R_{17} + R_{18}
\end{bmatrix}
$$

Compared with atomic pattern (1), these two patterns slightly reduce the number of field additions (gain of one addition every two multiplications). Moreover, atomic pattern (3) takes advantage of the squaring operation by replacing one multiplication out of two by a squaring.

In [27, Appendices] Longa expresses mixed affine-Jacobian addition formula as 6 atomic patterns (2) or (3) and fast doubling formula as 4 atomic patterns (2) or (3). It allows to perform an efficient left-to-right scalar multiplication using fast doubling and mixed affine-Jacobian addition protected with atomic patterns (2) or (3).

3.2 Atomic Left-to-Right Scalar Multiplication

We detail in the following why the Longa's left-to-right scalar multiplication using fast doubling and mixed affine-Jacobian addition is not compatible with our security constraints.

Defeating DSCA[5] requires the randomization of input point coordinates. This can be achieved by two means: projective coordinates randomization [12] and random curve isomorphism [23]. The first one allows to use the fast point doubling formula but prevents the use of mixed additions since input points $P, 3P, \ldots$ have their Z coordinate randomized. On the other hand the random curve isomorphism keeps input points in affine coordinates but randomizes a which thus imposes the use of the general doubling formula instead of the fast one.

Since Longa didn't investigate general doubling nor readdition, we present in Appendix A.1 the formulas to perform the former by using 5 atomic patterns (2) or (3) and in Appendix A.2 the formulas to perform the latter by using 7 atomic patterns (2). It seems very unlikely that one can express readdition using atomic pattern (3): since state-of-the-art readdition formula using the S–M trade-off requires 10 multiplications and 4 squarings, 3 other multiplications would have to be traded for squarings.

Therefore secure left-to-right scalar multiplication can be achieved either by using atomic pattern (2) and projective coordinates randomization which

---

[5] We include in DSCA the Template Attack on ECDSA from [29].

would involve fast doublings and readditions or by using atomic pattern (3) and random curve isomorphism which would involve general doublings and mixed additions.

3.3 Atomic Right-to-Left Mixed Scalar Multiplication

As suggested in [21] we protected Alg. 2 with atomicity. Since Longa's atomic patterns have not been designed for modified Jacobian doubling, we applied atomic pattern (1) to protect Alg. 2.

The decomposition of general Jacobian addition formula in 16 atomic patterns (1) is given in [9]. Since we haven't found it in the literature, we present in Appendix A.3 a decomposition of modified Jacobian doubling formula in 8 atomic patterns (1).

Projective coordinates randomization and random curve isomorphism countermeasures can both be applied to this solution.

3.4 Atomic Scalar Multiplication Algorithms Comparison

We compare in Table 3 the three previously proposed atomically protected algorithms. As discussed in Section 1.3 we fix $A/M = 0.2$ and $N/M = 0.1$. Costs are given as the average number of field multiplications per bit of scalar. Each cost is estimated for devices providing dedicated modular squaring – i.e. $S/M = 0.8$ – or not – i.e. $S/M = 1$. If extra memory is available, precomputations or postcomputations are respectively used to speed up left-to-right and right-to-left scalar multiplications. The pre/postcomputation cost is here not taken into account but is constant for every row of the chart.

It appears that in our context atomic left-to-right scalar multiplication using atomic pattern (2) with fast doubling and readditions is the fastest solution and is, on average for the 10 rows of Table 3, 10.5 % faster than atomic right-to-left mixed scalar multiplication using atomic pattern (1).

Table 3. Cost estimation in field multiplications per bit of the 3 atomically protected scalar multiplication algorithms with $A/M = 0.2$

Nb. of extra points	S/M	Left-to-right with (2)	Left-to-right with (3)	Right-to-left with (1)
0	0.8	17.7	18.2	20.0
	1	17.7	19.6	20.0
1	0.8	16.1	16.9	18.0
	1	16.1	18.2	18.0
2	0.8	15.6	16.5	17.3
	1	15.6	17.7	17.3
3	0.8	15.1	16.1	16.8
	1	15.1	17.4	16.8
4	0.8	14.9	16.0	16.6
	1	14.9	17.2	16.6

In the next section we present our contribution that aims at minimizing the atomicity cost by optimizing the atomic pattern. Then we apply it on the right-to-left mixed scalar multiplication algorithm since efficient patterns are already known for the two left-to-right variants.

4   Atomic Pattern Improvement

We propose here a twofold atomicity improvement method: firstly, we take advantage of the fact that a squaring can be faster than a multiplication. Secondly, we reduce the number of additions and negations used in atomic patterns in order to increase the efficiency of scalar multiplication.

4.1   First Part: Atomic Pattern Extension

As explained previously, our first idea is to reduce the efficiency loss due to field squarings turned into multiplications.

Method Presentation. Let O_1 and O_2 be two atomically written operations (point addition and doubling in our case) such that they require m and n atomic patterns respectively. Let us assume that a sub-operation o_1 from the atomic pattern (field multiplication in our case) could sometimes be replaced by another preferred sub-operation o_2 (such as field squaring). Let us eventually assume that O_1 requires at least m' sub-operations o_1 (along with $m - m'$ sub-operations o_2) and O_2 requires at least n' sub-operations o_1 (along with $n - n'$ sub-operations o_2).

Then, if $d = \gcd(m, n) > 1$, let e represents the greatest positive integer satisfying:

$$e \cdot \frac{m}{d} \leq m - m' \quad \text{and} \quad e \cdot \frac{n}{d} \leq n - n' \ . \tag{8}$$

Since 0 is obviously a solution, it is certain that e is defined. If $e > 0$ we can now apply the following method. Let a new pattern be defined with $d - e$ original atomic patterns followed by e atomic patterns with o_2 replacing o_1 – the order can be modified at convenience.

It is now possible to express operations O_1 and O_2 with m/d and n/d new patterns respectively. Using the new pattern in O_1 (resp. O_2) instead of the old one allows replacing $e \cdot m/d$ (resp. $e \cdot n/d$) sub-operations o_1 by o_2.

Application to Mixed Coordinates Scalar Multiplication. Applying this method to Alg. 2 yields the following result: O_1 being the Jacobian projective addition, O_2 the modified Jacobian projective doubling, o_1 the field multiplication and o_2 the field squaring, then $m{=}16$, $m'{=}11$, $n = 8$, $n' = 3$, $d = 8$ and $e = 2$. Therefore we define a new temporary atomic pattern composed of 8 patterns (1) where 2 multiplications are replaced by squarings. We thus have

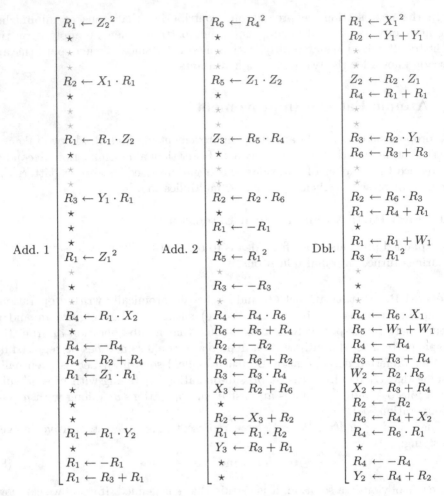

Fig. 2. Extended atomic pattern applied to Jacobian projective addition and modified Jacobian projective doubling

one fourth of the field multiplications carried out as field squarings. This extended pattern would have to be repeated twice for an addition and once for a doubling.

We applied this new approach in Fig. 2 where atomic general Jacobian addition and modified Jacobian doubling are rewritten in order to take advantage of the squarings. We denote by $\star$ the dummy field additions and negations that must be added to complete atomic patterns.

4.2 Second Part: Atomic Pattern Cleaning-Up

In a second step we aim at reducing the number of dummy field operations. In Fig. 2, we identified by $\star$ the operations that are never used in Add.1, Add.2

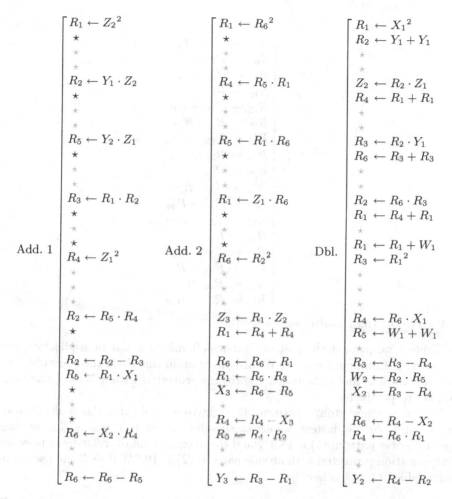

Fig. 3. Improved arrangement of field operations in extended atomic pattern from Fig. 2

and Dbl. These field operations may then be removed saving up 5 field additions and 3 field negations per pattern occurrence.

However, we found out that field operations could be rearranged in order to maximize the number of rows over the three columns composed of dummy operations only. We then merge negations and additions into subtractions when possible. This improvement is depicted in Fig. 3.

This final optimization now allows us to save up 6 field additions and to remove the 8 field negations per pattern occurrence. One may note that no more dummy operation remains in modified Jacobian doubling. We thus believe that our resulting atomic pattern (4) is optimal for this operation:

$$(4) \begin{bmatrix} R_1 & \leftarrow & R_2{}^2 \\ R_3 & \leftarrow & R_4 + R_5 \\ R_6 & \leftarrow & R_7 \cdot R_8 \\ R_9 & \leftarrow & R_{10} + R_{11} \\ R_{12} & \leftarrow & R_{13} \cdot R_{14} \\ R_{15} & \leftarrow & R_{16} + R_{17} \\ R_{18} & \leftarrow & R_{19} \cdot R_{20} \\ R_{21} & \leftarrow & R_{22} + R_{23} \\ R_{24} & \leftarrow & R_{25} + R_{26} \\ R_{27} & \leftarrow & R_{28}{}^2 \\ R_{29} & \leftarrow & R_{30} \cdot R_{31} \\ R_{32} & \leftarrow & R_{33} + R_{34} \\ R_{35} & \leftarrow & R_{36} - R_{37} \\ R_{38} & \leftarrow & R_{39} \cdot R_{40} \\ R_{41} & \leftarrow & R_{42} - R_{43} \\ R_{44} & \leftarrow & R_{45} - R_{46} \\ R_{47} & \leftarrow & R_{48} \cdot R_{49} \\ R_{50} & \leftarrow & R_{51} - R_{52} \end{bmatrix}$$

4.3   Theoretical Gain

In Table 4 we present the cost of right-to-left mixed scalar multiplication protected with atomic pattern (4). We also draw up in this chart the gains obtained over left-to-right and right-to-left algorithms protected with atomic patterns (2) and (1) respectively.

Due to our new atomic pattern (4), right-to-left mixed scalar multiplication turns out to be the fastest among these solutions in every cases. The average speed-up over pattern (1) is 18.3 % and the average gain over left-to-right scalar multiplication protected with atomic pattern (2) is 10.6 % if dedicated squaring is available or 7.0 % otherwise.

Table 4. Costs estimation in field multiplications per bit of Alg. 2 protected with improved pattern (4) and comparison with two others methods presented in Table 3 assuming $A/M = 0.2$

Nb. of extra points	S/M	Right-to-left with (4)	Gain over l.-to-r. with (2)	Gain over r.-to-l. with (1)
0	0.8	16.0 M	9.6 %	20.0 %
0	1	16.7 M	5.6 %	16.5 %
1	0.8	14.4 M	10.6 %	20.0 %
1	1	15.0 M	6.8 %	16.7 %
2	0.8	13.9 M	10.9 %	19.7 %
2	1	14.4 M	7.7 %	16.8 %
3	0.8	13.4 M	11.3 %	20.2 %
3	1	14.0 M	7.3 %	16.7 %
4	0.8	13.3 M	10.7 %	19.9 %
4	1	13.8 M	7.4 %	16.9 %

Table 5. Characteristics of our implementation of the atomically protected 192-bit scalar multiplication on an 8-bit chip with a 32-bit crypto-coprocessor

Timing	RAM size	Code size
29.6 ms	412 B	3.5 KB

4.4 Experimental Results

We have implemented Alg. 2 – without any window method – protected with the atomic pattern (1) on one hand and with our improved atomic pattern (4) on the other hand. We used a chip equipped with an 8-bit CPU running at 30 MHz and with a 32-bit crypto-coprocessor running at 50 MHz. In particular, this crypto-coprocessor provides a dedicated modular squaring. The characteristics of the corresponding implementation are given in Table 5. On the NIST P-192 curve [17] we obtained a practical speed-up of about 14.5 % to be compared to the predicted 20 %. This difference can be explained by the extra software processing required in the scalar multiplication loop management, especially the on-the-fly NAF decomposition of the scalar in an SSCA-resistant way.

When observing the side-channel leakage of our implementation we obtained the signal presented in Fig. 4. Atomic patterns comprising 8 modular multiplications and several additions/subtractions can easily be identified.

Fig. 4. Side-channel leakage observed during the execution of our scalar multiplication implementation showing a sequence of atomic patterns

5   Conclusion

In this paper, we propose a new atomic pattern for scalar multiplication on elliptic curves over $\mathbb{F}_p$ and detail our method for atomic pattern improvement. To achieve this goal, two ways are explored. Firstly we maximize the use of squarings to replace multiplications since the latter are slower. Secondly we minimize the use of field additions and negations since they induce a non-negligible penalty. In particular, we point out that the classical hypothesis taken by scalar multiplication designers to neglect the cost of additions/subtractions in $\mathbb{F}_p$ is not valid when focusing on embedded devices such as smart cards.

In this context our method provides an average 18.3 % improvement for the right-to-left mixed scalar multiplication from [21] protected with the atomic pattern from [9]. It also provides an average 10.6 % gain over the fastest algorithm identified before our contribution if dedicated squaring is available. Furthermore, though the topic of this paper is right-to-left scalar multiplication, our atomic pattern improvement method can be generically used to speed up atomically protected algorithms.

In conclusion we recommend that algorithm designers, addressing the scope of embedded devices, take into account additions and subtractions cost when these operations are heavily used in an algorithm. Moreover the issue of designing efficient atomic patterns should be considered when proposing non regular sensitive algorithms.

Acknowledgments

The authors are very grateful to Yannick Sierra for pointing them out the improvement using the subtractions leading to the efficient patterns of Fig. 3. The authors would also like to thank Christophe Clavier, Sean Commercial, Emmanuelle Dottax, Emmanuel Prouff, Matthieu Rivain and the anonymous referees of Cardis 2010 for their helpful comments on the preliminary versions of this paper.

References

1. ANSI X9.62–2005. Public Key Cryptography for The Financial Service Industry: The Elliptic Curve Digital Signature Algorithm (ECDSA). American National Standards Institute, November 16 (2005)
2. ANSI X9.63–2001. Public Key Cryptography for The Financial Service Industry: Key Agreement and Key Transport Using Elliptic Curve Cryptography. American National Standards Institute, November 20 (2001)
3. Arno, S., Wheeler, F.: Signed digit representations of minimal Hamming weight. IEEE Transactions on Computers 42(8), 1007–1009 (1993)
4. Bernstein, D.J., Birkner, P., Joye, M., Lange, T., Peters, C.: Twisted edwards curves. In: Vaudenay, S. (ed.) AFRICACRYPT 2008. LNCS, vol. 5023, pp. 389–405. Springer, Heidelberg (2008)
5. Bernstein, D.J., Lange, T.: Explicit-formulas database, http://www.hyperelliptic.org/EFD
6. Bernstein, D.J., Lange, T.: Faster addition and doubling on elliptic curves. Cryptology ePrint Archive, Report 2007/286 (2007), http://eprint.iacr.org/
7. Brier, E., Joye, M.: Weierstraß Elliptic Curves and Side-Channel Attacks. In: Naccache, D., Paillier, P. (eds.) PKC 2002. LNCS, vol. 2274, pp. 335–345. Springer, Heidelberg (2002)

8. Brown, M., Hankerson, D., López, J., Menezes, A.: Software Implementation of the NIST Elliptic Curves Over Prime Fields. In: Naccache, D. (ed.) CT-RSA 2001. LNCS, vol. 2020, pp. 250–265. Springer, Heidelberg (2001)
9. Chevallier-Mames, B., Ciet, M., Joye, M.: Low-cost Solutions for Preventing Simple Side-Channel Analysis: Side-Channel Atomicity. IEEE Transactions on Computers 53(6), 760–768 (2004)
10. Chevallier-Mames, B., Joye, M.: Procédé cryptographique protégé contre les attaques de type á canal caché. French patent, FR 28 38 210 (April 2002)
11. Cohen, H., Ono, T., Miyaji, A.: Efficient Elliptic Curve Exponentiation Using Mixed Coordinate. In: Ohta, K., Dingyi, P. (eds.) ASIACRYPT 1998. LNCS, vol. 1514, pp. 51–65. Springer, Heidelberg (1998)
12. Coron, J.-S.: Resistance against Differential Power Analysis for Elliptic Curve Cryptosystems. In: Koç, Ç.K., Paar, C. (eds.) CHES 1999. LNCS, vol. 1717, pp. 292–302. Springer, Heidelberg (1999)
13. Dimitrov, V., Imbert, L., Mishra, P.: Efficient and Secure Elliptic Curve Point Multiplication using Double-Base Chains. In: Roy, B. (ed.) ASIACRYPT 2005. LNCS, vol. 3788, pp. 59–78. Springer, Heidelberg (2005)
14. ECC Brainpool. ECC Brainpool Standard Curves and Curve Generation. BSI, v. 1.0 (2005), http://www.ecc-brainpool.org
15. ECC Brainpool. ECC Brainpool Standard Curves and Curve Generation. BSI, Internet Draft v. 3 (2009),
http://tools.ietf.org/html/draft-lochter-pkix-brainpool-ecc-03
16. Edwards, H.M.: A normal form for elliptic curves. Bulletin of the American Mathematical Society 44, 393–422 (2007)
17. FIPS PUB 186-3. Digital Signature Standard. National Institute of Standards and Technology, March 13 (2006), Draft
18. Großschädl, J., Avanzi, R.M., Savas, E., Tillich, S.: Energy-Efficient Software Implementation of Long Integer Modular Arithmetic. In: Rao, J.R., Sunar, B. (eds.) CHES 2005. LNCS, vol. 3659, pp. 75–90. Springer, Heidelberg (2005)
19. Hankerson, D., Menezes, A., Vanstone, S.: Guide to Elliptic Curve Cryptography, Springer Professional Computing Series (January 2003)
20. Hesse, O.: Uber die Elimination der Variabeln aus drei algebraischen Gleichungen vom zweiten Grade mit zwei Variabeln. Journal für die reine und angewandte Mathematik 10, 68–96 (1844)
21. Joye, M.: Fast Point Multiplication on Elliptic Curves Without Precomputation. In: von zur Gathen, J., Imaña, J.L., Koç, Ç.K. (eds.) WAIFI 2008. LNCS, vol. 5130, pp. 36–46. Springer, Heidelberg (2008)
22. Joye, M.: Highly regular m-ary powering ladders. In: Jacobson, M.J., Rijmen, V., Safavi-Naini, R. (eds.) SAC 2009. LNCS, pp. 135–147. Springer, Heidelberg (2009)
23. Joye, M., Tymen, C.: Protections against Differential Analysis for Elliptic Curve Cryptography. In: Koç, Ç.K., Naccache, D., Paar, C. (eds.) CHES 2001. LNCS, vol. 2162, pp. 386–400. Springer, Heidelberg (2001)
24. Joye, M., Yen, S.-M.: The Montgomery Powering Ladder. In: Kaliski Jr., B.S., Koç, Ç.K., Paar, C. (eds.) CHES 2002. LNCS, vol. 2523, pp. 291–302. Springer, Heidelberg (2003)
25. Kocher, P.: Timing Attacks on Implementations of Diffie-Hellman, RSA, DSS, and Other Systems. In: Koblitz, N. (ed.) CRYPTO 1996. LNCS, vol. 1109, pp. 104–113. Springer, Heidelberg (1996)
26. Kocher, P., Jaffe, J., Jun, B.: Differential Power Analysis. In: Wiener, M. (ed.) CRYPTO 1999. LNCS, vol. 1666, pp. 388–397. Springer, Heidelberg (1999)

27. Longa, P.: Accelerating the Scalar Multiplication on Elliptic Curve Cryptosystems over Prime Fields. PhD thesis, School of Information Technology and Engineering, University of Ottawa (2007)
28. Longa, P., Miri, A.: New Multibase Non-Adjacent Form Scalar Multiplication and its Application to Elliptic Curve Cryptosystems (extended version). Cryptology ePrint Archive, Report 2008/052 (2008), http://eprint.iacr.org/
29. Medwed, M., Oswald, E.: Template attacks on ECDSA. Cryptology ePrint Archive, Report 2008/081 (2008), http://eprint.iacr.org/
30. Meloni, N.: New point addition formulae for ECC applications. In: Carlet, C., Sunar, B. (eds.) WAIFI 2007. LNCS, vol. 4547, pp. 189–201. Springer, Heidelberg (2007)
31. Meloni, N., Hasan, M.A.: Elliptic Curve Scalar Multiplication Combining Yao's Algorithm and Double Bases. In: Clavier, C., Gaj, K. (eds.) CHES 2009. LNCS, vol. 5747, pp. 304–316. Springer, Heidelberg (2009)
32. Montgomery, P.: Speeding the Pollard and Elliptic Curve Methods of Factorization. Mathematics of Computation 48, 243–264 (1987)
33. SP 800-78-1. Cryptographic Algorithms and Key Sizes for Personal Identity Verification. National Institute of Standards and Technology (August 2007)
34. TR-03111. Elliptic Curve Cryptography Based on ISO 15946. Federal Office for Information Security (BSI), February 14 (2007)
35. Yao, A.C.-C.: On the Evaluation of Powers. SIAM Journal on Computing 5(1), 100–103 (1976)

A Atomic Formulas

A.1 Atomic General Doubling Using Pattern (2) or (3)

The decomposition of a general – i.e. for all a – doubling in Jacobian coordinates using atomic pattern (3) is depicted hereafter. The corresponding decomposition using atomic pattern (2) can straightforwardly be obtained by replacing every squaring by a multiplication using the same operand twice.

The input point is given as (X_1, Y_1, Z_1) and the result is written into the point (X_2, Y_2, Z_2). Four intermediate registers, R_1 to R_4, are used.

$$
1\begin{bmatrix} R_1 \leftarrow X_1{}^2 \\ \star \\ R_3 \leftarrow R_1 + R_1 \\ R_2 \leftarrow Z_1 \cdot Z_1 \\ \star \\ R_1 \leftarrow R_1 + R_3 \\ R_4 \leftarrow X_1 + X_1 \end{bmatrix}
\qquad
4\begin{bmatrix} R_2 \leftarrow R_1{}^2 \\ \star \\ \star \\ R_4 \leftarrow R_4 \cdot R_3 \\ R_4 \leftarrow -R_4 \\ R_2 \leftarrow R_2 + R_4 \\ X_2 \leftarrow R_2 + R_4 \end{bmatrix}
$$

$$
2\begin{bmatrix} R_2 \leftarrow R_2{}^2 \\ \star \\ \star \\ R_2 \leftarrow a \cdot R_2 \\ \star \\ R_1 \leftarrow R_1 + R_2 \\ R_2 \leftarrow Y_1 + Y_1 \end{bmatrix}
\qquad
5\begin{bmatrix} R_3 \leftarrow R_3{}^2 \\ R_1 \leftarrow -R_1 \\ R_4 \leftarrow X_2 + R_4 \\ R_1 \leftarrow R_1 \cdot R_4 \\ R_3 \leftarrow -R_3 \\ R_3 \leftarrow R_3 + R_3 \\ Y_2 \leftarrow R_3 + R_1 \end{bmatrix}
$$

$$
3\begin{bmatrix} R_3 \leftarrow Y_1{}^2 \\ \star \\ \star \\ Z_2 \leftarrow Z_1 \cdot R_2 \\ \star \\ R_3 \leftarrow R_3 + R_3 \\ \star \end{bmatrix}
$$

A.2   Atomic Readdition Using Pattern (2)

The decomposition of a readdition in Jacobian coordinates using atomic pattern (2) is depicted hereafter.

The input points are given as (X_1, Y_1, Z_1), (X_2, Y_2, Z_2) and the result is written into the point (X_3, Y_3, Z_3). Seven intermediate registers, R_1 to R_7, are used.

$$
1 \begin{bmatrix} R_1 \leftarrow Y_2 \cdot Z_1{}^3 \\ \star \\ \star \\ R_2 \leftarrow Y_1 \cdot Z_2 \\ \star \\ \star \\ \star \end{bmatrix}
\qquad
5 \begin{bmatrix} R_5 \leftarrow R_5 \cdot R_3 \\ \star \\ \star \\ R_3 \leftarrow Z_2 \cdot R_3 \\ \star \\ \star \\ \star \end{bmatrix}
$$

$$
2 \begin{bmatrix} R_3 \leftarrow Z_2 \cdot Z_2 \\ \star \\ \star \\ R_4 \leftarrow R_2 \cdot R_3 \\ R_5 \leftarrow -R_1 \\ R_4 \leftarrow R_4 + R_5 \\ \star \end{bmatrix}
\qquad
6 \begin{bmatrix} R_7 \leftarrow R_4 \cdot R_4 \\ \star \\ \star \\ Z_3 \leftarrow R_3 \cdot Z_1 \\ R_5 \leftarrow -R_5 \\ R_7 \leftarrow R_7 + R_6 \\ X_3 \leftarrow R_7 + R_5 \end{bmatrix}
$$

$$
3 \begin{bmatrix} R_2 \leftarrow X_2 \cdot Z_1{}^2 \\ \star \\ \star \\ R_3 \leftarrow X_1 \cdot R_3 \\ R_5 \leftarrow -R_2 \\ R_3 \leftarrow R_3 + R_5 \\ \star \end{bmatrix}
\qquad
7 \begin{bmatrix} R_3 \leftarrow R_1 \cdot R_5 \\ R_1 \leftarrow -X_3 \\ R_2 \leftarrow R_2 + R_1 \\ R_1 \leftarrow R_2 \cdot R_4 \\ \star \\ Y_3 \leftarrow R_1 + R_3 \\ \star \end{bmatrix}
$$

$$
4 \begin{bmatrix} R_5 \leftarrow R_3 \cdot R_3 \\ \star \\ \star \\ R_2 \leftarrow R_2 \cdot R_5 \\ R_6 \leftarrow -R_2 \\ R_6 \leftarrow R_6 + R_6 \\ \star \end{bmatrix}
$$

A.3 Atomic Modified Jacobian Coordinates Doubling Using Pattern (1)

The decomposition of a doubling in modified Jacobian coordinates using atomic pattern (1) is depicted hereafter.

The input point is given as (X_1, Y_1, Z_1) and the result is written into the point (X_2, Y_2, Z_2). Six intermediate registers, R_1 to R_6, are used.

$$
1 \begin{bmatrix} R_1 \leftarrow X_1 \cdot X_1 \\ R_2 \leftarrow Y_1 + Y_1 \\ \star \\ \star \end{bmatrix}
\qquad
5 \begin{bmatrix} R_3 \leftarrow R_1 \cdot R_1 \\ \star \\ \star \\ \star \end{bmatrix}
$$

$$
2 \begin{bmatrix} Z_2 \leftarrow R_2 \cdot Z_1 \\ R_4 \leftarrow R_1 + R_1 \\ \star \\ \star \end{bmatrix}
\qquad
6 \begin{bmatrix} R_4 \leftarrow R_6 \cdot X_1 \\ R_5 \leftarrow W_1 + W_1 \\ R_4 \leftarrow -R_4 \\ R_3 \leftarrow R_3 + R_4 \end{bmatrix}
$$

$$
3 \begin{bmatrix} R_3 \leftarrow R_2 \cdot Y_1 \\ R_6 \leftarrow R_3 + R_3 \\ \star \\ \star \end{bmatrix}
\qquad
7 \begin{bmatrix} W_2 \leftarrow R_2 \cdot R_5 \\ X_2 \leftarrow R_3 + R_4 \\ R_2 \leftarrow -R_2 \\ R_6 \leftarrow R_4 + X_2 \end{bmatrix}
$$

$$
4 \begin{bmatrix} R_2 \leftarrow R_6 \cdot R_3 \\ R_1 \leftarrow R_4 + R_1 \\ \star \\ R_1 \leftarrow R_1 + W_1 \end{bmatrix}
\qquad
8 \begin{bmatrix} R_4 \leftarrow R_6 \cdot R_1 \\ \star \\ R_4 \leftarrow -R_4 \\ Y_2 \leftarrow R_4 + R_2 \end{bmatrix}
$$

Key-Study to Execute Code Using Demand Paging and NAND Flash at Smart Card Scale

Geoffroy Cogniaux and Gilles Grimaud

LIFL, CNRS UMR 8022, University of Lille I. INRIA, Nord-Europe, France

Abstract. Nowadays, the desire to embed more applications in systems as small as Smart Cards or sensors is growing. However, physical limitations of these systems, like very small main memory, and their cost of production make it very difficult to achieve. One solution is to execute code from a secondary memory, cheaper, denser, but slower, as NAND Flash. Solutions based on Demand Paging and using a cache in main memory, began to be proposed and implemented in the domain of mobile phones, but consume too much RAM yet, compared to what a Smart Card can provide. In this paper, we show that we can dramatically increase performance by reducing the size of pages in the cache. This solution then allows a more intelligent access to the NAND. We also show that our solution allows to use Demand Paging within the limits of Smart Cards memories, where a conventional approach, offering too low bandwidth, makes code execution impossible from this kind of secondary memory. Finally, we present important future keys to optimize our proposal even more, and specially off-line code specialization aware of NAND characteristics and advanced cache properties.

1 Introduction

Nowadays, the desire to embed more applications in systems as small as Smart Cards or sensors is growing. However, challenges are not the same between a mobile phone and a Smart Card. Beyond the extreme physical constraints, as only a few kilobytes of RAM and not much more storage space for code, a Smart Card also has an extremely restrictive specification in regard to costs of production or energy consumption. It is not conceivable in these targets to run programs more expensive in space or energy only by inflating the hardware. The possible solution is to replace or at least extend the code storage capacity with another hardware with lower cost per bit of storage.

Generally, NOR flash is used as code storage space on systems such as Smart Cards. The NAND flash is another type of flash memory with different properties. This memory is also nonvolatile, has greater density, and therefore allows to embed more data than the NOR on a same silicon size, near 60%. The temptation is then huge to replace NOR by NAND. Unfortunately, the NAND, although coming with faster writings, is much slower to perform readings, and is not accessible byte per byte as NOR interface but per pages. This access mode causes incompressible latency and *a priori* excludes random accesses. NAND is then

D. Gollmann, J.-L. Lanet, J. Iguchi-Cartigny (Eds.): CARDIS 2010, LNCS 6035, pp. 102–117, 2010.

most often used to support a file system and so far, its development has mainly been driven for this purpose.

Executing code from memories such as NAND is made possible by the introduction of a cache in main memory or the use of SRAM buffers added directly into the NAND. This new category is called hybrid Flash. However, the presence of a dedicated RAM space is not sufficient to close the gaps between NAND and NOR. A cache manager will then have to be smart enough to hide the latency of the NAND and ensure fluidity when providing instructions to a processor or a virtual machine. In this context of paged memory, the Demand Paging is the most popular caching strategy because it offers the best balance between overall performance and reduced cache space. The idea of this method is to access slow hardware only in cases of extreme necessity and try to keep in cache as much data as possible, generally sorted by relevance of future uses. Of course, knowing if a cached data will be finally useful or not, is a non-trivial problem.

If hardware researches are working to provide more efficient device to reduce the latency of the NAND, at software level, greater efforts are usually done on the optimization of the page replacement policy in the cache. But in systems with tiny main memory, it remains to be seen how many bytes to sacrifice for a cache, in addition to the vital needs of the system. But beyond that, the main problem with these systems will be to know if this sacrifice will be enough to perform code execution from this slow memory.

The remaining of this paper is organized as follow: Section 2 describes research motivations and issues. Section 3 lists related works. Section 4 discusses a new way to use Demand Paging and NAND flash memory to use it in Smart Card too. Section 5 presents experimental results on reading performance. Finally, section 6 will discuss about best cache page size and its direct interactions with page content for future optimizations.

2   Motivations Around Smart Card and Flash Memories Characteristics

In this paper, we focus on very small embedded systems such as Smart Cards or sensors. This kind of devices has very restrictive specifications and hardware constraints aiming to reduce production cost and energy consumption dramatically. Despite their size, industrial trends would like to embed more applications and bigger programs in those targets.

Smart Card and sensors are mainly built around an 8 or 16 bits processor and generaly between 1 and 8KB of RAM. Code is then executed from flash memory such as NOR, reserving RAM for volatile data such as execution stack and variables. Thus, executing bigger applications will require more NOR, which would also be too expensive in energy, size and production cost. As an alternative, read-only code could be executed from a cheaper and denser flash memory such as NAND.

NOR is byte-wise and has a good and constant performance in random readings. With these properties, NOR can support XIP (execute-In-Place), to run programs directly, without any intermediate copy in main memory. The NAND flash has better writing performance and is cheaper and denser. It can store more informations on same die size and thus has a lower cost per bit. But NAND is much more slower in readings. NAND is block-wise [1]. The smallest read and write unit is the page that can store 512 or 2048 bytes. To read a byte randomly, the corresponding page must be first completly loaded in the hardware NAND data register. Only after this long time consuming operation, bytes can be fetched sequentially from the register until the wanted one is reached. In those conditions (Random worst case column of Table 1), NAND is not designed to support intensive random readings and is widely used to support file systems, designed with a per-block logic and almost always accessed sequentially.

Table 1. NAND characteristics aligned on a bus at 33MHz and 8bits wide

Device	Page Size	Latency	Byte Fetch	Page Fetch	Min[1]	Max[2]
K9F1208Q0B [3]	512 bytes	$15\mu s$	50ns	$25.6\mu s$	0.02	12.03
MT29F2G08A-ACWP [4]	2048 bytes	$25\mu s$	40ns	$81.94\mu s$	0.01	18.27
NOR Flash	-	-	40ns	-	-	23.84

Table 2. NAND characteristics aligned on a bus at 54MHz and 16bits wide

Device	Page Size	Latency	Byte Fetch	Page Fetch	Min[1]	Max[2]
K9F1208Q0B [3]	512 bytes	$15\mu s$	50ns	$25.6\mu s$	0.02	12.03
MT29F2G08A-ACWP [4]	2048 bytes	$25\mu s$	20ns	$40.9\mu s$	0.01	29.61
NOR Flash	-	-	9ns	-	-	108

[1] Worst Case: random reading bandwidth in MB/s
[2] Sequential reading Bandwidth in MB/s
[3] http://www.samsung.com
[4] http://www.micron.com

3 Related Works

The studies of code execution from NAND flash can be classified in four categories. In the first place, we can distinguish pure hardware solutions since NAND is not a well-adapted device to do random readings, and so far XIP [2, 3, 4, 5]. [6, 7, 8, 9, 10, 11, 12, 13] proposed software solutions using already available NAND, even if software is often limited to firmware here.

Besides, we can split both categories into two others: one aiming to propose an universal solution working with any program, and another one aiming to find best performance dedicating solutions to one program or one type of programs such as multimedia streaming.

In systems with limited SRAM size, copying the entire program in main memory is not possible. Instead, hardware and software researchers have worked on solutions using a cache managed by the Demand Paging strategy. It can be either in existing main memory or in SRAM integrated directly in the NAND device [2], resulting in a new one, now called hybrid NAND.

Generally, hardware based solutions are coming with a local SRAM cache managed by new circuits but many parts of the implementation are performed by the firmware. The main purpose to introduce a SRAM and a cache in the NAND device is to provide an interface similar to the NOR one, which is byte-wise and randomly accessible. But as explained in [10], in already available hybrid NAND such as OneNAND[TM] by Samsung[14], the integrated SRAM is not a cache yet, and doesn't offer enough performance to actually execute code[1]. If OneNAND offers a double buffers mechanism to access stored data more randomly by overlapping some internal NAND accesses and their latency, it doesn't hide all of them. [11, 15] propose a software-based solution to use this buffer as a true but secondary cache in relation with a higher level cache in main memory. When a NAND page is accessed more often than a static threshold, this page is promoted from in-NAND cache to main memory cache which allows faster accesses.

Most of the time, solutions aim at improving or adapting the replacement policy needed by the Demand Paging strategy because researches [16] showed that a gap always exists up to the theoretical best one, known as MIN [17]. When a cache is full and when the CPU tries to read instructions not present in cache yet, the new page loaded from the NAND must overwrite an existing one in the cache. Then, the replacement policy must decide which one to erase, hoping that this choice will be relevant for the future execution of the program. In the studied works, this choice may be based on priorities [2], pinning [9, 12], derived from well-known policies like LRU (Least Recently Used) [8, 9, 11],... , or using a completely new approach [4] by embedding a trace-based prediction tree within the NAND device, with good performance (being close to MIN behaviour) but with a RAM overhead, and universality lost.

All of these proposals have mobile phones as smallest devices. In this paper, we take an interest in extreme constraints of Smart Cards-sized devices with very small SRAM space to manage a cache (less than 4KB). We also want to evaluate performance behind very slow bus (33MHz, 8bits wide). Because in such devices, reserving SRAM bytes for a dedicated process represents a strong sacrifice, and buses are well-known bottlenecks. To successfully execute code from NAND-like memory, we will have to tune implementation to reduce this sacrifice, but as a first issue, it remains to be seen whether this sacrifice will be enough to reach abilities, before performance.

4   Demand Paging at Smart Card Scale

4.1   Conventional Demand Paging Issue in Smart Card

In conventional Demand Paging used in literature, a page in the cache has the same size that a physical NAND page, since reading a NAND page has a very

---

[1] Though it can execute a boot loader.

high cost, due to long access latency. An efficient Demand Paging and its replacement policy are aware of this problem and access the managed slow memory as less as possible.

Smart Cards, mobile sensors, and other small embedded systems have constraints that make conventional Demand Paging unusable in their context because of low performance. For instance, if we consider a system with only 2KB of RAM available for a cache, and a NAND with a page size of 2KB, there will be only one page in the cache. With this assumption, a replacement policy is useless, and the read bandwidth will be close to worst case of Table 1, unless executed program is only 2KB.

It can be said that the main problem with NAND is its long access latency. But, in our context, hiding latencies is not enough. We have explained there are two steps for bytes reading from NAND : a load phase and a sequential fetch phase. If the load phase has a good attention in research and industry, the second topic has not been well investigated yet, since, in mobile phone, authors considered good clock and bandwidth for buses. But, even if we have a NAND claiming to have a 108MB/s bandwidth and hiding all latencies, we will not have a real bandwidth faster than the bus one and copying a complete NAND page into SRAM cache may take a long time too (5th column of table 1).

4.2 Performance Is under Influence

A parameter may influence another and an accurate assessment must take these interactions into account. Into a graph of influence (Fig. 1), we listed and put physical and logical parameters face to intermediate results that are necessary for a proper assessment of our study. They can be classified into 4 categories:

- physical parameters related to hardware (rectangle boxes)
- logical parameters configuring the cache (inversed house boxes)
- development toolkit, languages, compilers, ... (ellipse boxes)
- intermediate statistics influencing the overall bandwidth (rounded boxes)

As shown in Fig. 1, page fault or MISS causes a series of transactions that affect the overall throughput. To make an instruction not present in cache available, the cache manager must load the new page into the hardware NAND data register, read the content of this register through the bus, then copy this page into the cache and finally actually read the requested instruction. (For short, in the remaining of this paper, we will refer to these four steps as *load*, *fetch*, *write*, and *read* steps). A MISS is itself influenced by the cache size (in pages count), the size of a cache page, the content of this page and of course the replacement policy. The Demand Paging is not only dependent on the way it is managed. If a replacement policy follows locality principle [18], only page size and page content create conditions for a better locality.

A compiled program is not a random series of instructions but follows some patterns of instructions and controls flows. The analysis of these patterns shows that a program has two interesting features grouped under the concept of the

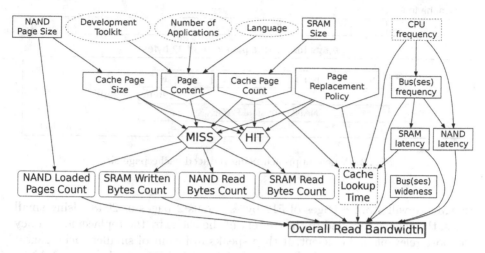

Fig. 1. Parameters influence graph

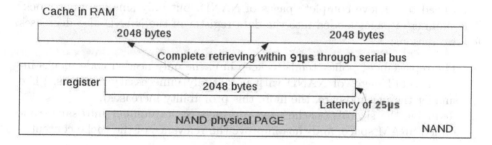

Fig. 2. Conventional approach of Demand Paging

locality principle [18]. A program tends to use instructions located in the same memory area. This is the principle of spatial locality and this area is therefore strongly related to the size of a page. A program also tends to reuse instructions that have already served in the recent past, typically in a loop. This is the temporal locality. To help a replacement policy to use more efficiently the temporal principle, blocks of code should be grouped by affinity, and therefore in the same page of NAND to avoid or reduce page faults.

4.3 Performance Improvement without Replacement Policy Change or Redesign

Regardless of the manner in which it is implemented and which policy is used, if we analyse the behaviour of the Demand Paging using NAND with small pages compared to NAND with big pages, we can see that the smallest achieves best performance. First because it has shorter access latency, and second because at the same cache size we can store more pages in it, for instance within 4KB of

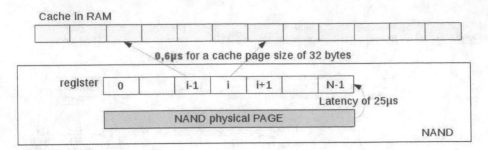

Fig. 3. A new approach using reduced cache page size

SRAM, we will store 8 pages of 512 bytes versus 2 pages of 2048. Using small pages, the changes applied to the content of the cache by the replacement policy are more relevant and efficient. It then speaks in favour of smaller cache pages.

If we reduce the size of a cache page, the number of bytes fetched from NAND, put on the bus, and then written into the SRAM cache decreases because there is no need to retrieve complete pages of NAND, but only smaller inner-block. The number of pages loaded into the data register of the NAND also decreases for two reasons:

1. The replacement policy tends to keep in cache only needed code blocks instead of full pages of NAND with potentially unnecessary methods. (The smaller the methods are, the more this probability increases).
2. Reducing the size of a cache page can increase its number into same consumed SRAM space, and thus improve the relevance of the cache content.

Reducing the cache page size introduces another advantage, completely useless until now if a page of cache and a page of NAND have the same size. Without hardware changes, we can now consider the data register as a real buffer. We have seen that for a conventional NAND (non-hybrid), it was sequentially accessible. Let us consider now a page of NAND with 512 bytes, a data register with the same capacity and a page cache size of 64 bytes, which divides the data register into 8 consecutive logical blocks. Three cases may arise after the fetch of the block number i of page number P and following a new page fault:

1. the page fault requests another page than P: we have to load the new page in the NAND register
2. the page fault requests block $i+j$ of P, then in that case there is no need to reload data register, we can fetch this block
3. the page fault requests the block $i-j$ of P, which causes a reload of the register, because we cannot turn back

j is here the number of block to skip to reach the wanted one. (We notice that all blocks between i and j will have to be fetched too)

Storing in memory the page number that is currently in the NAND register and the current block number is enough to distinguish the case (1) of the cases

(2) and (3), and up to avoid unnecessary register reloads which slow down overall performance.

5 Experiments

We investigated cache configurations independently of replacement policies and cache manager implementations, and different contexts such as native programs or Java programs. Our goal is to find solutions in case that replacement policies are useless, as described in Section 4.1, instead of redesigning a new one. Thus, we used LRU and MIN as references (which are the most common boundaries in cache studies), to instead investigate more specially NAND characteristics, cache configurations and crtitical Smart Card's hardware constraints such as the external bus frequency.

5.1 Experimental Setup

The results are from a new dedicated simulator based on the parameters described in Fig. 1. The simulation process happens in two stages. After providing the physical parameters to build a simulated architecture, a trace is replayed against it by applying the desired replacement policy, and then counting the MISS and HIT as well as collecting the necessary informations to compute the overall bandwidth in MB/s. We wanted to analyse and characterize the impact of pages sizes. Results are thus presented with the assumption that the simulator knew with a null cost if an instruction was already in the cache or not. It assumes a negligible overhead executing cache lookups since we will use finally a limited number of cache pages here. But it will be investigated in future works.

Traces of C programs (like Typeset from the MiBench benchmark suite) were obtained using Callgrind on Linux. The traces of Java programs have been generated by JITS (Java In The Small [19]), an instrumental JVM developed and maintained by the INRIA-POPS team[2]. Regarding the storage in NAND, we consider only what would be in the NOR: the *text* section of ELF binaries, and raw bytecode arrays of Java class files. They are in consecutive pages of NAND (if necessary, the same function can be distributed among several pages) as if they were copied by a programmer, in the order of the binary produced by the compiler.

5.2 Event-Driven Java Applications

We also needed a true Smart Card scale use-case, because most of benchmark programs come with big loops and/or deep dependencies on external libraries. At the same time, existing embedded systems benchmarks do not provide similar environment to those used in today's Smart Card. Systems such as JavaCard are based on event-driven multi-applicative environment (like Cardlets processing APDU).

---

[2] http://www.inria.fr/recherche/equipes/pops.en.html

The JITS platform is also one of them, when configured for sensors or Smart Cards. This suite of tools allows off-board code specialization to reduce the total memory footprint to strictly necessary Java classes and methods. Different from other embedded JVM, JITS allows the use of standard Java API instead of being limited to a specific subset, like in JavaCard. We then use the on-board JITS bytecodes interpreter, working in events fashion, which enables us to simulate parallel execution of several Java applications without the need to have a per-thread execution stack.

In our simulation, the JITS platform is configured for applications running on a Crossbow MicaZ target: 4KB of RAM, 128KB of NOR Flash. The applications deployed on the target then contain 56 classes and 119 methods for 6832 bytes of Java bytecodes, and requires 2.1 KB of RAM for volatile data such as stack, some basic Java objects and critical sections of code like the event manager. It leaves only 1.9 KB of RAM to physically store a cache on-board. In the simulator, we will consider that the JVM is in NOR, and Java bytecodes stored in a simulated NAND. The results reproduced here are from a trace of 1,534,880 Java bytecodes through 172,411 calls/returns of methods during the execution of 3 parallel event-driven applications, sampling data at different frequencies and then forwarding samples over the air network.

5.3   Experimental Results

Impact of NAND Pagesize and Buses Constraints. As a starting point, we explored conventional Demand Paging with cache page size aligned on NAND page size. Fig. 4(up) reports reading performance of the MiBench-Typeset applications after simulations of caches between 2 and 16KB, and using NAND flash with 512 or 2048 bytes per page. It shows that small pages outperforms large pages, even if it is no more an industrial trend to provide NAND with small pages. If we look at Fig. 4(bottom), with hardware reduced to Smart Card abilities (see Table 1), we are further from NOR performance. Code caching seems to require much RAM to hide weaknesses of NAND and buses, which is impossible in our targets.

Impact of Cache Page Size. Aiming at giving power back to replacement policy with another way, we investigated reduction of cache page size, discovering a new way to manage the NAND register. Fig. 5a shows, using a cache of 2KB, that performance is becoming closer to NOR. Fig. 5a reproduces simulations of our JITS sample with cache page size reduced by 2 each time. The first consequence is that cache page count increases. As described in Section 4.3, Fig. 5b shows with the same configurations as Fig. 5a, the impact on each page fault step : a decrease of *write* (due to reduction), and then a decrease of *fetch* and *load* (due to reduction and new register management).

With this new configuration, the gain is double:

- Either, at same cache size, we are improving reading performance.
- Or, at same reading performance, we are reducing dramatically the size of the cache.

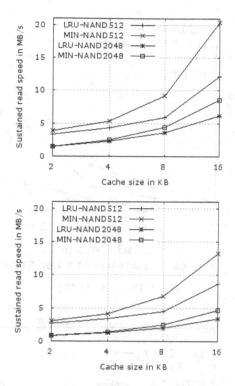

Fig. 4. Impact of NAND page size and bus speed on read Bandwidth, on a bus @54MHz-16bits (up) and on a bus @33MHz-8bits (bottom)

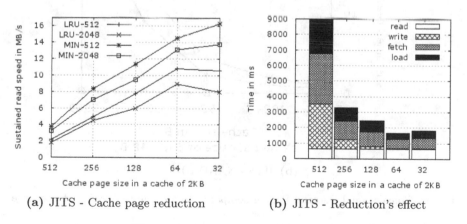

(a) JITS - Cache page reduction   (b) JITS - Reduction's effect

Fig. 5. Reduction of cache page size

If we take a look at our JITS application side (Fig. 6a for a 512 bytes NAND page size, Fig. 6b for a 2048 bytes NAND), we can show another very interesting advantage. These figures report reading performance using a cache page size of

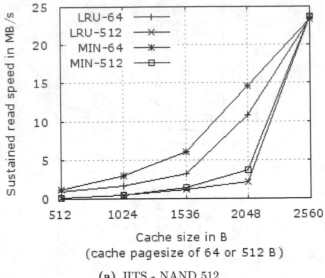

(a) JITS - NAND 512

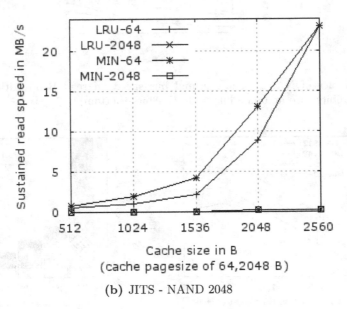

(b) JITS - NAND 2048

Fig. 6. Conventional Demand Paging compared to a cache with reduced page size

64 bytes. With a cache of 2KB (32 pages of 64 bytes), reading performance out-performs conventional Demand Paging, and even more, it makes code execution from a NAND with Demand Paging strategy possible (see Section 4.3). We are closer to NOR performance.

6 Discussion about the Best Cache Page Size

As shown in Fig. 5a, tuning the cache page size can improve overall performance. Unfortunately, the best cache page size is not unique, and may differ from programs to programs, and what is more, it may differ in a same program. For instance, the best cache page size for our JITS Java sample is 64 bytes when using LRU, though it is 32 when using MIN. To understand this difference, we have to distinguish two concurrent phenomenons, both getting better each other, but with some limits we will discuss here.

6.1 Buffer Effect

The first phenomenon, the buffer effect, has already been described above and refers to the new management of the NAND register. Based on it, a good page replacement policy is able to specialize the code on the fly, while searching and keeping only what it needs, without loading unnecessary instructions. Nevertheless, the limit to this specialization cannot be the instruction itself (ie, a cache page size of one byte), mainly because performance bottleneck would be transferred to lookups and indexing phases of the replacement policy algorithm.

6.2 Matching Code Granularity

The second phenomenon is based on code granularity concept and can set the limit of the first one, while explaining for example why a small cache page size can be better than another smaller one. In fact, a simple code specialization is already done by the page replacement policy. It means that finally, the policy splits code into two distinct categories: used and unused code. Following this, to keep efficiently data in cache, it will access NAND only to find useful code. If we help it with doing this distinction, overall performance will be improved.

At sources level, a program consists of classes and methods, or functions, depending on the programming languages. Once compiled, it then consists in series of basic blocks. A basic block is a group of several instructions, which will always be executed sequentialy because being between two jumping instructions (call/return, conditional jumps). With these bounds and to be efficient, a replacement policy should load an entire basic block when accessing its first instruction for the first time. Reducing cache page size to match the average size of a basic block as close as possible then gives better chance to the replacement policy to find more quickly useful sub-parts in a program, that may be spread over many pages into the NAND. For instance, the average basic block size (among only used basic blocks during simulation) of our JITS Java sample is about 60 bytes. That is the reason why the best cache page size for this sample is between 32 and 64 bytes. At this point, we can understand the impact of the noticed concurrent phenomenons. The best cache page size for LRU is 64 bytes, with the average code size aligned up to the cache page size. But MIN, having a better prediction mecanism than LRU, can take more advantage of the previously described buffer effect, and continue to have better performance with

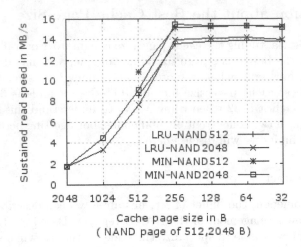

Fig. 7. MiBench-MAD - LRU and cache page reduction in a cache of 2KB

smaller and smaller cache page size. Its limit will be now the number of pages to maintain in cache and the time consumed by the replacement algorithm for looking up or indexing.

The MiBench-MAD benchmark (Fig. 7) shows that in fact the average basic block size is dominating the search for the best cache page size. MAD is a MP3 decoder calling, 90% of the time, two big functions. It puts the average size to 220 bytes. As shown in Fig. 7, best cache page size is still around this value. Nevertheless, with a higher value we see that we don't have the positive buffer as expected any more. Code granularity is thus as important as other cache parameters to tune an efficient cache system.

6.3   Toward a Better In-Binary Organization

We noticed in section 4.3 that a page fault can request a new block in the page already present in the NAND register. It results in a block jump (from block i to j). Getting j smaller than i is not an optimal situation because it causes the page to be reloaded. On the other hand, getting j greater than $i+1$ is neither a good situation because unnecessary bytes between block i and block $i+j$ will have to be fetched. Fig. 8 shows a spectrum of distance between i and j during our JITS sample (cases 2 and 3 described in section 4.3). A negative distance means that the same page had to be reloaded int the NAND register to read a block towards. A distance of 0 means that whereas the replacement has choosen to replace a block, it has finally needed the same block again resolving the next page fault. A distance of 31 means that the full NAND page had to be loaded and fetched, only to access its last logical block. Only 11.5% are in the optimal case where $j=i+1$, the only one without useless *fetches*.

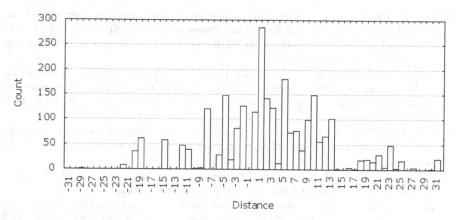

Fig. 8. JITS sample - Distance between two consecutive block requests using a cache of 2KB (32 pages of 64B)

In-binary organization is conditioned either by language, by compiler, or both. Fig. 8 speaks in favour of a control-flow analysis to group blocks by affinity of calls or sequences, directly in the binary.

7 Conclusion

We presented a new approach to parameterize the Demand Paging strategy to cache a slow secondary memory such as NAND flash in the context of Smart Card or embedded systems with the same size and the same constraints, such as slow buses and tiny main memory. Combined with an intelligent access to the NAND data register, reducing cache page size dramatically improves performance where conventional approach was close to worst case in term of bandwidth. We discussed about the optimality of our proposal, showing that the best cache page size were close to average size of used basic blocks. We noticed that this value could differ from programs to programs, and then may not always be shared between them to optimize all in once. We also pointed that the page replacement policy acted almost naturally as a on-the-fly code specializer. It means that running already Demand Paging-specialized code on this kind of targets may represent another interesting opportunity of gains.

References

[1] Micron Technical Note 29-19: NAND Flash 101 (2006)
[2] Park, C., Seo, J., Bae, S., Kim, H., Kim, S., Kim, B.: A low-cost memory architecture with nand xip for mobile embedded systems. In: CODES+ISSS 2003: Proceedings of the 1st IEEE/ACM/IFIP international conference on Hardware/software codesign and system synthesis, pp. 138–143. ACM, New York (2003)

[3] Lee, K., Orailoglu, A.: Application specific non-volatile primary memory for embedded systems. In: CODES/ISSS 2008: Proceedings of the 6th IEEE/ACM/IFIP international conference on Hardware/Software codesign and system synthesis, pp. 31–36. ACM, New York (2008)

[4] Lin, J.H., Chang, Y.H., Hsieh, J.W., Kuo, T.W., Yang, C.C.: A nor emulation strategy over nand flash memory. In: 13th IEEE International Conference on Embedded and Real-Time Computing Systems and Applications, RTCSA 2007, pp. 95–102 (2007)

[5] Lee, J.H., Park, G.H., Kim, S.D.: A new nand-type flash memory package with smart buffer system for spatial and temporal localities. Journal of Systems Architecture: the EUROMICRO Journal (2005)

[6] Lin, C.C., Chen, C.L., Tseng, C.H.: Source code arrangement of embedded java virtual machine for nand flash memory, pp. 152–157 (2007)

[7] In, J., Shin, I., Kim, H.: Swl: a search-while-load demand paging scheme with nand flash memory. In: LCTES 2007: Proceedings of the 2007 ACM SIGPLAN/SIGBED conference on Languages, compilers, and tools for embedded systems, pp. 217–226. ACM, New York (2007)

[8] Lachenmann, A., Marrón, P.J., Gauger, M., Minder, D., Saukh, O., Rothermel, K.: Removing the memory limitations of sensor networks with flash-based virtual memory. SIGOPS Oper. Syst. Rev. 41, 131–144 (2007)

[9] Kim, J.C., Lee, D., Lee, C.G., Kim, K., Ha, E.Y.: Real-time program execution on nand flash memory for portable media players. In: RTSS 2008: Proceedings of the 2008 Real-Time Systems Symposium, Washington, DC, USA, pp. 244–255. IEEE Computer Society, Los Alamitos (2008)

[10] Hyun, S., Lee, S., Ahn, S., Koh, K.: Improving the demand paging performance with nand-type flash memory. In: ICCSA 2008: Proceedings of the 2008 International Conference on Computational Sciences and Its Applications, Washington, DC, USA, pp. 157–163. IEEE Computer Society Press, Los Alamitos (2008)

[11] Joo, Y., Choi, Y., Park, C., Chung, S.W., Chung, E., Chang, N.: Demand paging for onenand™ flash execute-in-place. In: CODES+ISSS 2006: Proceedings of the 4th international conference on Hardware/software codesign and system synthesis, pp. 229–234. ACM, New York (2006)

[12] Park, C., Lim, J., Kwon, K., Lee, J., Min, S.L.: Compiler-assisted demand paging for embedded systems with flash memory. In: EMSOFT 2004: Proceedings of the 4th ACM international conference on Embedded software, pp. 114–124. ACM, New York (2004)

[13] Kim, S., Park, C., Ha, S.: Architecture exploration of nand flash-based multimedia card. In: DATE 2008: Proceedings of the conference on Design, automation and test in Europe, pp. 218–223. ACM, New York (2008)

[14] http://www.samsung.com (Onenand™ clock application note)

[15] Joo, Y., Choi, Y., Park, J., Park, C., Chung, S.W.: Energy and performance optimization ofdemand paging with onenand flash. IEEE Transactions on Computer-Aided Design of Integrated Circuits and Systems 27(11), 1969–1982 (2008)

[16] Al-Zoubi, H., Milenkovic, A., Milenkovic, M.: Performance evaluation of cache replacement policies for the spec cpu2000 benchmark suite. In: ACM-SE 42: Proceedings of the 42nd annual Southeast regional conference, pp. 267–272. ACM, New York (2004)

[17] Belady, L.A.: A study of replacement algorithms for virtual storage computers. IBM Systems Journal 5(2), 78–101 (1966)
[18] Denning, P.J.: The locality principle (2005)
[19] Courbot, A.: Efficient off-board deployment and customization of virtual machine based embedded systems. ACM Transactions on Embedded Computing Systems (2010)

Firewall Mechanism in a User Centric Smart Card Ownership Model

Raja Naeem Akram, Konstantinos Markantonakis, and Keith Mayes

Information Security Group Smart card Centre, Royal Holloway, University of London
Egham, Surrey, United Kingdom
{R.N.Akram,K.Markantonakis,Keith.Mayes}@rhul.ac.uk

Abstract. Multi-application smart card technology facilitates applications to securely share their data and functionality. The security enforcement and assurance in application sharing is provided by the smart card firewall. The firewall mechanism is well defined and studied in the Issuer Centric Smart Card Ownership Model (ICOM), in which a smart card is under total control of its issuer. However, it is not analysed in the User Centric Smart Card Ownership Model (UCOM) that delegates the smart card control to their users. In this paper, we present UCOM's security requirements for the firewall mechanism and propose a generic framework that satisfies them.

1 Introduction

The multi-application smart card initiative [1] ensures a secure and flexible execution environment for multiple applications from same or different organisations [2,3]. It facilitates the co-existence of interrelated and cooperative applications that augment each other's functionality. This enables applications to share their data as well as functionality with other applications, introducing a major security concern of unauthorised inter-application communication. The solution to this problem has been the smart card firewall.

The firewall acts as a supervisory authority on a smart card, monitoring inter-application communications [4]. The main aim is to ensure security and reliability of application sharing mechanisms even in adverse conditions such as caused by a malicious application, a developer's mistake or design oversight [5]. The firewall deployed in the Issuer Centric Smart Card Ownership (ICOM) is well defined [6, 7, 8, 9, 5] and studied [10, 11, 12, 13]. However, this is not the case for the firewall mechanism in the User Centric Smart Card Ownership Model (UCOM) [14], and it is the focus of this paper.

The widely adopted smart card based business model is the ICOM [14, 2, 15]. In this model, smart cards are under total control of the issuing organisation, referred to as the Card Issuer. Smart cards issued by a Card Issuer can host multiple applications and if required these can be from different organisations. Organisations that provide applications, but do not issue cards are referred to as Application Providers (or Service Providers) and they are reliant on establishing a business and trust relationship with Card Issuers. Card Issuers and Application

D. Gollmann, J.-L. Lanet, J. Iguchi-Cartigny (Eds.): CARDIS 2010, LNCS 6035, pp. 118–132, 2010.
© IFIP International Federation for Information Processing 2010

Providers also establish the necessary trust and assurance that the application will not harm the card platform and vice versa. Such an explicit business and trust relationship does not exist in the UCOM.

The UCOM gives the choice of applications to the users and they can request to have any application on their cards. The request is sent to the corresponding Service Provider (SP) in the UCOM. If the security assurance provided by the smart card along with its services and user credentials are valid then the SP leases its application(s) under certain terms and condition stipulated by the SP [14]. Leased application(s) are controlled only by their respective SPs and so this introduces unique issues regarding inter-application communications. In this paper, we will analyse the functional nature of the UCOM and its effects on the firewall mechanism and propose a framework that is suitable for secure operation.

In section two, we discuss the firewall mechanism within the multi-application smart card environment and how they are implemented in popular smart card platforms (e.g. Java Card [8] and Multos [9]). Section three describes unique issues presented to the firewall mechanism in the UCOM. In section four, a framework for a smart card firewall is presented that is suitable for the UCOM environment. In section five a case study briefly illustrates how the framework can be implemented, and finally section six provides the concluding remarks.

2 Multi-application Smart Card Platforms

In this section, we describe an application sharing mechanism in multi-application smart card platforms and how it is implement in Java Card and Multos.

2.1 An Application Sharing Mechanism

The most adopted business and operational scenario for the smart card based service model has been the ICOM [15]. For brevity, we will only discuss the application sharing (firewall) mechanism related to the ICOM in this section.

Multi-application smart cards facilitate co-operative schemes enabling optimised memory usage, with scope for data and service sharing between applications [15]. Therefore, a firewall mechanism should ensure application segregation while providing a secure and controlled way to allow applications to communicate data and share functionality. In the ICOM the issuer provides the platform security and reliability assurance, including the application segregation [7] that is necessary to avoid any on-card leakage of secret data.

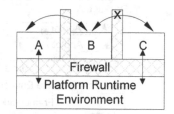

Fig. 1. A Generic Application Sharing Mechanism

A firewall is basically an access control mechanism that does not protect against information propagation [7] (which is beyond the scope of this paper). In addition to protecting applications; the firewall mechanism should also protect the platform by ensuring that applications can only access platform services through a well formed interface that cannot be used to subvert any protection of the platform.

To explain the firewall mechanism refer to simple example illustrated in figure 1. Consider that there are three applications: A, B, and C. The Application Providers of A and B have a trust relationship but Application Provider of C is not fully trusted by them. Application A specifies data and functionality that it wants to share with B, these are termed as shareable resources. The firewall facilitates the sharing with the help of the runtime environment. When B requests access to the resource of A, the firewall verifies the access credentials and if successful it allows the access. However, in the case of a request from the application C, the request will be denied.

The firewall should also segregate the platform runtime environment from the application space. To execute privileged services the application(s) could only make requests to the runtime environment through well formed Application Programming Interfaces (APIs). The firewall should ensure that this communication channel should not become a means to subvert the firewall in order to gain unauthorised access to resources from other applications.

2.2   Firewall Mechanism in Java Card

Java Card [4] is a smart card platform that supports a scaled down version of the popular Java language. The architecture of a Java Card is shown in figure 2.

The Java Card Runtime Environment (JCRE) sits on top of the smart card hardware and manages the on-card resources, applet execution and applet security [8]. The JCRE consists of APIs (e.g. `javacard.framework.APDU`, `Util` and `Shareable`) that an application can use to access JCRE services. The JCRE also has system classes that are integral to its functions and these classes are not visible to applications. Applets reside on top of the JCRE, and they are grouped together into packages.

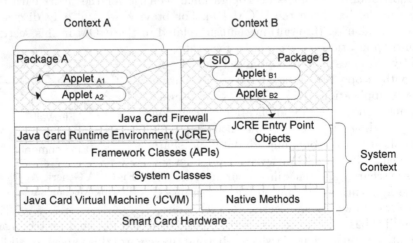

Fig. 2. Java Card Architecture

Each instance of an applet has a unique Application Identifier (AID) [8]. An instantiated representation of an applet is termed an object. Each object is associated with a context, including the JCRE objects (System Context). The Java Card Virtual Machine (JCVM) only allows an object to execute if the current "Active" context is the one from which it belongs. In figure 2, object of AppletB1 will only executes if the "Active" context is context B. The firewall restricts all cross context communication except for object sharing mechanisms: JCRE Entry Point Objects and Shareable Interface Objects (SIO). All applets in a package have the same context so there is no firewall between them.

The JCRE Entry Point Objects are instances of the Java Card APIs that can be used by applications to access platform services. These objects are accessible to all applets, and they enable non privileged (applets) applications to execute privileged commands. The JCRE Entry Point Objects are implemented by the Java Card manufacturer who is responsible for their security and reliability.

The SIO enables an application to share its resources with other authorised application(s). To utilise the SIO functionality, an application should extend the shareable interface (`javacard.framework.Shareable`) and the functionality implemented in the extended class will be shareable with other applets.

When an object requests either an SIO or JCRE Entry Point Object, the JCVM saves the current "Active" context and invokes the requested object along with the associated context. Therefore, a shareable object always executes in its own context, enabling it to access any applet from the package it belongs. By taking into account figure 2 when AppletA1 calls the SIO of AppletB1, the JCVM saves context A and invokes context B along with initiating the execution of the SIO. The SIO object can then call any method in package B. Furthermore, it can also call any JCRE Entry Point Object. When the SIO completes its execution, the JCVM restores the previous context (context A).

2.3   Firewall Mechanism in Multos

Compared to Java Card, Multos [9] takes a different approach to the smart card firewall. The Multos Card Operating System (COS) resides over the smart card hardware as illustrated in figure 3a. The Multos COS administers communication, resource management, and the virtual machine [9]. Applications do not have direct access to the Multos COS services, instead they utilise the Application Abstract Machine that is a set of standard APIs consisting of instructions and built-in functions. These APIs are used by applications to communicate with the COS and request privileged services. The top layer is the application space, and similar to Java Card the application segregation is implemented by the firewall.

In Multos, application delegation is implemented to facilitate application resource sharing. The application that initiates the process is called the delegator and the application that is initiated is called the delegate. The process of delegation works as described below and shown in figure 3b:

1. Application A (delegator) creates an APDU in the public memory and invokes the delegate command. The APDU consists of application B's AID, requested data or function and delegator's AID.

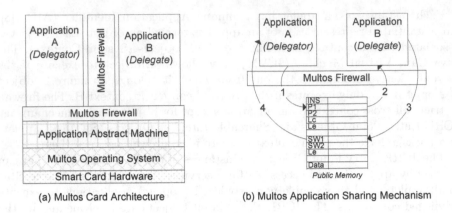

(a) Multos Card Architecture   (b) Multos Application Sharing Mechanism

Fig. 3. Multos Card Architecture and Firewall Mechanism

2. The Multos COS initiates the execution of B that looks for the APDU in the public memory. It reads the APDU and processes it.
3. On completion, B creates a response APDU within the public memory.
4. The Multos COS switches back to A that then retrieves B's APDU.

In both Java Card and Multos, additional measures are implemented in conjunction with the firewall mechanism to protect the platform. These measures include byte-code verification (on-card and off-card) [16,17], strict mechanism to install' applications [18] and virtual machine based security mechanisms [19,20].

3   User Centric Smart Card Ownership Model

In this section, we discuss the security and operational requirements for a firewall mechanism in the UCOM.

3.1   Application Sharing Requirements

The UCOM is expected to support a dynamic service environment with a wide range of application types. Therefore, the firewall mechanism should also reflect this dynamic nature [14].

Inter-application Communication. The UCOM firewall should facilitate a flexible mechanism that enables a server application[1] to implement a hierarchical access level firewall. In such a firewall, a server application assigns shareable resources according to different access levels. A client application[2] is initially assigned an access level although the server application can also revoke, upgrade, or demote the existing privileges of a client application, illustrated by figure 4.

---

[1] Server application: An application that provides shareable data or functionality to authorised applications.
[2] Client application: An application that requests the shareable resources of a server application. The notation to present this relationship is Server → Client.

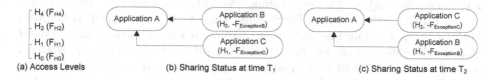

(a) Access Levels   (b) Sharing Status at time T_1 (c) Sharing Status at time T_2

Fig. 4. Hierarchical Access Level Firewall

Consider an application A that offers shareable data and functionality divided into different hierarchical levels. Requesting applications are only authorised to access data or functionality matching assigned level. In figure 4a, there are four hierarchical levels with H_0 the lowest and H_3 the most privileged level. The data and functionality associated with each level is denoted by the "F_{Level}". The "-$F_{Exception}$" is the negative permission, that lists the data or functionality that is not authorised to an application for the given access privileges. Application A keeps track of access levels along with -$F_{Exception}$" associated with each applications. Application B's access privileges (H_2, -$F_{ExceptionB}$) will be read as B has access to all data and function associated with level H_2 (F_{H2})and below (F_{H0} and F_{H1}) with an exception of data or functionality of "-$F_{ExceptionB}$'. B and C have access rights "H_2, -$F_{ExceptionB}$" and "H_1, -$F_{ExceptionC}$" respectively for A at time T_1. At some later time (T_2) A modifies the access privileges of B and C, demoting B to H_1 and upgrading C to H_2. In addition, the firewall mechanism will also allow the modification of the "-$F_{Exception}$".

Unlike the present Java Card or Multos firewalls, in the UCOM the sharing permissions will have limited lifetime and on expiry the client application(s) have to renegotiate the access permissions with the server application.

Application Sharing Delegation. A client application can delegate access to a server application (after authorisation) to another application on its behalf.

Consider the following scenario with three applications A, B, and C. There is an application sharing relationships A →B, and B →C; but none between A and C. Let us assume by way of example that application B gives royalty points if the cardholder uses A and these points are redeemable from C. Therefore, usage of A can lead to redeemable points (benefits) from C. At some point in time, the cardholder requests the deletion of application B and it requests the permission from A to delegate its sharing privileges to C. It is at the sole discretion of A's SP whether it would allow such an action or not. The SP of A may allow such action completely or impose conditions such as demoting the privileges to the lowest possible level for application C. Therefore from this point of time, C can access A on behalf of the B.

Application-Platform Communication. This requirement deals with bi-directional communication between an application and a smart card platform and it is sub-divided into two sections as listed below.

Application to Platform Communication. Platforms make their services available to applications either through Entry Point Objects [8] or standard APIs [9]. In both cases, applications may have access to more platform services than required that would not be desirable in the UCOM [14]. In the UCOM, applications are only given access to those platform services that are authorised by their SPs. The firewall ensures that an application cannot have access to any other services from the platform for which it is not authorised. This allows the SPs to control their applications' behaviours, especially in terms of on-card and off-card communication.

Platform to Application Communication. Java Card (like other multi-application smart cards) provides global access rights to the platform. The global access rights mean that an object of JCRE System Context can access any method (object) in any of the application contexts. However, the Java Card specification explicitly notes that the platform should only access certain methods (`select`, `process`, `deselect`, or `getShareableInterfaceObject`) from an applet context [8, see section 6.2.3]. In case of the UCOM, the firewall should ensure that a platform cannot have access to methods that are not sanctioned by the application SPs. Furthermore, it should enable an object or method to verify the requesting source. For example if the source is the platform, and it is trying to access an object or method not sanctioned by the corresponding SP, then it should throw a security exception.

Privacy Issues. In the UCOM, cardholders can have diverse applications on their smart cards, and each of these applications may represents their identity in some context. The firewall mechanism should not allow an application to discover the existence of other applications, because such a privilege could be abused to profile a user, perhaps for marketing or fraudulent purposes. In Java Card, `public static AID lookupAID` can be used to list the installed applications. It is not an issue in the ICOM as there is a central authority (card issuer) that has prior knowledge of installed applications and policed their functionality. However, it is a potential privacy threat in the UCOM.

4   Proposed Framework for the UCOM Firewall

In this section, the architecture of the proposed UCOM firewall is described along with explanation of its operations.

4.1   Overall Architecture

The UCOM is a smart card operating system and platform independent framework [14]. However, for brevity, clarity and intuitiveness we consider the Java Card firewall mechanism as the basis of our proposal. To illustrate the UCOM firewall, figure 5 shows a generic architectural view of the UCOM smart card that is principally similar to the Java Card (shown in figure 3).

The Runtime Environment (RE) Resource Manager controls the access to the RE Entry Point Objects that are used to access platform services. The resource

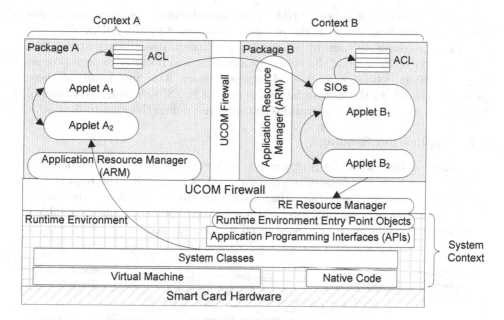

Fig. 5. Generic Architecture of User Centric Smart Card Firewall Mechanism

manager will enforce the security policy for applications as defined by the SPs, limiting the access to the platform resources as stipulated by the policy.

For each application (package), an Application Resource Manager (ARM) is introduced. This component will act as the authentication and resource allocation point. A client application will request a server application's ARM for shareable resources. The ARM will decide whether to grant the request based upon the client's credentials (associated privileges). At the time of application installation, the ARM also establishes a shareable interface connection with the platform, enabling it to access methods that are essential for the application execution. The platform can access any method in the application context only after authorisation from the application's SP. The ARM also receives information regarding the requesting application. If the request is from the system context for a method that is not allowed to be accessed by the platform, then the ARM will throw a security exception.

An Access Control List (ACL) is a private list and it is used to facilitate the implementation of the hierarchical access mechanism. It can be update remotely by the corresponding SP via the ARM, enabling the SP to change the behaviour of its application's sharing mechanism. The ACL holds the lists of granted permissions, received permissions (permissions to access other application's resources) and a cryptographic certificate revocation list of client applications. The structure of an ACL is under the sole discretion of its SP.

The operations of the UCOM firewall can be sub-divided into two distinctive phases. In phase one, a binding is established between the client and server applications. This process includes authentication of the client's credentials and access privileges by the server's ARM. In the second phase, the client application requests resources in line with the privileges sanctioned by the ARM.

To have a consistent view of the sharing mechanism over diverse application scenarios, the description of the application binding and resource request process are deliberately defined in high-level representations. The fine details of these processes are left to the individual preferences of the SPs. The UCOM firewall mechanism supports these operations but does not define the minute details.

4.2   Application Binding

This process deals with the first request by a client application for shareable resource(s) of a server application (phase one). Upon receiving the request, the server application first ascertains that the requesting application is the authorised application as it claims. After authentication, both applications establish a cryptographic binding that is used in all future requests.

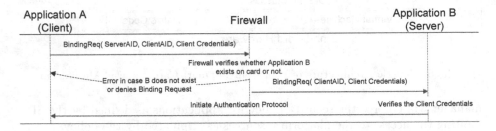

Fig. 6. Illustration of Application Binding Request Process

The process is illustrated in figure 6 and explained as below. Application A (client) sends a binding request message. This message consists of application B's (server) Application Identifier (AID), along with A's AID and credentials. The nature of the credentials can be at the sole discretion of the server application. However, to explain the process we use cryptographic certificates [21]. The SP of the server application, issues a cryptographic certificate to the client application's SP who in return issues individual (unique) certificates for its applications, certifying the unique public key pair of each client application. As the root authority (Certification Authority [21]) is the SP of a server application, any instance of the server application will be able to verify and accept it. On receiving the binding request the firewall mechanism looks up for the ServerAID to verify whether the application exists on the card or not. If it exists, the request would be forwarded to the corresponding ARM. Conversely, if the application does not exist, or server turns down the binding request, the firewall mechanism would throw an exception that would be same in both cases, to avoid a malicious application from potentially discovering the existence of an application on a card.

If the firewall forwards the request to the server application (Application B), it verifies the requesting application's credentials by initiating an authentication protocol. The outcome of the authentication protocol is generation and verification of a cryptographic (symmetric) binding key [22]. The client application will use this key in all future resource requests and in any related operation discussed in the subsequent sections. SPs should ensures that their authentication protocol is secure against application impersonation [22], and replay attacks [21].

4.3 Requesting Resource

A client application can request the server application's shareable resource as it required (subject to valid access permissions) as illustrated by figure 7.

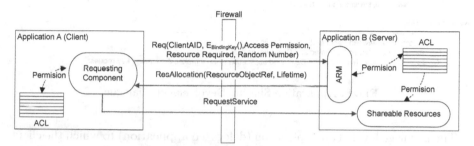

Fig. 7. Application Shareable Resource Access Request Process

The request message sent to the corresponding ARM consists of a ClientAID, an authenticator (message encrypted with binding key), access permission, required resource and a random number to provide freshness [21]. By verifying the authenticator, the ARM ascertains the origin of the message, i.e. the client application. Subsequently it checks the access permission for the client application (from the server application's ACL). If the client application is authorised to access the requested resource, the ARM would return the resource's object reference along with the sharing lifetime.

As described in section 3.1, the client application may have negative permission. To implement negative permission control each of the data or methods of the shareable resource is tagged with a unique ID. When the client application accesses a method from a shareable resource object, the unique ID of the method is compared with the negative permissions. If there is a match the method returns with an exception.

4.4 Privilege Modification

The SP of a server application can modify the privileges of a client application by updating the ACLs. The ARM of the server application verifies the initiator's (SP's) identity and credentials, before it allowing the update of the ACL(s). The implementation of the privilege modification is at the sole discretion of the SP. However, such an update could be similar to application update mechanism already deployed, notably Over-The-Air updates in (U)SIM application [23].

4.5   Application Sharing Delegation

This functionality of the UCOM firewall is subject to the sharing terms and conditions between the relevant SPs, which will grant or deny requests as appropriate.

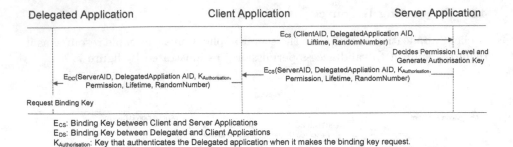

Fig. 8. Application Sharing Devolvement Dialogue

The privilege level of an application (delegated application) to which the client application delegates the resource-sharing does not have to be the same as itself. The privilege level of the delegated application is at the sole discretion of the server application's SP. The steps involved in the process of resource sharing delegation are listed below.

1. A client application requests a server application to delegate its resource-sharing privilege to another application.
2. According to the server application's policy, it can either keep the same level of privileges as the client application or demote the privileges for the delegated application. The server application generates a message encrypted by the binding key (Server→Client binding key) and sends it to the client application. The message contains Server AID, DelegatedApplication AID, Access permissions, Delegation lifetime and Delegation Request Key.
3. The client application decrypts the message and re-encrypts it with the Client→Delegated binding key and sends it to delegated application.
4. The delegated application uses it to authenticate itself to the server application and establishes a binding (section 4.2).

Once the delegation is completed, the client application cannot have access to the shareable resources, unless it requests the resource delegation to be terminated. The termination process is similar to the delegation process. Therefore, only one application (either client or delegated application) can access the shareable resources. The firewall mechanism ensures that once the resource delegation is terminated, the delegated application cannot have access to the resources.

4.6   Application-Platform Communication

At the time of installation, an application establishes bidirectional resource sharing with the platform. The application can access those platform APIs that are stipulated in the SP's application lease policy [14] and the platform obtains the shared resources of the application that are necessary to initiate the application execution. The platform security context does not have global access in UCOM based smart cards. This is to avoid any possible exploitation of the platform that could lead to the information leakage (data or code) from an application. The resource-sharing delegation is disabled in the platform-application communication and the firewall would deny such requests to avoid any illegal access to the APIs by an application through resource sharing delegation.

5   Case Study

In this section, a UCOM case study is discussed of an electronic purse application with special functionality. The described implementation is simply to illustrate the firewall mechanism.

5.1   Overall Scenario

In this scenario there are three applications, Electronic Purse, ABC Airline and XYZ Rentacar. The electronic purse application has a trust relationship with the other two applications but with different privilege levels. Whenever the cardholder uses the Electronic Purse application, royalty points can be earned for the airline application that can either be redeemed from the airline or from rent a car service. For brevity, the details are brief focusing only on the firewall mechanism.

The electronic purse application implements the shareable resources as illustrated by figure 9a. These resources have unique identifiers that are used to implement negative permission. The identifier is in the form of a byte value. For example, the byte gainRoyality() of the airline shareable resources, has the identifier "0x0001" represented by the private static byte gainRoyalityID. To enforce the negative permission, method identifiers are listed in the ACL that a method should check when it receives a request from the client applications.

Client Application	Hierarchical Level	Negative Permission	Delegated
ABC Airline	H₁	Non	false
XYZ Rentacar	H₀	Non	false
......	...	....	....

Hierarchical Levels:
H1: Access allowed to Airline and RentaCar Shareable Resources
H2: Access allowed to only RentaCar Shareable Resources

Electronic Purse (Server)

Shareable Resources
Airline Shareable Resources
byte gainRoyality()
boolean airlineService
(booking, payment)

RentaCar Shareable Resources
byte gainRoyality()
boolean rentACarService
(booking, payment)

(a) Electronic Purse Shareable Resouces

(b) ACL Implementation

Fig. 9. Electronic Purse Application Implementation

5.2 Implementation Examples

In this section, we will describe the details of the SP's dependent components of the UCOM based firewall mechanism, which are listed below:

Authentication Protocol. The protocol [24] is based on two steps. In the first step the protocol initiates the mutual authentication, and at the second step a symmetric key is mutually generated and shared.

Authenticator. It is an encrypted message that verifies the identity of a client application. The authenticator for the airline application is EBindingKeyABC(ABC-Identity | ResourceRequested | Random Number | Lifetime). The electronic purse application also calculates the authenticator, and if the results are the same then the ABC Airline request would be authenticated.

Application Sharing Delegation. The ABC airline application requests the resource sharing delegation. The electronic purse application only allows the delegated application to access the `gainRoyality()`. The resource sharing delegation process will upgrade the XYZ Rentacar application's privileges to H1 with negative permission for `private static byte airlineServicesID`.

This case study shows a simplistic view of an implementation of those firewall components that are left to a SP's discretion. The proposed framework provides a supporting platform that enables individual SPs to either implement their proprietary or well studied public algorithm to protect their shareable resources. This enables them to implement the crucial element of the firewall, and remove any possible ambiguity in different implementations (by card manufacturers).

6 Conclusion

In this paper, we discussed popular smart card based firewall mechanisms and how they work. Then we described the unique security requirements of the UCOM and presented an appropriate firewall mechanism extended from the Java Card firewall. During the research, the Multos based firewall mechanism was considered unsuitable for the open and dynamic environment that UCOM aims to support, because the security of the Multos firewall is reliant on the stringent application installation mechanism. In addition to implementing the traditional firewall controls, we also presented functionality that is lacking in the present popular firewall mechanism, but we consider them to be useful for the UCOM proposal. Future research directions will focus on implementation to test performance and practical feasibility of such proposals.

References

1. Deville, D., Galland, A., Grimaud, G., Jean, S.: Smart card operating systems: Past, present and future. In: Proceedings of the 5 th NORDU/USENIX Conference (2003)
2. Sauveron, D.: Multiapplication Smart Card: Towards an Open Smart Card? Inf. Secur. Tech. Rep. 14(2), 70–78 (2009)

3. Chaumette, S., Sauveron, D.: New Security Problems Raised by Open Multiapplication Smart Cards. LaBRI, Université Bordeaux 1 (2004), RR-1332-04
4. Chen, Z.: Java Card Technology for Smart Cards: Architecture and Programmer's Guide. Addison-Wesley Longman Publishing Co., Inc., Boston (2000)
5. Montgomery, M., Krishna, K.: Secure Object Sharing in Java Card. In: WOST 1999: Proceedings of the USENIX Workshop on Smartcard Technology, p. 14. USENIX Association, Berkeley (1999)
6. Éluard, M., Jensen, T.P., Denney, E.: An Operational Semantics of the Java Card Firewall. In: Attali, S., Jensen, T. (eds.) E-SMART 2001. LNCS, vol. 2140, pp. 95–110. Springer, Heidelberg (2001)
7. Bernardeschi, C., Martini, L.: Enforcement of Applet Boundaries in Java Card Systems. In: IASTED Conf. on Software Engineering and Applications, pp. 96–101 (2004)
8. Java Card Platform Specification; Application Programming Interface, Runtime Environment Specification, Virtual Machine Specification. Sun Microsystem Inc Std. Version 2.2.2 (March 2006), http://java.sun.com/javacard/specs.html
9. Multos: The Multos Specification, Online, Std., http://www.multos.com/
10. Huisman, M., Gurov, D., Sprenger, C., Chugunov, G.: Checking Absence of Illicit Applet Interactions: A Case Study. In: Wermelinger, M., Margaria-Steffen, T. (eds.) FASE 2004. LNCS, vol. 2984, pp. 84–98. Springer, Heidelberg (2004)
11. Mostowski, W., Poll, E.: Malicious Code on Java Card Smartcards: Attacks and Countermeasures. In: Grimaud, G., Standaert, F.-X. (eds.) CARDIS 2008. LNCS, vol. 5189, pp. 1–16. Springer, Heidelberg (2008)
12. Éluard, M., Jensen, T.: Secure Object Flow Analysis for Java Card. In: CARDIS 2002: Proceedings of the 5th conference on Smart Card Research and Advanced Application Conference, p. 11. USENIX Association, Berkeley (2002)
13. Bieber, P., Cazin, J., Marouani, A.E., Girard, P., Lanet, J.L., Wiels, V., Zanon, G.: The PACAP Prototype: A Tool for Detecting Java Card Illegal Flow. In: Attali, I., Jensen, T. (eds.) JavaCard 2000. LNCS, vol. 2041, pp. 25–37. Springer, Heidelberg (2001)
14. Akram, R.N., Markantonakis, K., Mayes, K.: Application Management Framework in User Centric Smart Card Ownership Model. In: Youm, H.Y., Jang, J. (eds.) WISA 2009. LNCS, vol. 5932, pp. 20–35. Springer, Heidelberg (2009)
15. Girard, P.: Which Security Policy for Multiplication Smart Cards? In: WOST 1999: Proceedings of the USENIX Workshop on Smartcard Technology, p. 3. USENIX Association, Berkeley (1999)
16. Basin, D.A., Friedrich, S., Posegga, J., Vogt, H.: Java Bytecode Verification by Model Checking. In: Halbwachs, N., Peled, D.A. (eds.) CAV 1999. LNCS, vol. 1633, pp. 491–494. Springer, Heidelberg (1999)
17. Basin, D.A., Friedrich, S., Gawkowski, M.: Verified Bytecode Model Checkers. In: Carreño, V.A., Muñoz, C.A., Tahar, S. (eds.) TPHOLs 2002. LNCS, vol. 2410, pp. 47–66. Springer, Heidelberg (2002)
18. Colby, C., Lee, P., Necula, G.C., Blau, F., Plesko, M., Cline, K.: A Certifying Compiler for Java. In: PLDI 2000: Proceedings of the ACM SIGPLAN 2000 conference on Programming language design and implementation, pp. 95–107. ACM, New York (2000)
19. Barthe, G., Dufay, G., Jakubiec, L., Melo de Sousa, S.: A Formal Correspondence between Offensive and Defensive JavaCard Virtual Machines. In: Cortesi, A. (ed.) VMCAI 2002. LNCS, vol. 2294, pp. 32–45. Springer, Heidelberg (2002)

20. Börger, E., Schulte, W.: Defining the Java Virtual Machine as Platform for Provably Correct Java Compilation. In: Brim, L., Gruska, J., Zlatuška, J. (eds.) MFCS 1998. LNCS, vol. 1450, pp. 17–35. Springer, Heidelberg (1998)
21. Schneier, B.: Applied cryptography: protocols, algorithms, and source code in C, 2nd edn. John Wiley & Sons, Inc., New York (1995)
22. Deville, D., Grimaud, G.: Building an "impossible" verifier on a java card. In: WIESS 2002: Proceedings of the 2nd conference on Industrial Experiences with Systems Software, p. 2. USENIX Association, Berkeley (2002)
23. Mayes, K., Markantonakis, K. (eds.): Smart Cards, Tokens, Security and Applications. Springer, Heidelberg (2008)
24. Markantonakis, K., Mayes, K.: A Secure Channel protocol for multi-application smart cards based on public key cryptography. In: Chadwick, D., Prennel, B. (eds.) CMS 2004 - Eight IFIP TC-6-11 Conference on Communications and Multimedia Security, pp. 79–96. Springer, Heidelberg (2004)

Combined Attacks and Countermeasures

Eric Vetillard and Anthony Ferrari

Trusted Labs, 790 Avenue Maurice Donat, 06250 Mougins, France

Abstract. Logical attacks on smart cards have been used for many years, but their attack potential is hindered by the processes used by issuers to verify the validity of code, in particular bytecode verification. More recently, the idea has emerged to combine logical attacks with a physical attack, in order to evade bytecode verification. We present practical work done recently on this topic, as well as some countermeasures that can be put in place against such attacks, and how they can be evaluated by security laboratories.

1 Forward

This paper presents theoretical work[1] related to the development of attacks that combine logical attacks on the card's software with physical attacks on the card's hardware. This particular piece of work has been performed on Java Card-based smart cards. However, we will see that the new attacks can be applied to other platforms, and Java Card has mostly been chosen because it is the most common interoperable smart card application platform.

2 Background

2.1 Physical Attacks

Smart cards have been subject to physical attacks since their inception. Attack techniques have evolved over time, and new attacks are being invented or enhanced all the time, either on the field (by hackers) or in security laboratories. However, most of the attacks fall in two main categories: observation attacks, whose goal is to observe the behavior of the card through some kind of side channel (timing, power consumption, electromagnetic signals, etc.), and perturbation attacks, whose goals is to modify the behavior of the card, usually by inducing a fault in the silicon.

Around 2000, observation attacks were greatly enhanced by the appearance of complex power analysis attacks, and in particular Differential Power Analysis (DPA, [6]). In the recent years, most developments have focused on fault induction attacks. When these attacks were invented, they were highly unpredictable, with low success rates. Recently, some laboratories have achieved very high success rates on very precise attacks, allowing attackers to design sophisticated attack paths.

---

[1] This work has been made possible by sponsorship from MasterCard International, and has been practically implemented through a collaboration with the EDSI laboratory, who performed the hardware attacks.

D. Gollmann, J.-L. Lanet, J. Iguchi-Cartigny (Eds.): CARDIS 2010, LNCS 6035, pp. 133–147, 2010.
© IFIP International Federation for Information Processing 2010

2.2 Logical Attacks

As smart cards grew more complex, so did their embedded software. In the end of the 1990's, a few systems appeared that allowed multiple applications to run on the same smart card. These systems, such as Multos and Java Card, introduced an additional abstraction layer, a virtual machine, which separated the smart card's system layer from its applications, and allowed the system layer to perform adequate security checks when running applications.

With the ability to load code, these systems also opened the possibility to load malicious code. This led to the development of logical attacks. Although such attacks can be applied on any system that allows code loading, the work has mostly focused on Java Card, for two reasons: first, it has always been an open system, whose specification is readily available; second, Java Card has become the dominant smart card middleware layer.

Commercial security evaluation laboratories, such as Trusted Labs, have used such attacks for several years in the evaluation of the security of smart cards. However, these attacks have remained confidential for a few years, even though the security of smart cards was studied [3] but recent work from the Radboud University Nijmegen [9] and from University of Limoges [7] have made some basic logical attacks publicly available.

There are mostly two categories of logical attacks that can be used on a system like Java Card:

- Illegal bytecode. The attack leverages the fact that Java Card cards are not able to verify that the bytecode that runs is valid (contrarily to other Java virtual machines, running on servers, workstations, or mobile phones). These attacks are quite powerful, and they achieve good results on many platforms.
- Bug exploitation. The attack uses legal bytecode that exploits a bug on the platform. Typical exploitable bugs are buffer overflow bugs, which result from missing checks, usually in lower layers of the card's software. Attack applications of this kind can be verified (their code is correct), and they can therefore be loaded on actual cards. However, they are specific to a given platform.

In both cases, there is a practical limitation today, as very few applications are actually downloaded into smart cards. In addition, the management of applications is restricted on deployed cards, which makes it difficult to load malicious code to perform actual attacks. Attacks based on illegal bytecode face an additional limitation, since application loading procedures usually require the verification of bytecode in order to detect such attacks.

In a typical attack path based on logical attacks, illegal bytecode is used in the attack design phase. Such code is loaded on development cards by the attacker, in order to determine the operational and security characteristics of the platform. At the same time, extensive testing is performed in order to identify an exploitable bug. If both parts are successful, the results are then combined to write an attack application that exploits a platform bug to perform an attack. Of course, since this last attack application exploits a bug, it is perfectly legal, and its bytecode can be successfully verified.

With such attacks, it is possible to cover all typical smart card threats: code and data disclosure, useful for reverse engineering; data modification; and even code modification and injection in some cases, usually successful. Ultimately, in some cases, confidential data disclosure can be achieved.

The illegal bytecode and the exploited bugs have varied effects, but the basic components are often the same:

- Type confusion. This is the most documented attack, which is used to transform integral values into references and vice-versa. The illegal references can then be used to access data illegally.
- Tampering with system data. Modifying an object's descriptor or a stack frame can be used to modify the execution context, and get access to data illegally.
- Illegal jump. Jumping illegally in the bytecode may allow a malicious application to jump into hidden attack code, or even dynamically loaded code, if the jump targets the content of an array.
- Buffer overflow/underflow. A very basic tool, which can be used on arrays, of course, and also on frames and on system buffers.

Of course, card designers have added countermeasures to their implementations, in order to make all of these attacks more difficult. Some of these countermeasures are actually part of the Java Card specification (or companion specifications), whereas some others have been designed by developers in order to make their platforms more robust:

- GlobalPlatform application management. This is a very basic countermeasure, as well as a highly efficient one. Most Java Card platforms also implement GlobalPlatform, which will require at least a cryptographic authentication before to allow any application management operation. This is of course a strong limitation for logical attackers.
- Java Card firewall. A Java Card platform hosts persistent data that belongs to several different applications. The firewall is a mechanism that ensures that an application cannot access another application's data, unless that data has been explicitly shared. The Java Card specification does not mandate any specific implementation, so the strength of the firewall greatly varies among platforms.
- Defensive virtual machines. Making a virtual machine defensive explicitly targets logical attacks, by making the virtual machine perform runtime checks that are redundant with the Java Card bytecode verification. The main issue is here performance, since adding redundancy at the virtual machine level has obvious costs.
- Advanced memory layouts. The first implementations of Java Card mostly used a flat memory model, in which user data was mixed with security attributes, and in which objects from different applications could be mixed. As memory grew and memory management became more complex, the layouts also changed, often becoming a countermeasure, in particular against system data disclosure.

- Classical countermeasures. Naturally, most classical countermeasures are used on Java Card platforms. Confidential objects are stored encrypted, and integrity-sensitive objects are implemented with enough redundancy.

With all these countermeasures, or even with a subset, it is in most cases difficult to identify an attack path based on logical attacks, except on the weakest platforms.

3   Mixing Physical and Logical Attacks

An idea that has been around for a while is to mix physical and logical attacks in order to build a successful attack path on a platform or application. In most cases, the high-level attacks is performed at the logical level, while physical attacks are used to thwart the countermeasures included on the platforms. Here are a few ways in which physical attacks can make logical attacks easier:

- GlobalPlatform attacks. One of the main limitations of logical attacks is that they are based on malicious code. This code cannot be loaded on cards by following standard content management procedures. By attacking GlobalPlatform's cryptographic mechanisms, physical attacks may allow a logical attack application to be loaded on a given platform. Since most platforms don't include on-card bytecode verification, if such attacks succeed on a platform, it becomes possible to include logical attacks in attack paths on such platforms.
- Memory dumps. It is possible to perform partial memory dumps using logical attacks during the reverse engineering phase; however, physical attacks provide ways to perform more complete memory dumps, in particular of the EEPROM.
- Execution trace analysis. It is possible, for instance by using power analysis [10], to figure out the sequence of instructions that is executed. Such attacks allow attackers to know precisely the sequence of bytecode instructions that runs, and to understand where to attack.

Similarly, logical attacks can make physical attacks easier, at least in a laboratory setting. The ability to load a well-known application, designed to be attacked, greatly simplifies the attacker's job. For instance, designing an attack on a counter is much easier on a platform where the attacker has the ability to reset the counter at will.

Overall, an attack scenario is likely to comprise many steps, in which logical and physical attacks will be mixed. In a typical laboratory scenario, we may start by getting a memory dump by a physical attack, then design a few logical attacks in order to get a better understanding of the platform's protections, and finally use a physical attack on a specific part of the code.

Over the years, we have developed a specific methodology for performing evaluations in which logical and physical attacks are mixed, by collaborating with several hardware labs. In a typical evaluation, we provide the code for the attack applications, as well as the guidelines for performing the attacks (how the attack point can be located, how the attack should be performed, and which results are expected). The hardware laboratory performs the attack (which often requires state-of-the-art techniques), and returns us the results. We then analyze the results obtained (for instance, a memory dump), and then provides the laboratory with new guidelines.

With such collaborations, it has been possible to exploit a wide range of software vulnerabilities, beyond traditional areas such as user authentication and cryptography.

4   Combined Attacks

It has now become possible to push the collaboration between hardware and software laboratories one step further, by designing attacks that can be applied in a systematic way on smart card application platforms. Such attacks have been designed by making the hypothesis that specific hardware attacks are possible, and by then determining the possible effect of these attacks on application middleware. The result of this analysis is a list of possible vulnerabilities, and an evaluation then consists in figuring out which ones are actually available on a given platform.

This approach has always been possible, but two factors have made it more interesting in the past few years:

- Attacks have become more accurate. In particular, the accuracy and success rate of fault induction attacks have greatly improved, making these attacks exploitable.
- Smart card software has become much more complex. Several application platforms are available, and the current shift to flash-based smart cards is going to make application platforms available even on low-end smart cards.

Barbu has applied this technique to Java Card 3.0 [1]. In the present paper, we apply it to classical Java Card 2.2 cards. We first make assumptions that are consistent with today's state-of-the-art on fault induction attacks [5], as follows:

- It is possible to perturb (with a good success rate) a mutable persistent memory read operation in order to replace the read value by a constant 00 value.
- It is possible to perturb (with a good success rate) a specific conditional jump instruction in order to "fix" its result and have it always jump in the same direction.

These assumptions are not unrealistic today, and they are likely to become even more realistic in the future. We will first present a few of the attack scenarios that become possible with such combined attacks.

4.1   Introducing a NOP

The first attack is based on a really simple fact: in Java Card, the opcode nop is represented by the value 00. Since application bytecode is read from mutable persistent memory, our first hypothesis implies that any opcode in the bytecode stream can be replaced by a nop opcode, with two possible consequences:

- If the replaced opcode has no parameters, the instruction it represents is skipped.
- If the replaced opcode has parameters, then its first parameter byte will be interpreted as an opcode, and the following bytes as its parameters.

We therefore see that this simple attack allow us not only to skip instructions, but also to introduce instructions at will in the bytecode stream.

The main interest of this attack is that it targets the main bytecode execution loop. This piece of code is critical for the performance of the platform, and it is therefore very difficult for developers to defend them with complex countermeasures.

4.2   Dropping the Firewall

The second attack focuses on the firewall checks, in order to allow an illegal access on an object through the firewall. In most object-related instructions, the firewall checks consist of a series of checks; the access is allowed if one of them succeeds.

For instance, the invocation of a virtual method is authorized if the object is owned by an applet in the currently active context, or if the object is designated as a Java Card RE Entry Point Object, or if the Java Card RE is the currently active context.

The attack here consists in using our second hypothesis to attack one of these checks, and to make it positive. The method invocation then becomes possible.

This main interest of this attack is that some platforms rely on encryption to protect the applications' assets, rather than on the firewall. In such applications, the firewall tests often include little redundancy, and can therefore be attacked.

4.3   Combining the Attacks

The attacks described above allow us to introduce unverified code in an application, (and in particular to forge a reference), and to "remove" the firewall tests on a reference access. By combining both attacks, and by also including traditional attacks, we are able to build interesting attack paths, such as the following one:

- Using a memory dump, determine the reference of a key object from a sensitive application, or a way to determine the value of that reference. This first part of the attack is performed in a "traditional" way on development cards, or partly on attacked cards, once a dump method has been discovered.

- In an apparently legal application, forge a copy of that reference. We will show in the practical results how this can be achieved by injecting a nop in an apparently normal program.
- Invoke the getKey() method, which returns the key value, on that reference, removing the firewall test. This can also be achieved by a simple attack, this time exploiting our attack on the firewall.
- Output the key value.

This is a very simple scenario, one that we have actually implemented. However, this is just one way of combining these attacks, leading to different attack paths. Our objective is here to show that, provided that perturbation attacks reach a certain quality threshold, an entire range of new attacks becomes available on open cards.

5   Experiments

Experiments have been conducted on a common Java Card platform, with a medium level of security. The targeted implementation is not considered as defensive, and its implementation of the Java Card firewall is rather simple, apparently without any significant redundancy. Quite likely, the typical firewall test consists in retrieving the object context from the object's header, and then comparing it with the current execution context, as required by the specification. This implementation is typical of cards developed by smaller vendors. Such cards can achieve security certifications, at least private ones, usually by relying on cryptography to protect the integrity and confidentiality of sensitive data.

Our experiments on the target platform have shown that it is very easy to identify the firewall test very precisely (it is easily identified as "the" test that fails when there is a firewall error). Breaking this test is therefore a rather simple task for a fault induction specialist, and the hardware laboratory has succeeded several times with good success rates (about 10%, without being detected).

With that result, on our target card, we have the ability to illegally access any object from any application, once we have obtained a reference to that object. The next step therefore consists in building a forged reference to an object. The way in which we can do that is to use another attack to transform an integral value into a reference. We will do that by writing a legal program, which can be transformed into an illegal one through a simple fault induction attack. The attack is based on the fact that the opcode for the nop bytecode is 00, and that we are able to replace a value read from EEPROM by a 00. Let's for instance consider the following code:

```
byte KEY_ARRAY_SIZE = 0x77;

Key getKey(short index){
    if (index<KEY_ARRAY_SIZE) {return keys[index];} else {return null;}}
```

This is a rather inconspicuous sequence of code, which simply performs a range check before to read a value from a local array of references. The bytecode sequence generated for this method is as follows:

```
00 1D      sload_1
01 10 77   bspush 0x77
03 6D 08   if_scmpge +08
05 AD 01   getfield_a_this objects
07 1D      sload_1
08 24      aaload
09 77      areturn
0A 01      aconst_null
0B 77      areturn
```

The attack simply consists in replacing the first bspush opcode by a nop opcode. The executed sequence then becomes:

```
00 1D      sload_1
01 00      nop
02 77      areturn
```

We have achieved our goal of transforming an integral value into a reference. In this particular case, we even have transformed a key index (possibly fetched directly from an incoming command) into a key object.

Once we have forged a reference, we simply need to invoke a method on it (for instance, the getKey() method), and to "remove" the firewall test.

We have implemented a similar scenario in practice, and we have actually been able to disclose the value of a key owned by another application with a success rate of about 5%. In addition, such an attack can be performed step by step, using different APDU commands. This greatly reduces the constraints on the hardware attack, because every fault induction attack can be performed independently of each other.

6   Protecting against the Attack

6.1   Preventing a Full Attack Path

We have shown and implemented an example of a combined attack that works on a basic implementation of Java Card. However, we are still missing some steps in order to industrialize the attack:

- The attack is able to disclose the value of a key whose reference is already known to the attacker. This implies that the attacker must also have the ability to analyze the target application, for instance by dumping the card's memory or analyzing the execution of code [10].
- The attack includes conspicuous code that would not go through a code review, even a basic one. In our example, the value of a key is sent unencrypted to the outside. This would raise questions from any code reviewer.

This dormant code is in fact equivalent to a Trojan horse, waiting to be activated.

Combined attacks allow a wide range of different attacks, but all the attacks that we have looked at have at least one of the following characteristics:

- They include a test whose result needs to be changed for the attack to succeed. This implies that the code that follows this test cannot be reached (dead code), or at least that it cannot be reached in a given case (dead path).
- They include a piece of code that conceals another one, which usually performs an unusual operation, or at least gives access to an unusual operation.

All these characteristics provide us with two leads to defend efficiently against such combined attacks: defensive virtual machines and application code analysis. We will review these two possibilities.

6.2 Defensive Virtual Machines

The idea behind a defensive virtual machine is that it will be under attack. It therefore includes countermeasures that make it hard to build a successful attack path. They do not defend against a specific and well-identified attack, but they rather reinforce the general robustness of the virtual machine.

- Firewall design. The Java Card specification only mandates a few simple checks to implement the firewall. It is also possible to implement the firewall using additional security mechanisms, such as memory encryption or MMU's.
- Redundant checks in the virtual machine. Bytecode verification makes most runtime checks useless under standard hypotheses. In a defensive virtual machine, the assumptions are weakened, and some checks are reintroduced. For instance, the virtual machine may verify that all jump targets are legal.

The difficulty in designing a defensive virtual machine is not in finding new countermeasures to include in the virtual machine, but rather to find a good compromise between security and performance. Each countermeasure has a cost (in memory, execution time, or both), which reduces the performance level of the card.

For instance, checking that the destination on a jump is in an appropriate range is very costly if performed on all jumps. However, this can be optimized by only checking the "long" jumps, which are used to jump over 128 bytes in one direction or another. Such jumps are far less frequent than short jumps, and they are far more likely to be involved in an attack, because they can reach a large part of memory.

Beyond local optimizations, the most difficult part in designing a defensive virtual machine is to build an impenetrable web of countermeasures, and to ensure that attackers are very likely to encounter one of the measures when designing new attacks. Some of the cards that we have evaluated greatly succeeded at this, making logical and combined attacks very hard to implement on their cards.

On the other hand, we also have evaluated many cards that are vulnerable to logical attacks, and whose sole protection against them is in the robustness of their GlobalPlatform implementation and the encryption of sensitive data. That means that such cards could be vulnerable to combined attacks, since the applications used in these attacks are valid and can be verified and legally loaded on a card.

6.3   Static Analysis

Application code analysis comes in complement to on-card runtime verifications (defensive virtual machines) and others hardware countermeasures, by statically ensuring a code being present on-card is not malicious. Static verification of programs is a very active research field, in particular around Java.

The Java bytecode verifier is the most commonly used static analysis tool. However, it is a very simple analyzer, and it remains possible to prove many more properties on Java bytecode. If it has been demonstrated that static verification could be performed on-card during code loading [8], bytecode verification remains traditionally performed off-card and has to be included in organizational countermeasures (bytecode verification and signature).

We have been working since 2002 on a tool that verifies the portability and security of Java Card applets. This tool has been used in many evaluations for the validation of numerous security rules e.g. tracing the use of critical APIs. Over the years, it has been extended mostly in collaborative research projects with information flow analysis [2] and security contract verification [4].

Static analysis tools for Java Card work by running analysed applications on an abstract virtual machine, and then checking that some rules can be verified. The abstraction can be quite precise, with an execution model that performs a global analysis of the code (in contrast to a method-local analysis), and a precise representation of the heap. This is possible because in Java Card, most of the objects are statically allocated, and the depth of invocations is limited by the small size of the Java stack.

We here suggest using a static analysis tool in order to identify applications that may contain Trojan horses to be used in combination with a physical attack as for instance

– Identify dead code and dead paths.
– Identify code that output secrets, in particular key values.
– Identify "unusual" constants.
– Identify unused variables.

7   Analysis

7.1   Can the Attacks Be Reproduced?

Yes, they can. On the logical part, implementing these attacks only requires a good level of expertise on smart card weaknesses and an in-depth knowledge about the implementation of Java runtime environments. On the physical part, implementing these attacks simply requires an ability to perform very precise fault induction attacks.

In both cases, few laboratories have the required skills in early 2009, and we don't know any laboratory that has both skills. Nevertheless, these skills are likely to become more common in the future.

7.2   Is Java Card Less Secure Than Other Systems?

In terms of resistance to attacks, there is no reason to believe that the Java Card platform is more sensitive than other platforms to our attacks. With the kind of precision that physical attacks can now achieve, all other existing middleware become vulnerable, as soon as they include the ability to load code.

However, a few factors make Java Card a common target for such attacks:

- Greater availability. Getting a development kit for a Java Card platform is quite easy, and the Java Card specification is also available to everybody.
- The "Windows effect". Just like Microsoft Windows, Java Card is today's dominant platform, so there are more incentives for attackers to develop an attack against Java Card.

This status may evolve with the gradual deployment of Java Card 3 platforms. The new platform includes new countermeasures, like mandatory bytecode verification, but it is also exposed to many new kinds of attacks. In addition, as it is new, it will be easier to find exploitable bugs, at least for a while.

About other platforms, the minimum requirement for being able to perform the attacks described here is to be able to develop an attack application and run it on a development platform, which must be similar enough to the platforms being actually deployed. In addition to traditional "open" Java Card-based smart cards, this covers the following cases:

- Any open card based on downloadable applications, such as BasicCard or Multos.
- Any closed card based on one of these open systems, provided that the application code runs in the same way on these cards.
- Any card OS that can be customized using an open API, as we can expect to find on flash-based smart cards.

Although they are nice-to-have features, the following are not absolute requirements for these new attacks to work:

- The ability to load applications on the attacked cards. Once an attack pattern is known, it is easiest to load an application that contains the pattern on an attacked card. However, it is also possible to analyze a closed card's code in order to find and exploit an instance of the attack pattern.
- A bytecode interpreter. The attack must be applied on a generic abstraction layer, but this layer does not need to be a bytecode interpreter. For instance, our firewall attack could work just as well on any memory management API that provides isolation between applications.

Of course, openness leads to an increase of the risk. However, developers of high-end open cards are likely to be aware of these risks and to include appropriate countermeasures, whereas developers of low-end closed cards are more likely to include very basic security measures, leaving more vulnerabilities available for exploitation.

7.3   Can Platforms Be Protected?

Of course, it is possible to include adequate protection in Java Card platforms. The main consequence of the new combinations of attacks described in the present paper is that some implementations become too vulnerable, and need to be replaced by alternative implementations. For instance, implementing fire-wall checks by a simple comparison between the current context and an object's owning context becomes almost impossible to protect.

The main challenge for platform developers will be to design new counter-measures that are efficient against combined logical and physical attacks, while providing an adequate performance level. This will in some cases require a significant redesign of the platform, with the introduction of new countermeasures.

However, this kind of situation occurs with all new attacks. For instance, in order to protect against DPA attacks [6], a well-known countermeasure consists in introducing counters that limit the number of uses of any given key. In that particular case, the countermeasure that protects a cryptographic implementation does not strengthen the cryptographic algorithm itself; it just makes the new attack unpractical.

7.4   What Security Measures for Certified Platforms?

In order to certify a platform in the context of this new attack, we need to look for suitable security measures on the platform, and to ensure that the proper assurance measures are taken in order to guarantee that these measures are theoretically suitable and that they have been correctly applied on the platform.

Reverse engineering is a key part of most attack paths, as the attackers need some information about the application and about the platform. Limiting the amount of information leaked from the platform then becomes an objective by itself. Protecting the confidentiality of the application bytecode remains difficult, since we have seen that power analysis allows significant disclosure. On the other hand, power analysis is very time-consuming, and it remains interesting to include protections against the more efficient alternative for reverse engineering: memory dumps. There are at least two interesting leads to get that protection:

- Protecting against classical physical memory dumps. The code targeted by memory dumps usually includes a transfer of memory (for instance, copying an array). These operations are not numerous. They should be carefully protected, and evaluations should verify the efficiency of the countermeasures.
- Protecting against logical memory dumps. Standard logical attacks are often used in the reverse engineering part, because they are very efficient (once an attack works, it is entirely deterministic, and it can be exploited in limited

time). The idea would here be to ensure that development cards, which are typically accessible to hackers, only accept verified bytecode. This can be achieved by embedding a bytecode verifier, or by embedding a mandatory DAP verification, and by having all applications verified and signed, either manually or automatically.

Another potential direction is to make the virtual machine more defensive, in particular regarding firewall checks. The objective is here to limit the potential harm made by an application to its own data. It is difficult to design systematic protections of the bytecode, mostly because of the high cost. For instance, adding redundancy to the main bytecode interpretation loop (for instance, to check the integrity of the opcode) will incur a significant performance cost. There are nevertheless a few leads:

- Protecting the firewall tests. The firewall tests are executed often, but only on object accesses. It is therefore possible to introduce some level of redundancy without paying a very high cost. The laboratories should focus on these tests, and perform fault induction tests on them.
- Protecting the virtual machine locally. Even if global countermeasures are very costly, it is possible to introduce some countermeasures that make the attacks more difficult, for instance performing some checks when running a nop opcode, which is very unusual in normal applications. The laboratories should look for such protections during evaluations.

The examples above are only instances of the checks to be performed. Yet, they show that in most cases, the countermeasures are indirect, and require a good understanding of combined attacks to be designed, implemented, and tested.

7.5   What Security Measures for Certified Applications?

In order to certify an application in the context of this new attack, the objective for a laboratory is to ensure that the application does not include any Trojan horse, and that it does not contain any code that has been designed to be attacked.

It is possible to introduce both intentional weaknesses and attack code in applications, even if it undergoes a security certification. Since such attacks require an insider job from the developer's staff, all countermeasures need to be implemented at the laboratory level. The laboratory therefore needs to consider bytecode-level attacks in their analysis of the application code. There are at least two things to watch:

- Analyze thoroughly unusual or useless code. If a piece of code does not seem to perform any interesting computation, it may be part of a Trojan Horse. Evaluators should be careful about this when performing a code review.
- Consider bytecode-level attacks. In addition to the obvious application weaknesses, which are visible at the application level, evaluators should be careful about bytecode-level attacks, which may either be voluntary or not.

The last point is very important. Although we have focused here on voluntary injection of vulnerable code, these attacks can be applied to any code, and they make it quite easy to modify the outcome of a program. Such fault induction attacks are already possible, but the attacks on bytecode may be easier to implement in some cases, for instance when attacking memory read operations has a good success rate.

7.6   Conclusion and Future Work

Logical attacks on smart cards have been available for many years. However, their practical application has been limited by the fact that, in order to be applied, they required an attack on the GlobalPlatform card content management commands, which are often difficult to implement.

With combined attacks, this work demonstrates that it becomes possible to implement a full attack path by combining logical attacks with a standard fault induction attack. Such combined attacks can therefore be implemented on platforms that were until now considered sufficiently safe.

We have shown a complete attack path based on combined attacks, which we have implemented on a classical platform. The results presented here remain incomplete, in the sense that we have mostly worked on code in which we have planted attack code without making significant efforts to conceal it. Therefore it would be of interest to work on attacks that can be concealed in a standard application, as well as to work on the exploitation of combined attacks on standard applications.

The platform on which we have performed the attacks has received many security certifications, while being known as sensitive to logical attacks. The availability of combined attacks raises the question of the requirements for certifications of open card platforms in the future. Evaluation laboratories should determine how these attacks should be considered in standard security evaluation programs.

Finally, another challenge raised by this paper consists in working on countermeasures against these attacks, and in particular on the detection of vulnerable code, totally or partially automated. Evaluation laboratories will however be confronted to a double problem:

- Certifying sensitive applications. In that case, laboratories have access to the application's code and specification, and significant resources are allocated to the evaluation. In such case, a partially automated analysis tool, identifying potential vulnerabilities is most useful, even if it possibly leads to false alarms.
- Scanning non-sensitive applications. In that case, laboratories only have access to the application's binary code, and the resources allocated to the evaluation are limited (a few hours). In such case, an automated tool that only detects obviously malicious code is needed.

Improvements of static analysis tools and application evaluation strategies have to be made to take combined attacks in consideration.

References

1. Barbu, G.: Fault attacks on a java card 3.0 virtual machine
2. Barthe, G., Beringer, L., Crégut, P., Grégoire, B., Hofmann, M., Müller, P., Poll, E., Puebla, G., Stark, I., Vétillard, E.: Mobius: Mobility, ubiquity, security. In: Montanari, U., Sannella, D., Bruni, R. (eds.) TGC 2006. LNCS, vol. 4661, pp. 10–29. Springer, Heidelberg (2007)
3. Chaumette, S., Hatchondo, I., Sauveron, D.: Jcat: An environment for attack and test on java card&trade. In: Proceedings of CCCT 2003 and 9th ISAS 2003, vol. 1, pp. 270–275 (2003)
4. Dragoni, N., Massacci, F., Schaefer, C., Walter, T., Vétillard, E.: A security-by-contracts architecture for pervasive services. In: Proceedings of 3rd Int'l Workshop on Security, Privacy and Trust in Ubiquitous Computing (SecPerU 2007). IEEE Press, Los Alamitos (2007)
5. ITSEC Joint Interpretation Library (JIL). Version 2.7. Application of Attack Potential to Smartcards (February 2009)
6. Kocher, P., Jaffe, J., Jun, B.: Differential power analysis. In: Wiener, M. (ed.) CRYPTO 1999. LNCS, vol. 1666, pp. 388–397. Springer, Heidelberg (1999)
7. Lanet, J.-L., Iguchi-Cartigny, J.: Developing a trojan applet in a smart card. Journal in Computer Virology 6(1) (2009)
8. Leroy, X.: Bytecode verification for java smart card. Software Practice & Experience 32, 319–340 (2002)
9. Mostowski, W., Poll, E.: Malicious code on java card smartcards: Attacks and countermeasures. In: Grimaud, G., Standaert, F.-X. (eds.) CARDIS 2008. LNCS, vol. 5189, pp. 1–16. Springer, Heidelberg (2008)
10. Vermoen, D., Witteman, M.F., Gaydadjiev, G.: Reverse engineering java card applets using power analysis. In: Sauveron, D., Markantonakis, K., Bilas, A., Quisquater, J.-J. (eds.) WISTP 2007. LNCS, vol. 4462, pp. 138–149. Springer, Heidelberg (2007)

Attacks on Java Card 3.0
Combining Fault and Logical Attacks

Guillaume Barbu[1,2], Hugues Thiebeauld[1], and Vincent Guerin[1]

[1] Oberthur Technologies - France
{g.barbu,h.thiebeauld,v.guerin}@oberthur.com
http://www.oberthur.com/
[2] Telecom ParisTech, Dep. ComElec, Groupe SEN - France
guillaume.barbu@telecom-paristech.fr
http://www.telecom-paristech.fr/

Abstract. Java Cards have been threatened so far by attacks using ill-formed applications which assume that the application bytecode is not verified. This assumption remained realistic as long as the bytecode verifier was commonly executed off-card and could thus be bypassed. Nevertheless it can no longer be applied to the Java Card 3 *Connected Edition* context where the bytecode verification is necessarily performed on-card. Therefore Java Card 3 *Connected Edition* seems to be immune against this kind of attacks. In this paper, we demonstrate that running ill-formed application does not necessarily mean loading and installing ill-formed application. For that purpose, we introduce a brand new kind of attack which combines fault injection and logical tampering. By these means, we describe two case studies taking place in the new Java Card 3 context. The first one shows how ill-formed applications can still be introduced and executed despite the on-card bytecode verifier. The second example leads to the modification of any method already installed on the card into any malicious bytecode. Finally we successfully mount these attacks on a recent device, emphasizing the necessity of taking into account these new threats when implementing Java Card 3 features.

Keywords: Java Card 3, Combined Attack, Fault Injection, Logical Attack.

1 Introduction

Nowadays Java Card technology is widely spread over the smartcard market for a large spectrum of applications, such as banking, identity or GSM. According to [19], more than 3.5 billion of Java Cards have been deployed worldwide so far, proving the needs in inter-operability, post-issuance loading, multi-application capability and security.

Fundamentally, smartcards are devoted to play a key role in secure transactions operating potentially in hostile environments. They are designed to resist to numerous attacks using both physical and logical techniques. Today fault attacks represent certainly the most powerful threat for smartcards. They consist in inducing a fault during a code execution as explained in [5] and then in

D. Gollmann, J.-L. Lanet, J. Iguchi-Cartigny (Eds.): CARDIS 2010, LNCS 6035, pp. 148–163, 2010.
© IFIP International Federation for Information Processing 2010

exploiting either a faulty computation result or an erroneous behavior to obtain information on secrets stored in the card. Although fault attacks have been mainly used in the literature from a cryptanalytic angle [2,6,3], their strength is to potentially stress every code layers embedded in a device. Practical details and comprehensive consequences could be found in [8].

Thanks to the inherent structure of the Java language, Java Cards have shown an improved robustness compared to native applications regarding fault attacks. However a device offering post-issuance loading and multi-application capability must also face to new threats associated to these features. Thus, the so-called malicious applets which are specifically developed by an attacker aiming at tampering with a Java Card device, should then be taken into consideration. Until now, all attacks based on malicious applet only used logical techniques to defeat the Java Cards security [24,17,13].

In this paper, we will introduce for the first time how a fault injection and a logical attack using a malicious applet can be combined to defeat a Java Card 3. The novelty of this paper is twofold. Firstly, such a combination has never been exploited until now. It turns out to be a very efficient way to tamper with a device like a Java Card. Secondly, we will show that even if the Java Card 3 standard appears to be very well designed with a real concern for security, it is still possible to attack devices embedding straightforward Java Card 3 implementations. We will also demonstrate that our attack is not purely theoretical, as it was successfully put into practice on a recent chip.

This paper is organized as follows : In Section 2, a brief reminder of Java Card 3 is exposed, with a special interest on the new features introduced by this standard. In Section 3, after a brief description of already published logical attacks on Java Card, we analyse if they are still relevant in the Java Card 3 context. In Section 4, we introduce a new kind of attacks combining fault injection and logical tampering. Two case studies are then exposed in Section 5 revealing how the security of a Java Card 3 device can be defeated. Finally, we discuss in Section 6 how to protect a platform against that kind of attack and how to handle the security to anticipate any weakness.

2   Brief Description of Java Card 3

This section aims at describing the context of the Java Card 3, with a special interest on the newly introduced features.

To follow the still growing requirements in embedded security, the Java Card 3.0 specification has been released [1]. For a best suitability, two editions are available: the *Classic* and the *Connected*.

2.1   Classic versus Connected Java Card 3.0 Editions

The *Classic Edition* stands for a moderate evolution of the previous Java Card 2.2.2 standard [22,20] and ensures a regular compatibility with classical applets and Java Card platforms deployed so far. Therefore all previous vulnerability analyses [24,17,13] applied on previous Java Card products remain valid on devices implementing *Classic Edition* Java Card 3.0.

The major evolution of Java Card 3 concerns the *Connected Edition* which represents a significant breakthrough compared to the previous Java Card standards. This latest release offers a myriad of new features and then opens up new opportunities for possible applications. This standard addresses the high-end range of devices and mainly targets the network field, where the smartcard plays a vital part in security.

The most interesting features introduced by Java Card 3.0 *Connected Edition* are:

- a strong evolution of the language, now closer to the standard java,
- a multi-threading capability,
- a connectivity adapted to the most common network standards (TCP/IP, HTTP(S)),
- an on-card class loader and linker.

For the sake of interest only the *Connected* version of Java Card 3.0 will be taken into consideration in the remainder of this paper.

2.2   Java Card 3.0: A Set of New Security Features

The complete specifications of the Java Card 3 *Connected Edition* have been revisited and enriched by new requirements to ensure a very high level of security.
The main security features concern:

- a context isolation mechanism, more commonly called the *application firewall*, ensuring that objects created in an application are not accessed by any other application,
- a mandatory On-Card Bytecode Verifier (OCBV) to prevent any ill-formed applet to be loaded and installed,
- a code isolation mechanism,
- optional security annotations to specifically define in the code particular sequences requiring a stronger security,
- secure communications such as Transport Layer Security,
- a security policy enforced by role-based and permission-based rules.

Why would the OCBV influence the Java Card security?

2.3   The ByteCode Verification

The bytecode verification [21] consists in checking the coherence of the CAP file before installing the applet on the card. Such operation turns out to be costly in term of code size, which can be critical for resources-restricted devices like smartcards. For this reason, up to the Java Card 3 standard, the specifications [21] allowed the possibility to execute this bytecode verification outside the card, which is the case for a majority of the Java Cards deployed so far.

To force this verification, Global Platform (GP) has specified the notion of Data Authentication Pattern (DAP). According to the Java Card configuration set by the issuer, an optional DAP verification can be requested during each new applet installation, consisting in checking the signature validity. The issuer or the application provider has then to sign the CAP file after processing the bytecode verification.

Considering the Java Card 3 *Connected Edition*, the loading and installation of ill-formed applets is now compromised since the bytecode verifier is now on card. Therefore it could be interesting to analyse the consequences of this new feature on the previously published attacks.

3   State of the Art of Java Card Software Attacks

In literature, previous works [24,17,13] attempting to attack Java Card devices assumed systematically that the attacker has the right to load an applet. Firstly, the context describing how one can load and install his own applet is recalled. And then, previous attacks are briefly described in order to analyse how they can be applied on Java Card 3 *Connected Edition*.

3.1   Loading an Applet: In the Jungle of Permission

The right to load an applet is not obvious in the reality of the field. To have this capability, an attacker has several possibilities:

1. The attacker owns the card manager key set, which means he plays the role of the issuer. No additional conditions are requested, the attacker is then able to load any package or install an applet without any further restrictions. It is the case for instance of white cards that anyone can buy on several web stores. Such cards are commonly provided with the card manager key set.
2. The attacker is in condition to load a package or install an applet by *Delegated Management* (only available from GP 2.1.1 [9]). That means the issuer has created on the card a kind of loading environment, called a *Security Domain*, providing loading, installation and extra secure communication features with certain privileges. The use of *Security Domains* requires ownership of some secret keys to achieve both authentication and communication through a secure messaging. Furthermore, loading and installing the applet by *Delegated Management* requires the INSTALL commands to be signed by the card's issuer.
3. The attacker is in condition to load a package or install an applet by *Authorized Management* (only available from GP 2.2 [10]). To do so, it is necessary that a *Security Domain* has been created beforehand by the issuer. The access to this *Security Domain* requires being authenticated and then owning the corresponding key set.

In conclusion, having the opportunity to load an applet on a Java Card is not obvious. This is simple indeed for everyone using white cards. However in that case, few assets are at stake, rendering the reach of any attack limited. Otherwise we can consider very unlikely the possibility for a basic attacker to load his own applet in normal conditions of use.

Nevertheless this assumption is necessary to consider any software attack. Therefore, in the following of this paper, we will assume:

H_0: **The attacker is able to load and install applications on card.**

3.2 Ill-Formed Applets: The Threat Number One

Until now, attacks threatening Java Cards are mainly divided into two categories:

- They exploit a weakness in the Virtual Machine (VM) implementation [24], or even a bug in the atomic operations [17]. These attacks are still valid in Java Card 3 *Connected Edition*. However, the number of such attacks is limited and can be easily addressed by developers without affecting the product performances.
- Another kind of attack concerned the execution of ill-formed applets. Such techniques are now considered as a classical attack (a brief description could be found in [7]). Their principle is to modify the CAP file in order to defeat security controls ensured typically by the firewall. They can be extremely powerful, as it was shown in [24], [17] and [13].

Why would the security of a Java Card be threatened by a CAP file modification?

Firstly, [24] and [17] have exposed how the type confusion could eventually lead to either Non Volatile Memory dump possibilities or to firewall circumventing. The success of their attacks was nevertheless conditioned by the absence of dynamic controls embedded in the platform, explaining why the attacks failed on some cards.

Secondly, [13] has described how changing a bytecode could provide the knowledge of manipulated references. This information was then exploited in a second step of the attack, consisting in changing the *Method Component* contained in the CAP file, improving an attack proposed by [12]. Finally [13] showed how a malicious applet's method could be replaced with a data array playing so the rule of a trojan horse, and giving the access in reading and writing to a large part of the memory space. Once again, the viability of this attack is mainly dependent on the implementation choices of the different cards tested.

Moreover, every ill-formed attack requires that the CAP file has not passed the bytecode verifier. As explained in Section 2.3, this assumption is not longer applicable on Java Card 3 *Connected Edition*. The direct consequence seems to be an apparent protection face to ill-formed applet attacks, and to most of others attacks published in literature so far.

However, this bytecode verification remains static, as it is executed once when the applet is being installed. The attack described in the next section will show why this "static" protection is not sufficient. We will demonstrate that logical attacks are still possible by combining them with a single fault injection during the application execution.

4   Combined Attack on Java Card 3.0, Theory and Practice

As explained in Section 3, it is now admitted that loading ill-formed application in order to get a type flaw is not an option anymore. In this section, we will firstly demonstrate that a combined attack can be an alternative to an ill-formed application loading. Then, we will show how this can be particulary dangerous for a Java Card 3.0 platform.

4.1   Attack Step 1: Combining Fault and Logical Attacks to Forge References

In this section we will firstly recall some basics about type conversion in Java. Then, we will demonstrate how a single physical disturbance of the code execution will enable us to induce a type confusion. This idea has been suggested in [17] and presented in [4] but neither any theoretical nor any practical examples have been published. Finally, we will show that the type confusion will permit to forge references and even possibly read and write their content, and this until the deletion of the application.

Recalls on Type Conversion
It is common knowledge that Java objects' types (classes) organization forms a hierarchy. Each class is a subclass of another class, except for the Object class on top of the hierarchy. This hierarchy enforces the principle of conversion which allows an object of type T1 to be used as if it were an object of type T2. A type conversion can be explicitly requested in the source code by the use of the cast operator: ().

For type safety reason, such conversions must be checked. Conversions proven incorrect at compile time result in a error. But, in most case, the check will happen at runtime *via* the checkcast instruction produced by the compiler and executed by the VM. Such an example is given below:

```
T1 t1;                          aload X
T2 t2 = (T2) t1;    ⇔          checkcast Y
                                astore Z
```

where X, Y and Z point respectively to t1, T2's class and t2.

The checkcast instruction takes as parameter the class into which the object (on top of the stack) is being converted. Its execution will merely consist in checking that the object is convertible into the given class regarding the class hierarchy. If the conversion is correct, the object reference is still on top of the stack at the end of the checkcast execution. Otherwise, a ClassCastException is thrown and the stack is cleared.

How a Faulty Conversion Leads to Reference Forgery
In [11], *Govindavajhala et al.* proposed a way to achieve type confusion and reference forgery on a virtual machine thanks to memory errors. Our approach, although slightly different, is inspired by their attack.

We consider the following classes[1]:

- public class A {byte b00,...,bFF;}   - public class B {short addr;}
- public class C {A a;}

Let us focus on the internal representation of instances of B and C classes (*cf.* Fig. 1). It is important to notice that both objects have the very same internal structure.

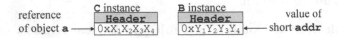

Fig. 1. Internal representation of instance of B and C

Imagine we can access an object either as an instance of B or C. Treating this object as a B instance, it is possible to set the value of its short field (b.addr = 0x1234;). And due to the internal structures of B and C classes, we have set the reference of the a field of this very object seen as an instance of C, as illustrated in Fig. 2.

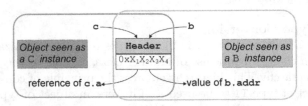

Fig. 2. Access to the same object either as B or C instance

Now let an application module containing the following extended applet (as well as classes A, B and C) be loaded, and this applet installed, on a recent chip embedding a straightforward implementation of the Java Card 3 *Connected Edition* specifications.

```
1. public class AttackExtApp extends Applet {
2.  B b; C c; boolean classFound;
3.  ... // Constructor (objects initialization), install method
4.  public void process(APDU apdu) {
5.   byte[] buffer = apdu.getBuffer();
6.   ...
7.   switch (buffer[ISO7816.OFFSET_INS]) {
8.    case INS_ILLEGAL_CAST:
9.     try {
10.     c = (C) ( (Object) b );
11.     return; // Success, return SW 0x9000
12.    } catch (ClassCastException e) {/*Failure, return SW 0x6F00*/}
13.    ... // more later defined instructions
14. } } }
```

---

[1] The size of a reference is implementation specific. Therefore the type of field **addr** in B could be either **short** or **int**.

Obviously, this application is well-formed and the OCBV will allow its loading and installation. However, the reader may have noticed the incorrect cast conversion of a B instance into a C instance (step 10)[2]. Checking the correctness of cast conversions is not in the scope of the OCBV, it is left to the `checkcast` execution, at runtime, which will prove this one incorrect.

In [23], *Vermoen et al.* successfully applied the principle of Power Analysis (PA) [14,15] to Java Cards in order to reverse engineer an applet. In our case, we will only rely on PA to monitor our application's execution, which is much less difficult.

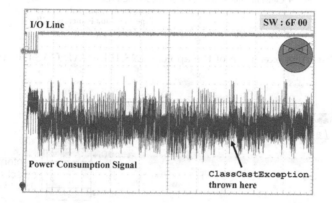

Fig. 3. Execution of the applet's INS_ILLEGAL_CAST instruction

By analysing this power consumption curve, we are able to determine the moment when the `ClassCastException` is thrown and thus when the `checkcast` is executed.

We are now going to disturb the execution at the precise moment when the `checkcast` is executed. For this purpose, we will use a laser equipment, targeting the back side of the chip. The following figure (Fig. 4) depicts the faulty execution of the same instruction.

We can see the instruction's execution is a little shorter than the regular execution in Fig. 3 (because the VM doesn't have to treat an exception raising) and the returned status word is the one expected when no error has occurred (90 00). The attack succeeded.

We are then able to access an actual B instance either as a B or a C object. Thus we can forge a's reference to any value (*via* `b.addr`), which in turn may let us read and write as many bytes as declared byte fields of class A (*cf.* Fig. 5.).

---

[2] The `Object` conversion is only meant to fool certain compilers. This conversion will probably not even be checked as each class is a subclass of `Object`.

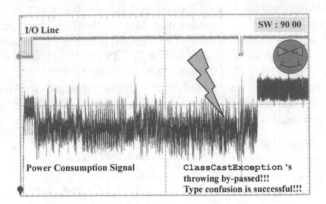

Fig. 4. Disturbed execution of the applet's INS_ILLEGAL_CAST instruction

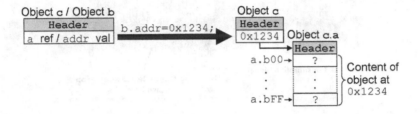

Fig. 5. Forgery of object a's reference

This can be done without requiring any additional disturbance. The sole security check we encountered has been permanently[3] neutralized by one single fault injection.

Can we then dump the whole VM heap? Surely not. Even forging references, access to an object that is not owned by our application and not shared must be forbidden by the application firewall, as specified in [21] and result in a SecurityException being thrown. Also, the behavior of the platform when trying to access bytes beyond the object's size, thanks to forgery, is not specified and is then typically implementation dependent.

Nevertheless, we are able to assign any reference to c.a and possibly read and write bytes c.a.bXY within the boundaries fixed by the application firewall and the VM implementation. This is roughly equivalent to the type-confusion-based attacks presented in Section 3 on Java Card 2.x platforms. However, we do not need ill-formed application loading nor specification/implementation flaws, the fault injection being the type confusion's cause.

---

[3] As long as our application is not deleted from the card.

4.2 Attack Step 2: Using our Reference Forgery Tool against a Java Card 3 Platform

We are now going to expose how the reference forgery tool presented in Section 4 can jeopardize a Java Card 3 *Connected Edition* platform thanks to the new dynamic features. We will start by setting our working hypothesis. Then we will explain how we can access and modify `Class` objects on the platform.

An Assumption about the `Class` Object

One of the features introduced by the Java Card 3 *Connected Edition* platform is on-card class loading. This can be used within an application thanks to the `java.lang.Class` class that has been added to the standard API [18] which specifies that *"Instances of the class `Class` represent classes and interfaces in a running Java application"*. `Class` objects are constructed by the class loading process, as defined in the standard Java VM specification [16], from the binary representation of these classes (the `.class` file). Working in a constrained environment, we cannot expect the `Class` object to be the exact copy of the `.class` file. Nevertheless we venture the following hypothesis:

H_1: **The bytecode of a class is stored in its `Class` instance.**

This assumption appears quite natural as the `Class` object aims at representing a running or ready-to-run class. Besides, if the `.class` file format can be optimized in some ways, the bytecode array itself cannot be modified without modifying the behavior of the methods it represents.

REMARK. *Another interesting point concerning `Class` object is that the specification requires root classes (applet, servlet, filter and listener classes), dynamically loadable classes and shareable interface classes of an application module to be loaded and linked during this application module loading. Thus we know that these instances of the class `Class` are constructed as soon as an application is loaded.*

Searching and Accessing `Class` Objects

Section 4 shows how we can forge reference of an `A` instance and access memory using its byte fields. This access will be executed on the platform respectively by the `getfield` and `putfield` instructions wether we try to get (read) or set (write) the byte value. A particularity of Java Card 3 *Connected Edition* is that its specification [21] allows access to implicitly transferable objects *via* `getfield` and `putfield` instructions. An implicitly transferable object is an object that is not bound to a specific java context.

Therefore, when an application requests access to such an object, the application firewall will grant the access instead of checking that the java context of the application matches the requested object's java context. In other words, such objects are not protected by the application firewall. The list of specified implicitly transferable classes [21] contains an interesting element: `java.lang.Class`.

To access a `Class` object (*i.e.* to forge b's reference to that of a `Class` object instance), we need to know the fully qualified name of this class and have the following instruction in the process method of our attack application:

```
1. case INS_SEARCH_CLASS:
2.    while (!classFound) {
3.      try {
4.        // Increment the forged reference
5.        b.addr++;
6.        // Convert the bytes given in APDU command into String
7.        String name = bytesToString(buffer, ISO7816.OFFSET_CDATA);
8.        // Is it a Class instance ?
9.        if (((Object) (c.a)) instanceof Class) {
10.         // Is it the Class instance we're looking for ?
11.         // Let us check its name
12.         if (((Class)((Object) (c.a))).getName().equals(name))
13.           classFound = true;
14.       }
15.    } catch (SecurityException se) {}
16.  }
```

REMARK. *In this instruction, we already take advantage of the implicitly transferable property of* Class *objects by using type conversion, the* instanceof *instruction and the* getName() *method on the forged reference (steps 9 and 12).*

Another way to achieve this could be to use the hashCode method of the Object class provided it is typically implemented as per [18]:

> "As much as is reasonably practical, the hashCode method defined by class Object does return distinct integers for distinct objects. (This is typically implemented by converting the internal address of the object into an integer, but this implementation technique is not required by the Java™ programming language.)"

Under H_1, and provided we can forge a's reference to a Class object's reference, then we can modify this class's bytecode array, regardless of the application it belongs to.

We expose in the following section two case studies of such an attack.

5   Applications of Our Combined Attack

In this section, we will present two case studies based on our combined attack proving we can execute ill-formed code despite the OCBV and modify any application installed on the card.

5.1   Case Study 1: Ill-Formed Code Injection

The OCBV prevents ill-formed applications from being loaded. This case study will show that our reference forgery tool enables an attacker to execute any sequence of bytecode instructions.

Imagine the attacker's application module contains an additional class with dummy methods filled with instructions ment to produce an easy to detect (and to modify) bytecode within the corresponding Class instance.

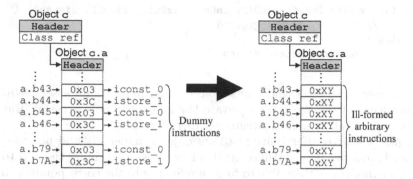

Fig. 6. Identification of dummyMethod and ill-formed code injection

To access his dummy Class object, he only has to use the INS_SEARCH_CLASS instruction with the proper class name (he obviously knows) to forge a's reference. He can then easily read the content of the Class object and detect the bytes corresponding to his dummy method. He can finally write the bytecode he wants, in disregard for any rule (Fig. 6).

This proves that under hypotheses H_0 and H_1, one can use the reference forgery tool to eventually have ill-formed code loaded on card despite the OCBV and without any additional fault injections.

REMARK. *Considering the state of the art, an application containing erroneous bytecode will not be more hazardous than the type-confusion we already got. Actually, we have the same chances to dump memory than with the attacks published in [24] and [17]. With a good knowledge of the Class object's structure we could also try to modify the static field resolution, as proposed in [12] and used in [13], to circumvent the application firewall. Nevertheless, this may enable future ill-formed-application-based attacks to target platform protected by OCBV.*

5.2   Case Study 2: Modifying Any Application Behavior

Unlike the previous case study, we will now fully take advantage of the implicitly transferable property of Class objects. Thanks to our reference forgery tool, the attacker is also able to modify any other applications regardless its context, endangering thus the whole platform integrity.

To illustrate how dangerous this can be, we study here the case of an application whose security relies on user/client authentication based on a signature scheme. The designers of this application being totally confident in the embedded signature scheme, since its implementation has been certified resistant against all kinds of side channel and fault attacks.

Therefore, somewhere in this application's code, the following lines will appear:

```
1. if (sig.verify(inBuff, inOff, inLen, sigBuff, sigOff, sigLen)) {
2.    ... // Success, access granted.
3. } else {
4.    ... // Failure, access denied.
5. }
```

Consider now an attacker who wants to access this application's assets. Without the knowledge of the signature's private key he cannot be successful. But the forgery tool will allow him to circumvent this obstacle.

Thanks to the transferability of `Class` objects, under H_1 and provided the attacker knows the fully qualified name of the class containing the call to the `verify` method, he is then able to forge a reference to the corresponding `Class` instance (still using the `INS_SEARCH_CLASS_OBJECT` instruction). He will then have access to its bytecode array.

Knowing the `verify` method's descriptor, he can deduce that a call to this method will consist in pushing the `sig`'s reference and all the arguments on the stack (`inBuff`, `inOff`, ...).

He can then identify the bytes involved in the call to the `verify` method in the bytecode array (Fig. 7).

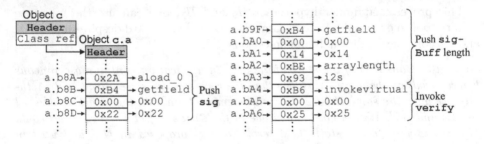

Fig. 7. The call of the `verify` method

Finally, he has just to set all these bytes to `0x00`, which corresponds to the `nop` instruction (*i.e.* no operation), except the last one, to which he assigns the value corresponding to `iconst_1`, pushing the value 1 on the stack (Fig. 8).

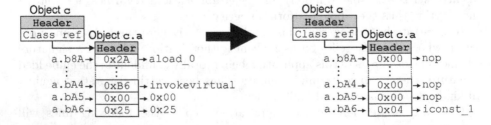

Fig. 8. Making the signature verification always successful

Operating this modification, the attacker changes the application's code as if its Java source code were the following:

```
1. if (true) {
2.    ... // Success, access granted.
3. } else {
4.    ... // Failure, access denied.
5. }
```

He has then granted access to the application's assets whatever the value of the signature.

This simple case study shows the potential threat such attacks can represent. Our application becomes a trojan horse capable of modifying other applications from the inside (as suggested in [13]). The number of possible attack *scenarii* is only limited by the attacker's imagination. Besides, although a good knowledge of the target application will ease the attack, we can eventually consider it as not necessary. If an attacker is able to read the content of all Class objects, identifying his target amongst those should not require huge efforts.

6 Security Concerns

The attacks described in Sections 4 and 4.2 reveal that some weaknesses in open platforms can defeat the whole security of a device. In a same vein, the attack described in [13] has shown that once a trojan horse had been setup, it could lead, in certain implementation conditions, to an access in both writing and reading to a large part of the memory, opening then plenty of possibilities to affect seriously the device reliability.

These examples illustrate that the open platform security relies on the implementation quality. Our attacks show that the Java Card 3 *Connected Edition* is not an exception. This new standard with all his additional features is not less secure than the previous versions, quite the reverse, and does not seem to contain any weakness. However to achieve a high level of security, even if a specification has been designed with a real concern for security, it must be associated to an appropriate security-oriented implementation. Therefore we can raise the question, how implementing the Java Card 3 specifications taking into account those threats?

Even if the chips appear to be more and more resistant with regard to fault injections, this risk should systematically be taken into consideration in the software, as an adequate complement. To achieve a resistant implementation, well-known countermeasures could be inserted, like execution flow controls, doubling sensitive operations and checking their coherency, variable redundancies, etc (*cf.* [8]). In the context of our attacks, the checkcast bytecode should then be considered as sensitive and handled accordingly.

Moreover, the success of the case studies described in Section 4.2 relies on an implementation choice: for optimization reason, as explained in Section 4.2, it was natural to associate the bytecode to the Class objects. However, it turns out to be a potential vulnerability regarding the logical attacks. It explains why the developer should often find the accurate balance between performance and security. A good know-how of the potential risks is then necessary to prevent any implementation weakness.

Last but not least, this attack has revealed that static controls could still be circumvented. We mean by static controls the controls performed for instance during the bytecode verification, ensuring the `.class` file is well-formed. However, once this verification achieved, the bytecode coherency is not checked during its execution. In other words, the installation of ill-formed applet is nearly impossible, but not its eventual execution. In normal conditions of use, the application needs obviously to be loaded and installed beforehand, the platform then looks secure. Nevertheless, for an attacker, once this first static verification bypassed, the platform does not ensure anymore an adequate protection, leading to a potential vulnerability. Finally the mandatory OCBV is a consequent security improvement, but it does not take the place of efficient dynamic controls performed during the VM execution.

7   Conclusion

In this paper, a new attack combining fault injection and logical tampering has been presented and applied on the Java Card 3 *Connected Edition*. We have demonstrated that this kind of attack is very efficient. It is thus possible to either alter any method regardless its java context or even to execute any bytecode, even ill-formed, bypassing the OCBV. Such vulnerabilities successfully applied on a device would affect dramatically its security.

Our attack is specific to Java Card 3.0 for two reasons. Firstly it held in a context of a mandatory OCBV, which is a specificity of the last Java Card specification. Secondly the possibility to handle `Class` objects, a newly introduced feature, was exploited.

Its practicability has been successfully demonstrated on a recent microcontroller, with a straightforward Java Card 3 implementation. These results have revealed the necessity of a secure implementation, even when specifications are designed to resist to the current state of the art attacks on smartcards.

Acknowledgement

The authors would like to thank Nicolas Bousquet, for his valuable suggestions during the design of the case studies presented in this paper, and Nicolas Morin, for his contribution to this work, putting the theoretical attack into practice. Additionally, thanks to Christophe Giraud and Philippe Hoogvorst for their helpful comments during this paper writing.

References

1. Allenbach, P.: Java Card 3: Classic Functionality Gets a Connectivity Boost (2009), http://java.sun.com/developer/technicalArticles/javacard/javacard3/
2. Anderson, R., Kuhn, M.: Tamper Resistance – a Cautionary Note. In: Proceedings of the 2nd USENIX Workshop on Electronic Commerce, pp. 1–11. USENIX Association (1996)

3. Aumüller, C., Bier, P., Fischer, W., Hofreiter, P., Seifert, J.P.: Fault Attacks on RSA with CRT: Concrete Results and Practical Countermeasures. In: Kaliski Jr., B.S., Koç, Ç.K., Paar, C. (eds.) CHES 2002. LNCS, vol. 2523, pp. 260–275. Springer, Heidelberg (2003)
4. Barbu, G.: Fault Attacks on Java Card 3 Virtual Machine. In: e-Smart 2009 (2009)
5. Bauduin, R.: Fault Attacks, an Intuitive Approach. In: Fault Diagnosis and Tolerance in Cryptography, FDTC 2006 (2006) (invited talk)
6. Boneh, D., DeMillo, R., Lipton, R.: On the Importance of Checking Cryptographic Protocols for Faults. In: Fumy, W. (ed.) EUROCRYPT 1997. LNCS, vol. 1233, pp. 37–51. Springer, Heidelberg (1997)
7. Common Criteria: Application of Attack Potential to Smartcards - Version 2.7, Rev.1 (2009)
8. Giraud, C., Thiebeauld, H.: A Survey on Fault Attacks. In: Smart Card Research and Advanced Application Conference (CARDIS 2004). LNCS, pp. 159–176. Springer, Heidelberg (2004)
9. GlobalPlatform Inc.: GlobalPlatform Card Specification 2.1.1. (2003)
10. GlobalPlatform Inc.: GlobalPlatform Card Specification 2.2. (2006)
11. Govindavajhala, S., Appel, A.: Using Memory Errors to Attack a Virtual Machine. In: IEEE Symposium on Security and Privacy, SP 2003 (2003)
12. Hyppönen, K.: Use of Cryptographic Codes for Bytecode Verification in Smartcard Environment. Master's thesis, University of Kuopio, Finland (2003)
13. Iguchi-Cartigny, J., Lanet, J.L.: Évaluation de l'injection de code malicieux dans une Java Card. In: Symposium sur la Sécurité des Technologies de l'Information et de la Communication, SSTIC 2009 (2009)
14. Kocher, P., Jaffe, J., Jun, B.: Introduction to Differential Power Analysis and Related Attacks. Technical report, Cryptography Research Inc. (1998)
15. Kocher, P., Jaffe, J., Jun, B.: Differential Power Analysis. In: Wiener, M. (ed.) CRYPTO 1999. LNCS, vol. 1666, pp. 388–397. Springer, Heidelberg (1999)
16. Lindholm, T., Yellin, F.: The Java Virtual Machine Specification, 2nd edn. Addison-Wesley, Reading (1999)
17. Mostowski, W., Poll, E.: Malicious Code on Java Card Smartcards: Attacks and Countermeasures. In: Grimaud, G., Standaert, F.-X. (eds.) CARDIS 2008. LNCS, vol. 5189, pp. 1–16. Springer, Heidelberg (2008)
18. Sun Microsystems Inc.: Application Programming Interface, Java Card Platform Version 3.0.1 Connected edn. (2009)
19. Sun Microsystems Inc.: Java Card Portal, http://java.sun.com/javacard/
20. Sun Microsystems Inc.: Runtime Environment Specification, Java Card Platform Version 2.2.2 (2006)
21. Sun Microsystems Inc.: Runtime Environment Specification, Java Card Platform Version 3.0.1 Connected edn. (2009)
22. Sun Microsystems Inc.: Virtual Machine Specification, Java Card Platform Version 2.2.2 (2006)
23. Vermoen, D., Witteman, M., Gaydadjiev, G.: Reverse Engineering Java Card Applet Using Power Analysis. In: Sauveron, D., Markantonakis, K., Bilas, A., Quisquater, J.-J. (eds.) WISTP 2007. LNCS, vol. 4462, pp. 138–149. Springer, Heidelberg (2007)
24. Witteman, M.: Java Card Security. Information Security Bulletin 8, 291–298 (2003)

Improved Fault Analysis of Signature Schemes

Christophe Giraud[1], Erik W. Knudsen[2], and Michael Tunstall[3]

[1] Oberthur Technologies,
4, allée du doyen Georges Brus, 33 600, Pessac, France
c.giraud@oberthur.com
[2] Alm. Brand,
Midtermolen 7, 2100 København Ø, Denmark
aberkn@almbrand.dk
[3] Department of Computer Science, University of Bristol,
Merchant Venturers Building, Woodland Road,
Bristol BS8 1UB, United Kingdom
tunstall@cs.bris.ac.uk

Abstract. At ACISP 2004, Giraud and Knudsen presented the first fault analysis of DSA, ECDSA, XTR-DSA, Schnorr and ElGamal signatures schemes that considered faults affecting one byte. They showed that 2304 faulty signatures would be expected to reduce the number of possible keys to 2^{40}, allowing a 160-bit private key to be recovered. In this paper we show that Giraud and Knudsen's fault attack is much more efficient than originally claimed. We prove that 34.3% less faulty signatures are required to recover a private key using the same fault model. We also show that their original way of expressing the fault model under a system of equations can be improved. A more precise expression allows us to obtain another improvement of up to 47.1%, depending on the values of the key byte affected.

Keywords: Fault analysis, Signature schemes, Smart card.

1 Introduction

Since their introduction in 1996 by Boneh, DeMillo and Lipton [3], fault attacks have been widely studied from both practical and theoretical points of view. This type of attack poses a serious threat that needs to be considered when implementing cryptographic algorithms on embedded devices [2]. Once a suitable mechanism for injecting a fault is found, fault attacks would allow an attacker to break any cryptographic implementation faster than any other kind of attacks. The following examples speak for themselves: a DES secret key can be revealed by using two faulty ciphertexts [4,10], an 128-bit AES secret key can be recovered by using one faulty ciphertext [16] and CRT RSA private parameters can be obtained by using one faulty signature [13,11]. In the particular case of DSA [8], ECDSA [8], XTR-DSA [14], Schnorr [17] and ElGamal [7] signature schemes, fault attacks are not as efficient. Indeed, if an attacker is able to induce an error on a single bit, the most efficient attacks on such schemes can recover the

D. Gollmann, J.-L. Lanet, J. Iguchi-Cartigny (Eds.): CARDIS 2010, LNCS 6035, pp. 164–181, 2010.

corresponding private keys by using one faulty signature per bit of the private key [1,6]. However, injecting a fault that would only affect one bit would be very difficult to put into practice. Giraud and Knudsen extended previous attacks to use a more realistic model where faults where considered that would affect one byte [9]. By using this fault model, they claimed that one would be able to recover a 160-bit private key by using 2304 faulty signatures and then conducting an exhaustive search amongst 2^{40} possible keys.

In this paper, we analyse the attack proposed by Giraud and Knudsen [9] in more detail, and we show that their attack is much more efficient than originally claimed. Our improved analysis is two-fold. Firstly, under the same assumptions used in [9], we prove that the average number of trials required to conduct an exhaustive search is 2^{30} and not 2^{39} as implicitly indicated in [9]. Consequently, under the same attack model used in [9] we show that an attacker needs 34.3% less faulty signatures to recover a 160-bit private key. Secondly, we improve the detail of the system of equations representing the fault model. This more precise definition allows us to significantly improve the results given in [9], especially if the key is composed of bytes close to 0 or 255. In such a case, the improvement can be up to 47.1%.

The rest of this paper is organised as follows. In Section 2, we recall the previous fault attacks which have been published on signature schemes. In Section 3, we compute the average number of guesses to conduct an exhaustive search if performing a fault attack by using the fault model presented in [9]. In Section 4, we present a more accurate system of equations representing the fault model used in [9]. This allows us to improve the original result and to show that the efficiency of this attack is dependant on the key value. Finally, Section 5 investigates if there is an optimal method to perform the exhaustive search.

2   Previous Work

The first fault attack on signature schemes was proposed in [5] on the RSA using the Chinese Remainder Theorem (CRT). It was shown that a CRT RSA private key could be derived if one fault was injected during the generation of a signature. This attack requires an attacker to obtain two signatures for the same message M, where one signature is correct and the other one is faulty. By computing the gcd of the modulus N and the difference between the correct and the faulty signature, the attacker would obtain one private factor of the modulus. This attack was extended in [13,11] by using only one signature generation.

A fault attack on RSA, where the CRT is not used, is defined in [1]. Again the attack compares the result of generating signatures from the same message with, and without faults. While a signature is being generated an attacker generates a fault causing one bit of the private exponent d to be changed, resulting in a faulty signature S'. Assuming that the i-th bit of d is complemented, then, as described in [1], we have:

$$\frac{S'}{S} \equiv M^{d'-d} \equiv \begin{cases} M^{2^i} & (\text{mod } N) & \text{if the } i\text{-th bit of } d = 0, \\ \frac{1}{M^{2^i}} & (\text{mod } N) & \text{if the } i\text{-th bit of } d = 1. \end{cases} \tag{1}$$

where S is the correct signature. In [1] it was also shown that this attack can be applied to other signature schemes, such as ElGamal, Schnorr and DSA.

In [12] it was shown that this attack can be improved by raising the formula to the power of the public exponent v, giving:

$$\frac{S'^v}{M} \equiv \begin{cases} (M^v)^{2^i} & (\mathrm{mod}\ N) & \text{if the } i\text{-th bit of } d = 0, \\ \frac{1}{(M^v)^{2^i}} & (\mathrm{mod}\ N) & \text{if the } i\text{-th bit of } d = 1. \end{cases} \tag{2}$$

In this case it is not necessary to know the correct signature S.

An attacker can compute $\frac{S'^v}{M}$ mod N for all the possible one-bit fault errors in d. This requires a total of $\log_2 d$ trials to completely derive d if an attacker is able to dictate which bit of d is complemented.

This was extended by Giraud and Knudsen in [9] to consider faults that affect one byte of an exponent. Let us now describe this extension where, to avoid any ambiguity, the fault needs to be treated as an integer difference between a correct exponent byte and a corrupted exponent byte. As above, we define the private key as d and d' as the corresponding corrupt private key. We define d_j and d'_j as the jth byte of d and d' respectively, a fault on the ith byte will therefore produce:

$$\begin{cases} d'_j = d_j, & \forall j \neq i \\ d'_j = d_j + e, \text{ if } j = i \end{cases} \tag{3}$$

with $d_j, d'_j \in \{0, \dots, 255\}$ and $e \in \{-255, \dots, 255\}$ where $e = 0$ corresponds to no error. For each fault on one byte of d, the attacker will deduce the position i of the corrupted byte since it is the only value for j which satisfies $d_j \neq d'_j$. He will then compute the corresponding value of e by subtracting d'_i with d_i. By definition, the possible values for e are:

$$e \in \{-d_i, \dots, 255 - d_i\}\ . \tag{4}$$

If two faults are observed, e and $\widehat{e}$, the possible values of d_i can be restricted to n values where:

$$e < \widehat{e} : \widehat{e} - e = 256 - n\,, \tag{5}$$

which means that:

$$-e \leq d_i \leq -e + (n-1)\ . \tag{6}$$

In [9] it is shown that the number of faulty signatures required to observe two faults with a significant enough difference to reduce d_i to a certain number of hypotheses can be defined. The average number of faults required to reduce the possible values to x values, for $x \in \{1, \dots, 8\}$, are shown in Table 1.

In the next section, we present another way of analysing the efficiency of the attack described in [9]. Indeed, whatever the number of candidates left, the most important information is the average number of guesses the attacker needs to do to recover the value of the secret key.

Table 1. Expected number of faulty signatures required to reduce the number of possible values for one key byte [9]

Maximum[1] number of candidates left for d_i	Expected number of faulty signatures required
1	384.0
2	213.3
3	149.3
4	115.2
5	93.9
6	79.2
7	68.6
8	60.4

3   A More Practical Analysis

The analysis in [9] defines the average number of faulty signatures that are required to reduce the number of possible values for d_i to a given number of hypotheses. It is then suggested that the private key can be found using an exhaustive search. However, the expected number of guesses an attacker would have to conduct is not defined in [9]. This information is of uttermost importance when analysing the efficiency of the attack. For example, it is shown in [9] that a 2^{160} key space is reduced to at most 2^{40} by using 2304 faulty signatures. Therefore, one could assume that expected number of guesses in the exhaustive search is 2^{39}, but this is not the case as it will be seen in this section. In the following, we derive the expected number of guesses for a given number of induced faults under the same assumptions defined in [9].

3.1   Notation

After inducing t faults γ_i for $i \in \{1, \cdots, t\}$, we define the Min statistic by:

$$\text{min} = \text{Min}(\gamma_1, \ldots, \gamma_t) \; , \tag{7}$$

and the Max statistic by:

$$\text{max} = \text{Max}(\gamma_1, \ldots, \gamma_t) \; . \tag{8}$$

3.2   Expected Search Time

By denoting by N the number of possible values for the variable we disturb (in our case $N = 256$ since we disturb one byte), we summarise the attack described in [9] as follows:

---

[1] In [9], it is written "Average number of candidates left" but their formula gives the average number of faulty signatures required to reduced the number of candidates to *at most n*. Therefore we need to replace "Average" by "Maximum".

"Induce t faults on a variable $K \in \{0, \cdots, N-1\}$ which results in observed values min and max with difference $f = \max - \min$. Then guess between the $N - f$ remaining candidates at random."

Theorem 1 gives the probability of guessing the correct key in the gth guess using this algorithm:

Theorem 1. *Let a variable $K \in \{0, \cdots, N-1\}$ with value a be given. The probability of the number of guesses X being equal to g using the ACISP Algorithm with t faulty signatures uniformly distributed is given by:*

$$\Pr(X = g | K = a) = \Pr(max = a - g + 1 | K = a)$$
$$= \left(\frac{N-g+1}{N}\right)^t - \left(\frac{N-g}{N}\right)^t \tag{9}$$

Using Theorem 1, we can compute the expected waiting time as:

Corollary 1. *The expected size of an exhaustive search by using the algorithm described in [9] is:*

$$\sum_{s=1}^{N} \left(\frac{s}{N}\right)^t .$$

The proofs of Theorem 1 and Corollary 1 are given in Appendix A[2].

By using Corollary 1 with $N = 256$, we can compute the expected number of faulty signatures to reduce the number of guesses to x, for $x \in \{2, \ldots, 8\}$, as shown in Table 2.

Table 2. Expected number of faulty signatures required to reduce the expected number of guesses to x, for $x \in \{2, \ldots, 8\}$

Expected number of guesses for d_i	Number of faulty signatures performed
2	176.5
3	102.8
4	72.7
5	56.2
6	45.7
7	38.5
8	33.2

We can, therefore, demonstrate using Corollary 1 that using 2304 faulty signatures to attack a 160-bit key (i.e. 115.2 faulty signatures per key byte) implies that the expected number of guesses required to conduct an exhaustive search is $\left(\sum_{s=1}^{256} \left(\frac{s}{256}\right)^{115.2}\right)^{20} \approx 2^{30}$ and not 2^{39} as implicitly indicated in [9].

---

[2] In Appendix A.1, we present a simpler proof of [9, Theorem 1] than the one in the aforementioned article.

Moreover, under the same attack model as in [9] (i.e. an attacker being able to inject faults on one byte and being able to perform 2^{39} signatures during the exhaustive search to find the correct key), we compute by using Corollary 1 that only 1513.3 faulty signatures are required[3] to recover a 160-bit private key. It is therefore an improvement of 34.3% compared to what was announced in [9].

The analysis presented in [9] and in this section are based on Relations (4) and (6). However, we show in the next section that these Relations can be refined, leading to an improvement of the corresponding analyses.

4 Improving the Analysis

In this section we will discuss some improvements to the analysis given in [9]. This is based on a more precise definition of the fault model and subsequent interpretation.

4.1 Reducing the Number of Possible Values for the Error

In this section, we present two remarks that allow us to improve the number of faulty signatures required.

Firstly, as described above, we have:

$$d_i + e = d_i' \tag{10}$$

with $d_i, d_i' \in \{0, \ldots, 255\}$ and $e \in \{-255, \ldots, 255\}$. In [9], Relation (10) leads them to the following relation:

$$-e \leq d_i \leq 255 - e \tag{11}$$

However, we can reduce this interval of possible values for d_i by taking into account that $d_i \in \{0, \ldots, 255\}$. This leads us to the following relation:

$$\mathrm{Max}(0, -e) \leq d_i \leq \mathrm{Min}(255, 255 - e), \tag{12}$$

One may note that this restriction only significantly improves the analysis when the key byte value is close to 0 or to 255.

Another way to slightly improve the analysis of [9] is to notice that they take into account the case $e = 0$ when computing their probabilities. As this case corresponds to not inflicting any error, the resulting signature will be correct and can then be excluded. We can, therefore, define the error e as:

$$e \in \{-d_i, \ldots, 255 - d_i\} \setminus \{0\}, \tag{13}$$

which further allows us to reduce the number of faulty signatures required.

In the next section, we redo the analysis done in [9] and in Section (3) by using Relations (12) and (13) instead of Relations (6) and (4) respectively.

---

[3] To obtain $\left(\sum_{s=1}^{256} \left(\frac{s}{256}\right)^t\right)^{20} \approx 2^{39}$, we need to use $t = 75.66$ faulty signatures per byte.

4.2   The Expected Number of Faults Required

To compute the statistically expected number of faults that will need to be observed we can model the system using a series of geometric distributions (see Appendix B). In this section we assume that an attacker wants to reduce the number of possible hypotheses for a given byte to less than α. That is, the results of this analysis can be directly compared to those presented in [9].

The simplest case will be where the key byte is equal to zero or 255. Assuming that the effect of a fault is uniformly distributed, the probability of a given event allowing this is $\alpha/255$. So, we can say that attacker would expect to reduce the hypotheses to less than α after $255/\alpha$ observed faults.

This is no longer the case if we consider other key values as observations can occur that are improved upon with subsequent observations. An attacker will be interested in observing a fault such that $e \in \{-k, \ldots, -k+\alpha\}$ or $e \in \{255 - k - \alpha, \ldots, 255 - k\}$, for some key byte k. This is because these values can be combined to make a list of less than, or equal to, α hypotheses. For any event an attacker would expect to observe a value form these groups with a probability of $\frac{2\alpha}{255}$, and therefore would expect this to occur after $\frac{255}{2\alpha}$ observed faults.

For each of the 2α possible faults there will be a certain number of faults that will be of interest to an attacker. For each of the possible faults the number of faults that improve the amount of information can be noted. The probability of observing a further fault of interest can be computed and another expectation derived from this. This can be continued for each possible combination of observations for a given α and the average expected number of observations can be computed.

For key values close to zero or 255 the initial two groups $\{-k, \ldots, -k+\alpha\}$ or $\{255 - k - \alpha, \ldots, 255 - k\}$ will be modified since an attacker will know the value when no fault is applied, i.e. $e = 0$. This means that the average expectation across all the possible key values will lead to the expected number of faults.

If, for example, we consider the case where $\alpha = 2$. For simplicity, we will also assume that the key byte value is $\in \{2, \ldots, 253\}$, i.e. the value of the key byte will not interfere with the analysis. Using the above method the expected number of observations X_1 is computed as

$$E(X_1) = \frac{255}{4} + \frac{1}{4} \cdot \frac{255}{2} + \frac{1}{4}\left(\frac{255}{3} + \frac{2}{3} \cdot \frac{255}{2}\right) + \frac{1}{4} \cdot \frac{255}{2} + \frac{1}{4}\left(\frac{255}{3} + \frac{2}{3} \cdot \frac{255}{2}\right)$$
$$= 212.5 \,,$$

where E is a function that returns the statistical expectation.

If the key byte value is $\in \{1, 254\}$, then the known value for no fault being injected will be part of the process. Using the above method the expected number of observations X_2 is computed as

$$E(X_2) = \frac{255}{3} + \frac{1}{3} \cdot \frac{255}{2} + \frac{1}{3} \cdot \frac{255}{2}$$
$$= 170 \,.$$

If the key byte value is $\in \{0, 255\}$, then we only need one observation of interest to reduce the number of possible values to the required amount. Using the above method the expected number of observations X_3 is computed as

$$E(X_3) = \frac{255}{2} = 127.5 \ .$$

The expectation for a uniformly distributed key $\in \{0, \ldots, 255\}$ is a weighted mean of the above expectations. The expected number of faults required X therefore becomes

$$E(X) = \frac{252\, E(X_1) + 2\, E(X_2) + 2\, E(X_3)}{256} = 211.5 \ .$$

The results of computing the above for $\alpha \in \{1, \ldots, 8\}$ is shown in Table 3 (all rounded to one decimal place).

Table 3. Expected number of guesses for one key byte depending on the number of faulty signatures

Maximum number of hypotheses for d_i	Expected number of faulty signatures
1	381.5
2	211.5
3	147.8
4	113.8
5	92.5
6	77.9
7	67.3
8	59.2

One can note that the improvement in Table 3 is minimal compared to Table 1 (1.3% on average). The improvements discussed in Section 4.1 only have a significant impact when a the value of a key byte is close to 0 or to 255. Figure 1 shows the key value dependency of this improvement when using 114 faulty signatures. In such a case, the improvement is of 39.2% if the key byte is equal to 0 or 255. Moreover, the smallest the number of faulty signatures we use, the biggest the improvement is. For instance, we obtain an improvement of 49.3% when using 10 faulty signatures if the key byte is equal to 0 or 255.

4.3   The Expected Size of an Exhaustive Search

The analysis described in the previous section is limited in the same way as the analysis described in [9]. The number of faults required is that needed to reduce the number of faults to less than a given value. In this section we define the expected number of faults required to produce an exhaustive search of a given size.

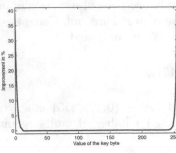

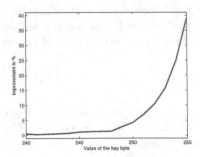

Fig. 1.a. Global view   Fig. 1.b. Zoom on Fig. 1.a

Fig. 1. Improvement of the analysis on the number of remaining candidates depending of the key byte value when using 114 faulty signatures

We first define the probability that a set of t observations will span X different values, for $X \in \{1, \ldots, N-1\}$ (in our case $N = 256$). Trivially, we can say that

$$\Pr(X = 1) = \frac{N-1}{(N-1)^t} \tag{14}$$

since the probability of all t observations having the same value is $\frac{1}{(N-1)^t}$ for each possible value of X.

For $X = 2$,

$$\Pr(X = 2) = \frac{2\,S(t,2)\,(N-2)}{(N-1)^t} \tag{15}$$

where we define $S(n, i)$ as a function that returns the Stirling numbers of the second kind. That is, the number of ways of partitioning n elements into i non-empty sets. Given that our sets are unique this needs to be multiplied by 2. Furthermore, there are $(N-2)$ possible sets where $X = 2$.

Computing the expectation becomes more complex for $X > 2$ since the sets representing the minimum and maximum possible values need to be non-empty, but the values in between can be empty. In order to compute the number of possible combinations that will span x different values we consider that the values fall into two sets. The first set represents the minimum and maximum values (there will be a minimum of two observations in this set). The second set represents the values in between the minimum and maximum observation and can contain empty sets.

We consider t faults that span x different values, where $t > 2$ and $x > 2$. These faults will be distributed between the two sets defined above. The set representing the minimum and maximum values contains i observations, where i is $\in \{2, \ldots, t\}$, then the number of combinations that are possible for a given i will be $2\,S(i, 2)$, as described above. The remaining observations will be in the other set where the number of combinations will be $(x-2)^{t-i}$. We can note that this number of combinations will only take into account one particular set of

i observations from t faults. This means that there will be $\binom{t}{i}$ possible ways of choosing i observations. This leads to

$$\Pr(X = x \,|\, x > 2) = \frac{(N - x) \sum_{i=2}^{t} 2\, S(i, 2)\, (x - 2)^{t-i} \binom{t}{i}}{(N - 1)^t}, \tag{16}$$

where we note that there are $(N - x)$ possible combinations where $X = x$.

The list of key hypotheses that can be excluded will also depend on the value of the byte affected by the fault being injected. The probability of a set of observations having a particular difference between the maximum and minimum observation x for a specific key value k is

$$\Pr(X = x \,|\, k = z) = \frac{\Pr(X = x)}{256}, \tag{17}$$

where we assume that the z is $\in \{0, \ldots, 255\}$, i.e. 256 possible values.

However, the expectation cannot be computed directly from this probability. This is because the signature where no fault is injected is known, i.e. an observation where the fault induced is equal to zero. For a minimum observation M_1 and a maximum observation M_2, spanning x values, we can define:

$$\text{Min}(M_1, 0)$$
$$\text{Max}(0, M_2)$$

For a given M_1 and M_2 the number of values that are actually spanned will be equal to $\text{Max}(0, M_2) - \text{Min}(M_1, 0)$, and the number of remaining hypotheses is equal to $N - 1 - \text{Max}(0, M_2) + \text{Min}(M_1, 0)$. Therefore, the probability given above for $\Pr(X = x \,|\, k = z)$ needs to be divided by $N - x$ to produce the probability for specific values of M_1 and M_2.

The expected number of remaining hypotheses $E(Y)$ can be computed as

$$E(Y) = \sum_{z=0}^{N-1} \sum_{x=1}^{N-1} \sum_{\substack{m \,\in\, \Phi \\ m + x - 1 \,\in\, \Phi}} (N - \text{Max}(0, m + x - 1) + \text{Min}(m, 0)) \frac{\Pr(X = x \,|\, k = z)}{N - x},$$

where we use the notation defined above (cf. (14), (15), (16) and (17)). In addition we denote m as the minimum observation in a set of observations that span x values. The values that m and $m + x - 1$ can take are in Φ, where Φ is the set $\{-z, \ldots, N - z - x\} \setminus \{0\}$.

If we assume the actual key value is uniformly distributed between the remaining hypotheses h then the expected number of tests required to find a key byte is computed as $(h + 1)/2$. For a fault in one by these values are shown in Table 4, rounded to one decimal place.

In order to allow the results of the improvement to be directly compared to the results described in Section 3, we used the formula for $E(Y)$ to compute the expected number of faulty signatures required to reduce the number of guesses between 2 and 8, cf. Table 5.

Table 4. Expected number of hypotheses and guesses required to determine a given key byte

t	$E(\#$ of Remaining Hypotheses)	$E(\#$ of Tests)
1	170.3	85.7
2	127.7	64.3
3	102.1	51.6
4	85.1	43.0
5	72.9	37.0
6	63.7	32.4
7	56.7	28.8
8	51.0	26.0
9	46.4	23.7
10	42.5	21.8

Table 5. Expected number of faulty signatures required to reduce the expected number of guesses to x, for $x \in \{1, \dots, 8\}$

Expected number of guesses for d_i	Number of faulty signatures required
2	174.8
3	101.4
4	71.4
5	55.0
6	44.5
7	37.4
8	32.1

By observing Table 5, one can see that the improvement is minimal compared to Table 2 (2.1% on average). It only has a significant impact when the value of a key byte is close to 0 or 255. Figure 2 shows this improvement when using 73 faulty signatures. In such a case, the improvement is of 37.6% if the key byte is equal to 0 or 255. Moreover, the smallest the number of faulty signatures we use, the biggest the improvement is. For instance, we obtain an improvement of 48.1% when using 10 faulty signatures.

The analysis conducted in this section shows that using the same attack model used in [9][4] and considering a random 160-bit key (resp. a 160-bit key that consists of bytes equal to 0 or 255), we would need 1488^5 (resp. 800^6) faulty ciphertexts to recover the entire key. In the latter case, we have an improvement of 47.1% comparing to the result presented in Section 3.

---

[4] That is, by using byte-fault model and a expected number guesses of 2^{39}.

[5] To obtain $E(Y)^{20} \approx 2^{39}$ with $N = 256$, we need to use $t = 74.4$ faulty signatures per key byte.

[6] To obtain $E(Y)^{20} \approx 2^{39}$ with $N = 256$, $z \in \{0, 255\}$ and by dividing $\Pr(X = x)$ by 2 instead of 256 to obtain $\Pr(X = x \mid k = z)$, we need to use $t = 40$ faulty signatures per key byte.

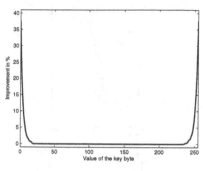
Fig. 2.a. Global view

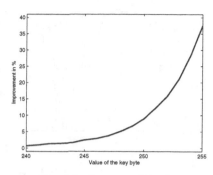
Fig. 2.b. Zoom on Fig. 2.a

Fig. 2. Improvement of the analysis on the number of guesses depending of the key byte value when using 73 faulty signatures

5   The Exhaustive Search

In [9], no detail is given on how to obtain the correct value of the key amongst the possible values that are defined by the analysis. If, for example, there are 4^{20} (2^{40}) possible values for a private key, we can say that one would expect to conduct 2^{39} trials, on average, to identify the correct value amongst the 4^{20} possible values. In this section we demonstrate that there is no best method of searching through the hypotheses that are produced by the analyses described in this paper.

We define a series of t faults γ_i for $i \in \{1, \ldots, t\}$, which we assume are drawn from a distribution that is uniform over the integers in $\{\eta, \ldots, 255 - \eta\} \setminus \{0\}$, where η is an unknown integer $\in \{0, \ldots, 255\}$. In order to rank a given value of η, we divide the interval into s intervals. For simplicity, we assume that the intervals are evenly spaced. Let x_i denote the number of the observed γ which fall within the i-th interval, so we have

$$x_1 + \cdots + x_s = t \ . \tag{18}$$

Given that the faults induced are uniformly distributed, then

$$E(x_1) = \cdots = E(x_s) = \frac{t}{s} \ , \tag{19}$$

where E is a function that returns the statistical expectation.

This can be used to conduct a frequency test. That is, we compute a statistic λ, where

$$\lambda = \sum_{i=1}^{s} \frac{(O(x_i) - E(x_i))^2}{E(x_i)} \ , \tag{20}$$

and O is a function that returns the number of observed faults in a particular interval. Then $\lambda \sim \chi^2(s - 1)$ and can be used to test the null hypothesis that η is a given value for each possible value $\in \{0, \ldots, 255\}$. For a given λ the P-value

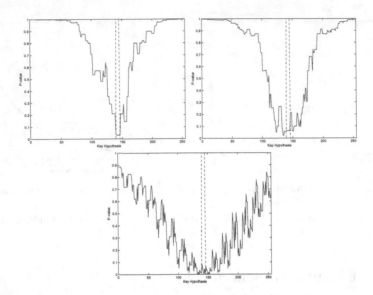

Fig. 3. Returned P-values plotted for all possible values for one byte for $s = 3, 5, 15$ (top left, top right and bottom middle respectively). The dashed lines represent the boundaries identified by the minimum and maximum observed fault.

can be computed which is a value between 0 and 1, where the larger the value the more evidence is provided against a hypothesis for η (typically values above 0.95 or 0.99 are used as a boundary, above which it can be stated that there is no evidence to support a given null hypothesis).

A set of 32 simulated observations were generated where η was, arbitrarily, set to 140. The above statistical test was then conducted for $s \in \{3, 5, 15\}$, i.e. small divisors of 255. In Figure 3 we show the resulting P-values for all the possible hypotheses for η. The dashed lines represent the boundaries that can be deduced by observing the maximum and minimum possible values (see Equation (12)).

One could assume that the P-value between the two lines could be used to determine which values of η are most likely and use this to optimise the exhaustive search required once the possible values for a private key have been reduced to a certain amount. However, this is not the case.

The test described above where the number of faults was set to values $\in \{1, \dots, 64\}$, where 10 000 tests were conducted for each value. In each case the distribution of the number of tests required in an exhaustive search was identical to that produced by simply starting with the least (or most) significant hypothesis and incrementing (or decrementing) the hypothesis for each test.

This is because the number of observed faults is not enough to give a good indication of the distribution to which they belong. If enough faults were observed to give a strong indication of the correct value of η, it would be expected that the minimum and maximum observation would also identify η without requiring any further computation.

6   Conclusion

In this paper, we show that the fault attack described by Giraud and Knudsen at ACISP 2004 is much more efficient than originally claimed. We proved that, using the same attack model, we need 34.3% less faulty signatures to recover a 160-bit private key. Furthermore, by improving the fault model expression, we show that for some key values we obtain another improvement of up to 47.1%. Finally, we show that there is no optimal way of performing the exhaustive search in order to reduce the computation complexity of this step.

In summary, Giraud and Knudsen claim that they need 2304 faulty signatures to recover a 160-bit private key, but in this paper we prove that one would only need between 800 and 1488 faulty signatures to recover such a key, using the same model and expected size of the required exhaustive search.

Acknowledgments

The authors would like to thank Frédéric Amiel for initiating this work and Emmanuel Prouff for his helpful comments on the preliminary version of this paper. The work described in this paper has been supported in part by the European Commission IST Programme under Contract IST-2002-507932 ECRYPT and EPSRC grant EP/F039638/1.

References

1. Bao, F., Deng, R., Han, Y., Jeng, A., Narasimhalu, A.D., Ngair, T.-H.: Breaking Public Key Cryptosystems an Tamper Resistance Devices in the Presence of Transient Fault. In: Christianson, B., Lomas, M (eds.) Security Protocols 1997. LNCS, vol. 1361, pp. 115–124. Springer, Heidelberg (1998)
2. Bar-El, H., Choukri, H., Naccache, D., Tunstall, M., Whelan, C.: The Sorcerer's Apprentice Guide to Fault Attacks. IEEE 94(2), 370–382 (2006)
3. Bellcore. New Threat Model Breaks Crypto Codes. Press Release (September 1996)
4. Biham, E., Shamir, A.: Differential Fault Analysis of Secret Key Cryptosystem. In: Kaliski Jr., B.S. (ed.) CRYPTO 1997. LNCS, vol. 1294, pp. 513–525. Springer, Heidelberg (1997)
5. Boneh, D., DeMillo, R., Lipton, R.: On the Importance of Checking Cryptographic Protocols for Faults. In: Fumy, W. (ed.) EUROCRYPT 1997. LNCS, vol. 1233, pp. 37–51. Springer, Heidelberg (1997)
6. Dottax, E.: Fault Attacks on NESSIE Signature and Identification Schemes. Technical report, NESSIE (October 2002)
7. ElGamal, T.: A Public-Key Cryptosystems and a Signature Scheme based on Discret Logarithms. IEEE Transaction on Information Theory 31(4), 172–469 (1985)
8. FIPS PUB 186-3. Digital Signature Standard. National Institute of Standards and Technology, Draft (March 2006)
9. Giraud, C., Knudsen, E.: Fault Attacks on Signature Schemes. In: Wang, H., Pieprzyk, J., Varadharajan, V. (eds.) ACISP 2004. LNCS, vol. 3108, pp. 478–491. Springer, Heidelberg (2004)

10. Giraud, C., Thiebeauld, H.: A Survey on Fault Attacks. In: Quisquater, J.-J., Paradinas, P., Deswarte, Y., Kalam, A.E. (eds.) Smart Card Research and Advanced Applications VI – CARDIS 2004, pp. 159–176. Kluwer Academic Publishers, Dordrecht (2004)
11. Joye, M., Lenstra, A., Quisquater, J.-J.: Chinese Remaindering Based Cryptosystems in the Presence of Faults. Journal of Cryptology 12(4), 241–245 (1999)
12. Joye, M., Quisquater, J.-J., Bao, F., Deng, R.: RSA-type Signatures in the Presence of Transient Faults. In: Darnell, M.J. (ed.) Cryptography and Coding 1997. LNCS, vol. 1355, pp. 155–160. Springer, Heidelberg (1997)
13. Lenstra, A.: Memo on RSA Signature Generation in the Presence of Faults. Manuscript (1996)
14. Lenstra, A., Verheul, E.: An Overview of the XTR Public Key System. In: Alster, K., Urbanowicz, J., Williams, H. (eds.) Public Key Cryptography and Computational Number Theory, de Gruyter, pp. 151–180 (2000)
15. Naccache, D., Nguyen, P., Tunstall, M., Whelan, C.: Experimenting with Faults, Lattices and the DSA. In: Vaudenay, S. (ed.) PKC 2005. LNCS, vol. 3386, pp. 16–28. Springer, Heidelberg (2005)
16. Saha, D., Mukhopadhyay, D., RoyChowdhury, D.: A Diagonal Fault Attack on the Advanced Encryption Standard. Cryptology ePrint Archive, Report 2009/581 (2009), http://eprint.iacr.org/
17. Schnorr, C.: Efficient Identification and Signatures for Smart Cards. In: Brassard, G. (ed.) CRYPTO 1989. LNCS, vol. 435, pp. 239–252. Springer, Heidelberg (1990)

A   Proof of Theorem 1 and Corollary 1

A.1   Distributions

Theorem 2. *Let a random variable X be given, which is uniformly discrete on the interval 1 to N:*

$$\forall 1 \leq x \leq N : P(X \leq x) = \frac{x}{N}$$

and define the function G as:

$$\forall 1 \leq x \leq N : G(x) := P(X_1, \cdots, X_t \leq x) = P(X \leq x)^t = \left(\frac{x}{N}\right)^t.$$

The following hold:

i. *For $a - (N-1) \leq m \leq a$:*

$$P(max = m | K = a) = \left(\frac{N + m - a}{N}\right)^t + \left(\frac{N - 1 + m - a}{N}\right)^t$$

$$P(min = m | K = a) = \left(\frac{a + 1 - m}{N}\right)^t + \left(\frac{a - m}{N}\right)^t$$

ii. *For $d \geq 2$ and $a - (N-1) \leq m \leq a - d$:*

$$P(min = m, max = m + d | K = a) = P(max = a - (N-1) + d | K = a)$$
$$- P(max = a - N + d | K = a)$$

iii. For $d \geq 2$:

$$P(max - min = d) = (N - d)(P(max = d + 1) - P(max = d))$$
$$P(d \leq max - min) = 1 - (N - d + 1)G(d) + (N - d)G(d - 1)$$

The latter result is the same as the result from [9]:

$$P(T_n \leq t) = P(d \leq max - min) = 1 - (N - d + 1)G(d) + (N - d)G(d - 1)$$

Proof (Theorem 2.i).

$$P(max \leq a) = P(X_1, \cdots, X_t \leq a)$$
$$= \prod_{i=1}^{t} P(X_i \leq a)$$
$$= P(X \leq x)^t$$
$$= G(a)$$
$$P(min \leq a) = 1 - P(min > a)$$
$$= 1 - P(a + 1 \leq X_1, \cdots, X_t)$$
$$= 1 - G(N - a)$$
$$P(max = a) = P(max \leq a) - P(max \leq a - 1)$$
$$= G(a) - G(a - 1)$$
$$P(min = a) = P(min \leq a) - P(min \leq a - 1)$$
$$= G(N - a + 1) - G(N - a)$$

□

Proof (Theorem 2.ii). For $d \geq 0$ and $1 \leq a \leq N - d$:

$$P(min \geq a, max \leq a + d) = P(a \leq X_1, \cdots, X_t \leq a + d)$$
$$= P(1 \leq X_1, \cdots, X_t \leq d + 1)$$
$$= G(d + 1)$$

For $d \geq 2$ and $1 \leq a \leq N - d$:

$$P(min = a, max = a + d) = P(a \leq X_1, \cdots, X_t \leq a + d)$$
$$+ P(a + 1 \leq X_1, \cdots, X_t \leq a + d - 1)$$
$$- P(a \leq X_1, \cdots, X_t \leq a + d - 1)$$
$$- P(a + 1 \leq X_1, \cdots, X_t \leq a + d)$$
$$= G(d + 1) - G(d) - (G(d) - G(d - 1))$$
$$= P(max = d + 1) - P(max = d)$$

□

Proof (Theorem 2.iii).

$$P(max - min = d) = \sum_{a=1}^{N-d} P(min = a, max = d + a)$$
$$= \sum_{a=1}^{N-d} (P(min = d + 1) - P(max = d))$$
$$= (N - d)(P(max = d + 1) - P(max = d))$$

$$P(d \le max - min) = P(d \le max - min \le N - 1) = \sum_{a=d}^{N-1} P(max - min = a)$$

$$= \sum_{a=d}^{N-1} (N - a)(P(max = a + 1) - P(max = a))$$

$$= \sum_{a=d+1}^{N} (N - a + 1)P(max = a) - \sum_{a=d}^{N-1} (N - a)P(max = a)$$

$$= \sum_{a=d+1}^{N-1} P(max = a) + P(max = N) - (N - d)P(max = d)$$

$$= P(d + 1 \le max) - (N - d)P(max = d)$$

$$= 1 - G(d) - (N - d)(G(d) - G(d - 1))$$

$$= 1 - (N - d + 1)G(d) + (N - d)G(d - 1)$$

If we substitute $N = 256$ and $d = N - n = 256 - n$ we get the result from [9, Theorem 1]:

$$P(T_n \le t) = P(256 - n \le max - min \le 255)$$
$$= 1 - (n + 1)G(256 - n) + nG(255 - n)$$
$$= 1 - (n + 1)\left(\frac{256 - n}{256}\right)^t + n\left(\frac{255 - n}{256}\right)^t$$

but the derivation here is much simpler than the one in the aforementioned article. $\square$

A.2   Generic Formula for Making the Correct Guess

Lemma 1. *With the notation:*

$$A = "NumGuess = n"$$
$$B_{m,d} = "min = m, max = m + d"$$
$$C = "K = a"$$

The probability of guessing the correct key in the gth guess can be expressed as

$$P(NumbGuess = g|K = a) = \sum_{d=0}^{N-g}(P(max = d) - P(max = d - 1))$$
$$\times \sum_{m=a-(N-1)}^{a-d} P(A|B_{m,d} \cap C)$$

Proof. Notice that

$$P(A \cap B|C) = \frac{P(A \cap B \cap C)}{P(C)} = \frac{P(A|B \cap C)P(B \cap C)}{P(C)} = P(A|B \cap C)P(B|C)$$

and

$$P(A|C) = P(\cup_{m,d}(A \cap B_{m,d})|C) = \sum_{m,d} P((A \cap B_{m,d})|C) = \sum_{m,d} P(A|B_{m,d} \cap C)P(B_{m,d}|C)$$

Now we can write:

$$P(NumbGuess = g|K = a) = \sum_{d=0}^{N-g} \sum_{m=a-(N-1)}^{a-d} P(A|B_{m,d} \cap C)P(B_{m,d}|C)$$

and we know from Theorem 2.ii that

$$P(B_{m,d}|C) = P(max = d) - P(max = d - 1)$$

Insertion concludes the proof.   □

A.3   Proofs of Theorem 1 and Corollary 1

Proof (Theorem 1). Having observed $min = m$ and $max = m + d$, [9] is content with noting that the number of remaining candidates equals $N - d$ and therefore

$$P(A|B_{m,d} \cap C) = \frac{1}{N - d}$$

The claim follows by insertion in the formula of Lemma 1.   □

Proof (Corollary 1). The expected is given by the formula

$$\sum_{s=1}^{N} sP(NumbGuess = g|K = a) = \sum_{s=1}^{N} s \left(\left(\frac{N - s + 1}{N} \right)^t - \left(\frac{N - s}{N} \right)^t \right)$$

which reduces to the claimed formula.   □

B   The Geometric Distribution

A geometric distribution is produced when we consider a system

$$\Pr(X = x) = (1 - p)^{x-1} p$$

That is, a geometric distribution is produced when there will be $x - 1$ failures before a successful event (that occurs with probability p) and the system stops.

We note that a geometric series, for $-1 < r < 1$ gives

$$g(x) = \sum_{k=0}^{\infty} a r^k = \frac{a}{1 - r},$$

and the first differential is

$$g'(x) = \sum_{k=1}^{\infty} a k r^{k-1} = \frac{a}{(1 - r)^2} .$$

If X has a geometric distribution and $0 < p < 1$, then the expectation of X is given by

$$E(X) = \sum_{x=1}^{\infty} x q^{x-1} p = \frac{p}{(1 - q)^2} = \frac{1}{p},$$

using the above formula for $g'(x)$ with $a = p$ and $r = q$.

When Clocks Fail:
On Critical Paths and Clock Faults

Michel Agoyan[1], Jean-Max Dutertre[2],
David Naccache[1,3], Bruno Robisson[1], and Assia Tria[1]

[1] CEA-LETI
Centre microélectronique de Provence G. Charpak
Département SAS
80 Avenue de Mimet, F-13120 Gardanne, France
{michel.agoyan,bruno.robisson,assia.tria}@cea.fr
[2] École nationale supérieure des Mines de Saint-Étienne
Centre microélectronique de Provence G. Charpak
Département SAS
80 Avenue de Mimet, F-13120 Gardanne, France
dutertre@emse.fr
[3] École normale supérieure, Département d'informatique, Équipe de cryptographie,
45 rue d'Ulm, F-75230 Paris CEDEX 05, France
david.naccache@ens.fr

Abstract. Whilst clock fault attacks are known to be a serious security threat, an in-depth explanation of such faults still seems to be put in order.

This work provides a theoretical analysis, backed by practical experiments, explaining when and how clock faults occur. Understanding and modeling the chain of events following a transient clock alteration allows to accurately predict faulty circuit behavior. A prediction fully confirmed by injecting variable-duration faults at predetermined clock cycles.

We illustrate the process by successfully attacking an FPGA AES implementation using a DLL-based FPGA platform (one-bit fault attack).

1 Introduction

Fault attacks consist in modifying an electronic circuit's behavior to achieve malicious goals [2,3]. Fault attacks exist in numerous variants ranging from a simple alteration of a round counter during symmetric encryption [4] to mathematical Differential Fault Attacks (DFA) where secret information is obtained by comparing (differentiating) correct and faulty encryption results [6,12].

Faults can be caused by a variety of intrusive and non-intrusive means [1] such as lasers [16], electromagnetic perturbations [10,13], voltage variations [9] or clock glitches [7].

In this work we present a new clock alteration technique for *scenarii* in which the attacker is given access to the target's clock. We start by explaining and modeling the chain of events causing the faulty behavior. This theoretical analysis

D. Gollmann, J.-L. Lanet, J. Iguchi-Cartigny (Eds.): CARDIS 2010, LNCS 6035, pp. 182–193, 2010.

perfectly reflects experimental observations and allowed the injection of precise single-bit faults into a chip running the AES algorithm (an actual implementation of the attack described in [8]).

After introducing the model, we will overview the fault injector's design, the target chip's structure and the way in which the injector was used to extract AES keys.

2 Why Clock Faults Occur?

We inject faults by violating *synchrony*, a basic assumption under which traditional digital ICs operate. In essence, most[1] ICs execute calculations by processing data by combinatorial logic blocks separated by D flip-flop register banks sharing the same clock (figure 1).

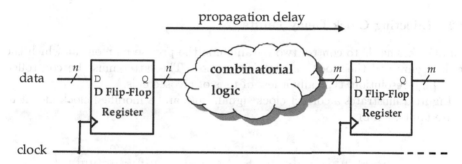

Fig. 1. Synchronous Representation of Digital ICs

Data is usually latched by registers at raising clock edges. Between two such edges, the computed data travels between registers and gets modified by the intermediate combinatorial logic blocks. The time needed to propagate data through combinatorial logic is called *propagation delay*. The propagation delay and a second delay element, inherent to the use of D flip-flop, called *set-up time*, define the circuit's maximal operating frequency (nominal circuit period). Indeed, to ensure proper circuit operation, the clock period must be strictly greater than the maximal propagation delay in concerned circuit (this maximal propagation delay is called *critical path*) plus the registers' set-up time. In other words:

$$T_{\text{clock}} > t_{\text{critical}} + t_{\text{set-up}} \tag{1}$$

As a matter of fact any data bit entering a register is the result of a combinatorial calculation involving several previous register output bits. The transformation of the previous registers' output into the next register's input bit takes a determined delay. This delay depends on the the logic performed as well as on the data transiting through the logic. In addition, propagation time varies with circuit temperature and power supply voltage.

---

[1] ICs that do not assume synchrony exist but we do not consider these in this work.

2.1   Overclocking

Overclocking consists in decreasing the clock period (or, put differently, increasing clock frequency). If setup delays are not respected, the D flip-flop's input is not given sufficient time to reach the latch. Causing faulty data to be latched instead. This led several authors to use overclocking as fault injection means [9,15].

A decreased clock period can potentially affect logical paths whose propagation times exceed the decreased clock period minus the set-up time. From the attacker's perspective, the ability to control precisely the clock period is crucial for inducing faults with precision. Note that temperature and power supply changes may also be used to exert such control.

Fault attacks consist in injecting faults at precise moments. To avoid injecting faults continuously, overclocking must be brief and transient. The fault injection technique described in the next section allows doing so.

2.2   Injecting Clock Delay Faults

An attacker needs to control two parameters: the precise moment at which the fault occurs and the clock anomaly's duration. The latter must be controlled with high resolution, typically a few of tens of picoseconds.

Figure 2 illustrates a correct clock signal, CLK, and a modified clock meant to cause faults, FAULTY_CLK.

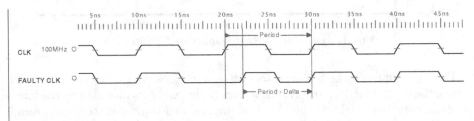

Fig. 2. Normal (CLK) vs. Faulty (FAULTY_CLK) Clock Signals

The two waveforms differ only between the delimiters positioned at 20ns and 30ns. During that interval, the FAULTY_CLK's period is reduced by Δ ns. The Δ time decrement causes a set-up time violation fault. Note that the extension by Δ of the preceding clock cycle's low state has no adverse effect.

Generating FAULTY_CLK with sufficient accuracy and precision is a challenging task. To do so, we use the embedded Delay Locked Loop (DLL) of a recent FPGA family (Xilinx Virtex 5). Two clocks (CLK_DELAYED i) with programmable skews are generated from CLK. The skews of the CLK_DELAYED i signals, denoted δ_i, are programmable. FAULTY_CLK is obtained by switching between the CLK_DELAYED i using a TRIGGER signal. Figure 3 depicts this process in further details.

If CLK_DELAYED 2 is delayed by δ_2 time units, CLK_DELAYED 1 must be delayed by $\delta_1 = \frac{\delta_2}{2}$ to preserve a 50% duty cycle at FAULTY_CLK's transient fault interval.

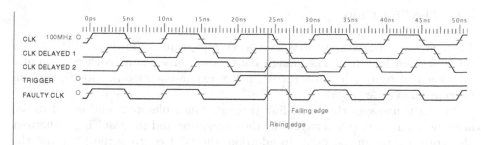

Fig. 3. Faulty (FAULTY_CLK) Clock Signal Generation

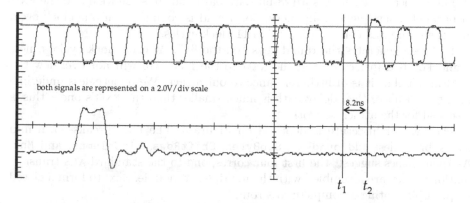

Fig. 4. FAULTY_CLK (uppermost signal) and AES_START (lowermost signal)

The device assembles FAULTY_CLK by combining CLK_DELAYED 2's raising edge and CLK_DELAYED 1's falling edge. This is controlled by the signal TRIGGER that positions the perturbation in time. The accurracy at which FAULTY_CLK's shape can be controlled (in our setting 35ps) depends on δ_t, the smallest elementary delay that the DLL is able to provide. We will refer to FAULTY_CLK's altered signal chunk as the *faulting period* (in Figure 3, the interval between 24ns and 30ns).

An oscilloscope screen-shot of FAULTY_CLK is shown on Figure 4 (uppermost signal). Here, CLK's period (10ns) was reduced to $[t_1, t_2] = 49\delta_t \simeq 8.2$ns in FAULTY_CLK. The lowermost signal's high level indicates the AES' start. The implementation completes an encryption round in one cycle. Hence, the diagram shows a fault injection at the ninth round (*cf.* section 3.2).

As we write these lines, a Xilinx Virtex 5 development board costs less than $1000.

3   Clock Fault DFA on AES

We tested the attack setup on a concrete AES implementation. The following sections describe the target chip, the attack's theoretical principle ([8]) and report practical experiment results.

3.1   The Test Chip

The test chip (Xilinx Spartan 3AN FPGA) implements a hardware 128-bit AES [11,5] written in VHDL. The design consists of three main blocks: a communication and control module (CCM), a key expansion module (KEM), and an encryption module (ENM).

The CCM manages the serial link through which plaintext and key material are input. The start signal triggering the encryption and the resulting ciphertext also transit through the CCM. In addition, the CCM controls the KEM and the ENM's operations during encryption.

The implementation uses a 128-bit data path and runs the KEM and the ENM in parallel. Consequently, an encryption round is completed in one clock cycle and the entire AES computation takes 11 clock cycles.

The KEM generates the round keys "on the fly". At each clock cycle, a new round key is transferred from the KEM to the ENM. We will not overview the KEM in detail as it is of little relevance to our attack. We nonetheless underline that the KEM's critical delay path is much smaller than the ENM's one – this is essential for the attack to work.

The ENM architecture is depicted on Figure 5. The ENM breaks-down into five submodules: AddRoundKey, SubBytes, ShiftRows, MixColumns, and Mux. As their names suggest, the first four correspond to the standard AES transformations. They are assembled with the multiplexer module, Mux, to form a closed loop, implementing a complete AES round.

The Mux module opens the loop for plaintext acquisition during the initial round and closes it afterwards. The AddRoundKey module has a dedicated bus (ciphertext) through which ciphertext is output after the final round. The MixColumns module is bypassed during the final round. SubBytes is the only clocked module (all the others being purely combinatorial blocks). This allows, as mentioned before, to complete an encryption round in one clock cycle. This loop architecture features a long data propagation path. Consequently, the

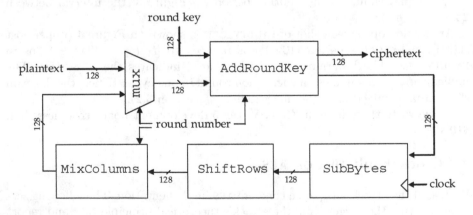

Fig. 5. AES Structure

design's critical delay path is located in the ENM. The nominal clock frequency of this AES implementation is 100 MHz.

3.2 Giraud's One-Bit Attack

This section recalls Giraud's DFA [8] (hereafter "Giraud's one-bit attack"). The attack is based on the restrictive assumption that the opponent can inject one-bit faults. We use the following notations:

M^i the algorithm's state at the end of round i
K^i i-th round key number
C a correct ciphertext
D a faulty ciphertext

The attacker injects a single bit fault into one byte of state M^9 just before the final round's SubBytes operation. This allows to retrieve the last round key K^{10}.

Consider the i-th state byte just before the final round M_i^9. The corresponding byte index in the ciphertext is ShiftRows(i). As per the AES' specifications, for all $i \in \{0, \ldots, 15\}$:

$$C_{\text{ShiftRows}(i)} = \text{SubBytes}(M_i^9) \oplus K^{10}_{\text{ShiftRows}(i)} \tag{2}$$

If a one-bit fault $e,^2$ is injected into the j-th byte of M^9, we obtain at index j:

$$D_{\text{ShiftRows}(j)} = \text{SubBytes}(M_j^9 \oplus e) \oplus K^{10}_{\text{ShiftRows}(j)} \tag{3}$$

and for index $i \in \{0, \ldots, 15\}\backslash\{j\}$:

$$D_{\text{ShiftRows}(i)} = \text{SubBytes}(M_i^9) \oplus K^{10}_{\text{ShiftRows}(i)} \tag{4}$$

Hence, a comparison (differentiation) between the correct and the faulty ciphertexts leaks information both on the fault's position and on the AES key. For $i \in \{0, \ldots, 15\}\backslash\{j\}$, equations 2 and 4 yield:

$$C_{\text{ShiftRows}(i)} = D_{\text{ShiftRows}(i)} \tag{5}$$

This allows to identify the faulty byte's index j because the only index for which $C \oplus D$ is nonzero is ShiftRows(j). Moreover, at index j, equations 2 and 3 yield:

$$C_{\text{ShiftRows}(j)} \oplus D_{\text{ShiftRows}(j)} = \text{SubBytes}(M_j^9) \oplus \text{SubBytes}(M_j^9 \oplus e) \tag{6}$$

Equation 6 is then solved for the eight possible values of e (the only hypothesis made on e is that $e = 2^i$ for some i). This provides a set of candidates for M_j^9.

At this point, new one-bit fault injections targeting the same byte are required to reduce the solution set to one item, namely M_j^9. The probability to find M_j^9 in three attempts (i.e. three different faults) is $\simeq 99\%$.

---

[2] That is: $e = 2^i$ for $i = 0, \ldots, 7$.

$K^{10}_{\text{ShiftRows}(j)}$ is then calculated from M^9_j, using equation 2:

$$K^{10}_{\text{ShiftRows}(j)} = C_{\text{ShiftRows}(i)} \oplus \text{SubBytes}(M^9_j) \tag{7}$$

Equation 7 shows that the attack works independently on each round key byte. Indeed, no MixColumns transformation follows the fault injection and MixColumns is the only transformation capable of propagating faults among bytes. Consequently, the whole round key K^{10} can be progressively retrieved by the attacker. Finally, knowing K^{10}, the secret key K is found by reversing the key expansion algorithm.

3.3   The Attack Process

The experimental set-up (Figure 6) consists in a test chip board (TCB), a clock fault generator (CFG) and a computer.

The TCB embeds the AES implementation described in the previous section. Its clock is provided by the CFG. The secret key, the plaintext and the encryption start signal are transmitted to the TCB from the computer *via* a serial link. As encryption ends, the ciphertext is offloaded *via* the serial link. The TCB provides a trigger signal to the CFG indicating the exact beginning of the encryption process. This is done to ease synchrony between fault injection and AES rounds. Note that the trigger could be replaced by the inspection of power consumption (SPA) to precisely locate the AES rounds in time.

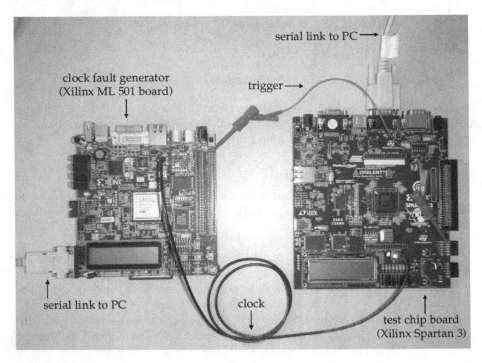

Fig. 6. Experimental Set-up

The CFG generates a 100 MHz clock signal continuously fed into the TCB. When the trigger signal indicates that encryption was started, a countdown is started. As the countdown ends a faulting period is produced during round nine, as required by Giraud's one-bit attack. The serial link between the computer and the CFG is used to define the exact value of the faulting period decrement Δ.

The computer runs a test campaign as described in Algorithm 1.

Algorithm 1. Test Campaign Pseudo-Code

---

send the key K and the plaintext M to the test chip.
$\Delta \leftarrow 0$.
while (clock_period $> \Delta$) **do**
    encrypt and retrieve the ciphertext
    $\Delta \leftarrow \Delta + \delta_t$
end while

The generation of a faulting period is automatic and hence not explicitly mentioned in the pseudo-code. Indeed, the trigger signal sent from the TCB to the CFG indicates the encryption's launch and causes a faulting period generation during the ninth round as shown in Figure 4. As the faulting period gradually decreases, more set-up time violation faults appear in the calculation process. The resulting faulty ciphertexts are ordered by decreasing faulting periods. Then, faulty ciphertexts are successively compared with the correct ciphertext. This allows identifying the faulty bytes (Eq. 6 and Eq. 7). In addition, for each ciphertext byte, a list of induced faults is built in order of appearance. Assuming that the first injected fault stems from a one-bit fault induced just before the last SubBytes, we build the corresponding set of guessed bytes for K^{10} from equations 6 and 7. For the test campaign described in Algorithm 1, we obtain a set of guesses for every byte of K^{10}. To reduce progressively these sets to singletons we inject different one-bit faults repeating the test campaigns with the same key but with different plaintexts. Indeed, each data bit arriving to the SubBytes's registers possesses its own logic path and propagation time (section 2). This propagation time highly depends on the data handled during encryption. Consequently, plaintext changes modify all propagation times. As propagation times vary, the injected one-bit faults differ with a 7/8 probability at the byte level.

As a result, one needs at least three (and sometimes four) test campaigns (same key and different plaintexts) to retrieve the entire round key. Finally, K is obtained by reversing the key expansion process.

3.4   Experimental Results

A first experiment targeting the final AES round was conducted to test the CFG. We implemented successfully Giraud's one-bit attack as well as its extension to two bits.

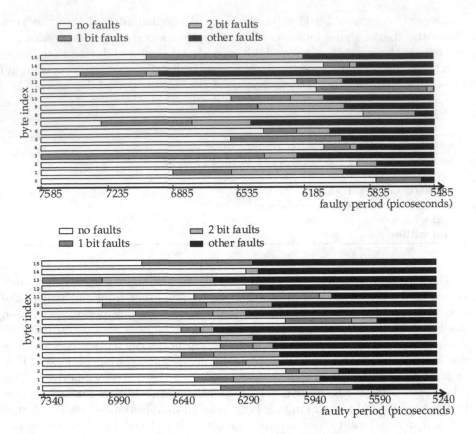

Fig. 7. Two fault injection experiments: same key, different plaintexts

Injecting multiple-bit faults. To test the hypothesis that a decrease in the faulting period causes more internal faults, we targeted the AES' tenth round while progressively increasing Δ.

As expected, the comparison of correct and faulty ciphertexts reveals that the device progressively transits from normal operation to multi-bit faults. This is done by exhibiting none, one-bit, two-bit and multiple-bit faults as described in Figure 7. Note that the above is not an attack but an experimental fault characterization experiment where the AES plays the role of a big propagation delay cause.

Figure 7 reports fault characterization experiments conducted with a constant key and two different plaintexts.

Figure 7 shows the faults' timing and nature as a function of the faulting period's duration (the horizontal axis). Each horizontal bar, associated with a byte number, uses a color code to reflect the nature of faults (no fault, one-bit fault, two-bits fault, more than two bits fault) and their point of appearance in time. The first one-bit fault occurs in byte 3 for a faulting period of 7585 ps ($= 10000 - 69 \times 35$ ps), and the last fault appears on byte 0 for a 5800 ps faulting

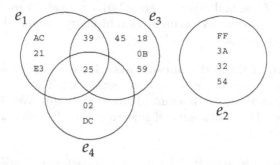

Fig. 8. Reducing the number of bytes candidates

period. With the exception of bytes 2 and 8, the first fault is always a one-bit fault. This is compatible with the theoretical fault genesis model introduced at the beginning of this paper. Figure 8 shows how the number of byte candidates is progressively reduced. Each of the four sets in the example is associated with a different one-bit fault e_i (for $i \in \{1, 2, 3, 4\}$). Here, the correct round key byte, 0x25, is found at the intersection of sets associated with e_1, e_3 and e_4. The fact that the set associated with e_2 stands apart indicates that the one-bit fault assumption about e_2 was wrong. Leaving aside e_2, the set of guesses is reduced by successive sets intersections until a singleton containing the round key byte is reached. However, taking into account set e_2 requires the more complex intersection process described in Algorithm 2.

Algorithm 2. Determining the correct key byte

$i \leftarrow 2$
$S \leftarrow e_1$
while $(|S| \neq 1)$ **do**
   if $S \cap e_i = \emptyset$ **then**
      $S = S \cup e_i$
   else
      $S = S \cap e_i$
   end if
   $i \leftarrow i + 1$
end while
return the single element of S as the correct key byte.

The probability of injecting successively a one-bit and a two-bit fault when reducing the faulty period can be estimated from Figure 7, where bytes 8, 5, 2 and 0 are counter-examples. Many examples seem to indicate that this probability is greater than 70% (experimentally).

The probability to cause successively one-bit, two-bit, and three-bit faults seems to be 50% (experimentally). These statistics were obtained thanks to the very small value of the faulty-period granularity, namely 35ps. This resolution seems to allow the progressive accumulation of faulty propagation paths as the faulting period is decreased.

Implementation of Giraud's one-bit attack. We wrote a script that plays the elementary test campaign described in section 3.3. The test was run several tens of times, for at least five different plaintexts per run. We always found the correct round key. The probability of injecting one-bit faults was found to be greater or equal to 90%.

Extension to two-bit attack. The ability to inject and identify two-bit faults has prompted us to extend the attack. Note that two-bit attacks can defeat one-bit parity check countermeasures. To that end, we need to solve equation 6 with the assumption that e is a two-bit fault. The only adverse effect is an increase in the cardinality of potential solution sets. The experiment was successful: 13 to 14 round key bytes were found on average with the automated test campaign. This allowed to exhaustive-search the whole key.

Repeating the campaign with many different plaintexts, we were always able to inject two-bit fault at every byte location, even if we never succeeded in injecting two-bit faults simultaneously on all bytes.

4   Conclusion

This paper describes a new fault injection technique based on clock reshaping during a precise cycle to cause setup time violation faults. The new technique would be a good candidate to benchmark safe-error [17] or differential behaviorial [14] analysis.

This technique is inexpensive, efficient and non-intrusive. As such, it underlines the importance of further research in countermeasure design.

References

1. Bar-El, H., Choukri, H., Naccache, D., Tunstall, M., Whelan, C.: The sorcerer's apprentice guide to fault attacks. Special Issue on Cryptography and Security 94(2), 370–382 (2006)
2. Biham, E., Shamir, A.: Differential fault analysis of secret key cryptosystems. In: Kaliski Jr., B.S. (ed.) CRYPTO 1997. LNCS, vol. 1294, pp. 513–525. Springer, Heidelberg (1997)
3. Boneth, D., DeMillo, R.A., Lipton, R.J.: On the importance of checking cryptographic protocols for faults. In: Fumy, W. (ed.) EUROCRYPT 1997. LNCS, vol. 1233, pp. 37–51. Springer, Heidelberg (1997)
4. Choukri, H., Tunstall, M.: Round reduction using faults. In: Proc. Second Int'l Workshop Fault Diagnosis and Tolerance in Cryptography, FDTC 2005 (2005)
5. Daemen, J., Rijmen, V.: Rijndael, Aes proposal (1998)
6. Dusart, P., Letourneux, G., Vivolo, O.: Differential fault analysis on aes. In: Zhou, J., Yung, M., Han, Y. (eds.) ACNS 2003. LNCS, vol. 2846, pp. 293–306. Springer, Heidelberg (2003)

7. Fukunaga, T., Takahashi, J.: Practical fault attack on a cryptographic lsi with iso/iec 18033-3 block ciphers. In: Proc. of the 2009 Workshop on Fault Diagnosis and Tolerance in Cryptography, FDTC 2009, pp. 84–92 (2009)

8. Giraud, C.: DFA on AES. In: Dobbertin, H., Rijmen, V., Sowa, A. (eds.) AES 2005. LNCS, vol. 3373, pp. 27–41. Springer, Heidelberg (2005)

9. Guilley, S., Sauvage, L., Danger, J.-L., Selmane, N., Pacalet, R.: Silicon-level solutions to counteract passive and active attacks. In: FDTC 2008: Proceedings of the 2008 5th Workshop on Fault Diagnosis and Tolerance in Cryptography, pp. 3–17 (2008)

10. Hutter, M., Schmidt, J.-M.: Optical and em fault-attacks on crt-based rsa: Concrete results. In: Proceedings of the 15th Austrian Workhop on Microelectronics (2007)

11. NIST. Announcing the Advanced Encryption Standard (AES). Federal Information Processing Standards Publication No. 197, November 26 (2001)

12. Piret, G., Quisquater, J.-J.: A differential fault attack technique against spn structures, with application to the aes and khazad. In: Walter, C.D., Koç, Ç.K., Paar, C. (eds.) CHES 2003. LNCS, vol. 2779, pp. 77–88. Springer, Heidelberg (2003)

13. Quisquater, J.J., Samyde, D.: Eddy current for magnetic analysis with active sensor. In: Proceedings of ESmart 2002, Eurosmart, pp. 185–194 (2002)

14. Robisson, B., Manet, P.: Differential behavioral analysis. In: Paillier, P., Verbauwhede, I. (eds.) CHES 2007. LNCS, vol. 4727, pp. 413–426. Springer, Heidelberg (2007)

15. Selmane, N., Guilley, S., Danger, J.-L.: Practical setup time violation attacks on AES. In: EDCC-7 2008: Proceedings of the 2008 Seventh European Dependable Computing Conference, pp. 91–96 (2008)

16. Skorobogatov, S.P., Anderson, R.J.: Optical fault induction attacks. In: Kaliski Jr., B.S., Koç, Ç.K., Paar, C. (eds.) CHES 2002. LNCS, vol. 2523, pp. 2–12. Springer, Heidelberg (2003)

17. Yen, S.-M., Joye, M.: Checking before output may not be enough against fault-based cryptanalysis. IEEE Transactions on Computers 49, 967–970 (2000)

Modeling Privacy for Off-Line RFID Systems*

Flavio D. Garcia** and Peter van Rossum

Institute for Computing and Information Sciences,
Radboud University Nijmegen, The Netherlands
{flaviog,petervr}@cs.ru.nl

Abstract. This paper establishes a novel model for RFID schemes
where readers are not continuously connected to the back office, but only
periodically. Furthermore, adversaries are not only capable of compromising tags, but also of compromising readers. This more properly models large scale deployment of RFID technology such as in public transport
ticketing systems and supply-chain management systems. In this model
we define notions of security (only legitimate tags can authenticate) and
of privacy (no adversary is capable of tracking legitimate tags). We show
that privacy is always lost at the moment that a reader is compromised
and we develop notions of forward and backward privacy with respect to
reader corruption. This models the property that tags cannot be traced,
under mild additional assumptions, for the time slots before and after
reader corruption. We exhibit two protocols that only use hashing that
achieve these security and privacy notions and give proofs in the random
oracle model.

1 Introduction

During the last decade, the use of RFID technology has expanded enormously.
It is currently deployed in electronic passports, tags for consumer goods, public
transport ticketing systems, race timing, and countless other applications.

The widespread use of RFID has raised privacy concerns. Since most RFID
tags will send a unique identifier to every reader that attempts to communicate
with it, an adversary could build an "RFID profile" of an individual, i.e., the
collection of unique identifiers of the RFID tags that the individual usually
carries. This profile could be used to track this person, or to infer behavior such
as spending or traveling patterns, jeopardizing this person's privacy.

For simple RFID applications (for instance the tagging of products in stores
to enable RFID based cash registers), the privacy problems could be solved

* The work described in this paper has been partially supported by the Euro-
pean Commission through the ICT program under contract ICT-2007-216676
ECRYPT II.
** Partially supported by the research program Sentinels (www.sentinels.nl), project
PEARL (7639). Sentinels is being financed by Technology Foundation STW, the
Netherlands Organization for Scientific Research (NWO), and the Dutch Ministry
of Economic Affairs.

D. Gollmann, J.-L. Lanet, J. Iguchi-Cartigny (Eds.): CARDIS 2010, LNCS 6035, pp. 194–208, 2010.
© IFIP International Federation for Information Processing 2010

by sending the kill-command to the RFID tags (upon leaving the store). This, however, is useless for situations such as access control, where legitimate readers need to verify the authenticity of tags.

Various RFID schemes using cryptographic techniques that guarantee both security (authenticity of accepted tags) and privacy have been proposed. Because RFID tags are low-cost and low-power devices, they are limited in the type of cryptography that can be used. In particular, it is not possible to use public key cryptography in a way that is both cheap and fast enough. Additionally, most RFID tags are not tamper-resistant and do not have the ability to keep time, since they lack an independent energy source.

Protocols that have been proposed to achieve both security and privacy are, among others, OSK/AO [OSK03, AO05], NIBY [NIBY06], and YA-TRAP [Tsu06]. In the literature, RFID schemes are typically modeled as a multi-threaded reader that enjoys an always-active secure communication channel with the back office [JW07, Vau07, Avo05]. Although this approach is simple and practical, it cannot model several widely deployed RFID systems nowadays.

In practice, in a number of large-scale RFID systems, readers remain off-line most of the time and have only periodic connection with the central back office. During that connection, the readers and the back office synchronize. Typical examples of this configuration are transport ticketing systems such as the London Oyster card and the Dutch OV-chipkaart, where readers in buses and trains connect to a central database during the night and remain off-line during the day. This configuration enforces the migration of sensitive information from the back office to the readers, since readers now have to be able to decide by themselves whether to grant access to a passenger or not, to name an example. This configuration brings new security threats: readers might de-synchronize with other readers, tags or with the back office itself. Besides that, if an attacker steals or tampers with a reader that now contains sensitive information it should not compromise the security and privacy of the whole system. Concurrently and independently this issue has also been studied by Avoine et al. in [ALM09]; both results were presented at RFIDSec'09.

Our contribution. In this paper, we propose to explicitly model the existence of multiple readers, that, just as tags, can be compromised by the adversary and their secret information obtained. With respect to tag corruption, we consider a "forward" notion of privacy: if a tag is corrupted in the future, its past behavior is still private. With respect to reader corruption, we consider both a "forward" and a "backward" notion of privacy: if a reader is corrupted in the future, privacy of past communication should still be guaranteed, but also if some reader has been corrupted in the past, privacy should still be guaranteed in the future. See Figures 1 and 2.

Because readers only periodically connect to the back office, one cannot expect to retain privacy of tags (or security of the system) at the moment a reader is destroyed. More precisely, during a time slot (a period between two successive synchronizations of the whole system) in which a reader gets corrupted, security and privacy cannot be guaranteed. There is the additional point that tags do

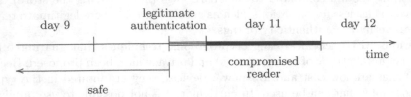

Fig. 1. Self-stabilizing Forward Privacy

not have an intrinsic notion of time. For forward privacy, since the adversary can corrupt a reader in the future, privacy is only guaranteed if the last communication of the tag (before the time slot where reader corruption takes place) is with a legitimate reader. When there is no reader corruption, this condition is not necessary and our notion of forward privacy reduces to the standard one.

For backward privacy, note that a corrupted reader will always be able to communicate with a tag that has not communicated with the system since the reader corruption took place. It is not until a tag communicates with a legitimate reader that one can expect to regain privacy guarantees.

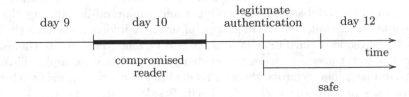

Fig. 2. Self-stabilizing Backward Privacy

We formulate three notions of privacy: forward privacy with respect to tag corruption, self-stabilizing forward privacy with respect to reader destruction, and self-stabilizing backward privacy with respect to reader destruction. "Self-stabilizing" refers to the fact that privacy is not immediately guaranteed outside the time slot where reader destruction takes place, but only after communicating with a legitimate reader.

As in [Vau07], we consider several classes of adversaries (depending on their ability to corrupt or destroy tags, destroy readers, or see the result of an authentication protocol between a tag and a reader) and the privacy (and security) notions are parameterized by the class of adversaries under consideration. We model the privacy requirements as in [JW07]. An attacker generates two uncorrupted tags. Later, he get access to only one of them and has to guess which one it is. The privacy requirement is that he only guesses correctly with probability negligibly larger than $\frac{1}{2}$. The difference between the three privacy notions is expressed in the different capabilities the adversary has. For privacy with respect to tag corruption, the adversary cannot destroy readers. For self-stabilizing forward privacy with respect to reader destruction, the adversary can only corrupt readers after being given access to the challenge tag. For self-stabilizing backward privacy with respect to reader corruption, it can only corrupt readers before it is given access to the challenge tag.

Finally, we analyze three protocols. First, because we have slightly modified the notion of privacy from the literature combining ideas from [JW07] and [Vau07], we present a slightly modified version of the OSK protocol that obtains security and privacy with respect to tag corruption. We then describe two other protocols, using only hashing, that additionally achieve self-stabilizing forward and backward privacy with respect to reader corruption. In all three cases, we prove the security and privacy of the scheme in the random oracle model.

Structure of the paper. In Section 2 we formally model an RFID system with off-line readers. We model adversaries, as usual, as probabilistic polynomial-time algorithms that interact with an RFID system by means of oracles. In Section 3, we define the notions of security and privacy, using a game-based approach. Section 4 describes the three protocols achieving our security and privacy notions and the proofs in the random oracle model. Finally, Section 5 concludes.

2   System Model

To model this scenario, consider a scheme where readers have a secure communication channel with the back office that is only active during synchronization. We assume that readers are single threaded, i.e., can only have one active protocol instance with a tag at a time. After running a protocol with a tag, the reader has an output that is typically the identity of the tag. New readers and tags can be added to the system at will. The formal definition follows.

Definition 2.1 (RFID scheme). *An RFID scheme Π consists of:*

- *a probabilistic polynomial-time algorithm* SetupSystem *that takes as input the security parameter 1^η and outputs the public key pair (sk, pk) of the system.*
- *a probabilistic polynomial-time algorithm* SetupReader *that takes as input the secret key of the system sk and outputs the initial state of the reader s and the reader's secret k.*
- *a probabilistic polynomial-time algorithm* SetupTag *that takes as input the secret key of the system sk and outputs the initial state of the tag s and the tag's secret k.*
- *a polynomial-time interactive protocol* Sync *between the readers and the back-office.*
- *a polynomial-time interactive protocol between a reader and a tag, where the reader returns* Output. *Output is typically the identity of the tag.*

An adversary is a probabilistic polynomial-time algorithm that interacts with the system by means of different oracles. The environment keeps track of the state of each element in the system and answers the oracle queries according to the protocol. Besides adding new tags and readers to the system and being able to communicate with them, an adversary can also corrupt tags. This models techniques like differential power analysis and chip slicing. By corrupting a tag an adversary retrieves its internal state. Something similar happens with readers, although in this case we assume that the system can detect that. In the example of the transport ticketing system we assume that the company would detect if a bus gets stolen or a missing gate at the metro station. An adversary can also initiate the synchronization protocol which models waiting until the next time-period. Additionally, an adversary might be capable of seeing the result of an authentication attempt by external means, for instance, by looking whether a door opens or not. The formal definition of adversary follows.

Definition 2.2 (Adversary). *An* adversary *is a probabilistic polynomial-time algorithm that takes as input the system public key pk and has access to the following oracles:*

- CreateReader($\mathcal{R}$) *creates a new reader by calling* SetupReader(sk) *and updates the state of the back-office. This new reader is referenced as* $\mathcal{R}$.
- DestroyReader($\mathcal{R}$) *destroys reader* $\mathcal{R}$ *and returns its internal state s to the adversary. After calling* DestroyReader, *oracle calls with this reference are no longer valid.*
- CreateTag($\mathcal{T}$) *creates a new tag* $\mathcal{T}$ *by calling* SetupTag(sk) *and updates the state of the back-office. This new tag is referenced as* $\mathcal{T}$.
- CorruptTag($\mathcal{T}$) *returns the internal state s of the tag* $\mathcal{T}$.
- Launch($\mathcal{R}$) *attempts to initiate a new protocol instance at reader* $\mathcal{R}$. *If* $\mathcal{R}$ *has already an active protocol instance then* Launch *fails and returns zero. Otherwise it starts a new protocol instance and returns one.*
- Send(m, A) *sends a message m to the entity A and returns its response m'. The entity A can either be a reader* $\mathcal{R}$ *or a tag* $\mathcal{T}$.
- Result($\mathcal{R}$) *outputs whether or not the output of the last finished protocol instance at reader* $\mathcal{R}$ *is not* $\bot$, *i.e.,* Output $\neq \bot$.
- Sync() *initiates the interactive protocol* Sync *between the readers and the back-office.*

Definition 2.3. *We denote by* $\mathcal{O}$ *the set of oracles* {CreateReader, CreateTag, CorruptTag, Launch, Send, Sync, Result} *and* $\mathcal{O}^+ = \mathcal{O} \cup$ {DestroyReader}.

3   Security Definitions

This section elaborates on the security and privacy definitions from the literature, adapting them to our model. Then, it also discusses (when applicable) the relations among them.

   The main goal of an RFID system is security, which means that readers are able to authenticate legitimate tags. Throughout this paper we focus on privacy. For the sake of self containment, we include here the following security definition which is an adapted version of the security definition proposed in [Vau07].

Definition 3.1 (Security). *An RFID scheme is secure if for all adversaries $\mathcal{A}$ and for all readers $\mathcal{R}$, the probability that $\mathcal{R}$ outputs the identity of a legitimate tag while the last finished protocol instance at reader $\mathcal{R}$ and this tag did not have any matching conversation, is a negligible function of η. Matching conversation here means that $\mathcal{R}$ and the tag (successfully) executed the authentication protocol.*

Next we define privacy with respect to tag corruption. We compose the definitions of Juels and Weis [JW07] and Vaudenay [Vau07] since each of them has its advantages: the former is indistinguishability based, which makes it more practical; the latter has the drawback of being simulation based but is stronger and allows for a variety of adversaries with custom capabilities. Privacy is defined in an IND-CCA like fashion where the adversary tries to win the privacy game. In this game, the environment creates system parameters by calling SetupSystem. Then it gives the public key of the system pk to the adversary $\mathcal{A}_0$. This adversary has access to the set of oracles $\mathcal{O}$. Eventually, $\mathcal{A}_0$ must output two uncorrupted challenge tags $\mathcal{T}_0^\star$ and $\mathcal{T}_1^\star$. Then, the environment chooses a random bit b and gives the adversary $\mathcal{A}_1$ access to $\mathcal{T}_b^\star$. At this point, the original references to $\mathcal{T}_0^\star$ and $\mathcal{T}_1^\star$ are no longer valid. Again, the adversary has access to all oracles $\mathcal{O}$. Finally, the adversary outputs a guess bit b'. The adversary wins the game if $b = b'$. The formal definition follows.

Definition 3.2 (Privacy game)

$$
\begin{array}{l}
\textbf{Priv-Game}_{\Pi,\mathcal{A}}(\eta) : \\
\quad (sk, pk) \leftarrow \mathsf{SetupSystem}(1^\eta) \\
\quad \mathcal{T}_0^\star, \mathcal{T}_1^\star \leftarrow \mathcal{A}_0^{\mathcal{O}}(pk) \\
\quad b \leftarrow \{0,1\} \\
\quad b' \leftarrow \mathcal{A}_1^{\mathcal{O}}(\mathcal{T}_b^\star) \\
\quad \textbf{win if } b = b'.
\end{array}
$$

The challenge tags $\mathcal{T}_0^\star$ and $\mathcal{T}_1^\star$ must be uncorrupted, which means that no CorruptTag($\mathcal{T}_{\{0,1\}}^\star$) query has been made. Adversaries implicitly pass state.

In general, it is hard to define a realistic adversarial model as different applications have different requirements. Following the lines of Vaudenay [Vau07], we consider different classes of adversaries depending on their capabilities. The notions of forward, weak and narrow adversaries are due to Vaudenay. Intuitively, a *forward* adversary is an adversary that observes communication between tags and readers and later on acquires one of these tags and tries to link it with some of the past sessions, compromising its privacy. If the adversary succeeds to do so, with non-negligible probability, we say that is a *winning* adversary. A *weak* adversary is an adversary that is unable to corrupt tags. In real life scenarios it is often realistic to assume that an adversary can see the outcome of an authentication attempt. For instance, this is the case of transport ticketing systems where an adversary could observe whether the gate of the metro opens or not, for a specific tag. An adversary that is unable to do so is called *narrow*.

We introduce the notion of *reader-destructive* adversary which is a forward adversary, additionally empowered with a DestroyReader oracle.

Definition 3.3 (Types of adversaries). *An adversary who has access to all oracles $\mathcal{O}$ is called* forward. *Note that $\mathcal{A}_1$ is allowed to perform* CorruptTag *queries on $T_b^\star$. An adversary is called* weak *if it does not perform any* CorruptTag *query. An adversary is called* narrow *if it does not perform any* Result *query. An adversary is called* reader-destructive *if it additionally has access to a* DestroyReader *oracle.*

Remark 3.4. Note that this notion of forward adversary is stronger than the one proposed by Vaudenay and closer to the notion of Juels and Weis.

Definition 3.5 (Privacy). *Let C be a class of adversaries in {forward, weak, narrow}. An RFID scheme is said to be C-private if for all probabilistic polynomial-time adversaries $\mathcal{A} = (\mathcal{A}_0, \mathcal{A}_1) \in C$*

$$\mathbb{P}[\boldsymbol{Priv\text{-}Game}_{\Pi,\mathcal{A}}(\eta)] - 1/2$$

is a negligible function of η.

Next, we want to generalize this privacy definition to the off-line setting, where readers can be subdued. A first attempt would be to take Definition 3.5 and additionally empower the adversary with a DestroyReader oracle. Unfortunately, the resulting definition is not achievable since the following adversary wins the privacy game with probability one, regardless of the particular scheme.

```
𝒜₀^{𝒪⁺}(pk):
    CreateReader(ℛ)
    CreateTag(T₀⋆)
    CreateTag(T₁⋆)
    Sync()
    s ← DestroyReader(ℛ)
    id ← Execute(s, T₀⋆)
    return T₀⋆, T₁⋆

𝒜₁^{𝒪⁺}(T_b⋆):
    if id = Execute(s, T_b⋆) then return 0
    else return 1
```

where Execute$(s, \mathcal{T})$ runs the authentication protocol with tag $\mathcal{T}$ using s as the internal state of the reader.

A setup with off-line readers is inherently insecure during the time-period where reader destruction takes place. The following definition captures the notion of self-stabilizing forward privacy with respect to reader destruction. Intuitively, is the same definition as before. However, before reader destruction takes place, we must guarantee that readers and tags have the same notion of time. This is achieved by having the tags communicate with a legitimate reader followed by a Sync, without the adversary interfering. This means that once the time moves forward, the privacy of past sessions is ensured, even if the adversary retrieves the internal state of a reader, see Figure 3.

Definition 3.6 (Self-stabilizing forward privacy game)

$$
\begin{aligned}
&\textbf{\textit{SS-Fwd-Priv-Game}}_{\Pi,\mathcal{A}}(\eta) \;: \\
&(sk, pk) \leftarrow \mathsf{SetupSystem}(1^\eta) \\
&\mathcal{T}_0^\star, \mathcal{T}_1^\star \leftarrow \mathcal{A}_0^{\mathcal{O}}(pk) \\
&b \leftarrow \{0,1\} \\
&\mathcal{R}_0^\star, \mathcal{R}_1^\star \leftarrow \mathcal{A}_1^{\mathcal{O}}(\mathcal{T}_b^\star) \\
&\mathsf{Execute}(\mathcal{R}_0^\star, \mathcal{T}_0^\star) \\
&\mathsf{Execute}(\mathcal{R}_1^\star, \mathcal{T}_1^\star) \\
&\mathsf{Sync}() \\
&b' \leftarrow \mathcal{A}_2^{\mathcal{O}^+}(\mathcal{T}_b^\star) \\
&\textbf{\textit{winif}} \text{ if } b = b'.
\end{aligned}
$$

where $\mathsf{Execute}(\mathcal{R}, \mathcal{T})$ runs the authentication protocol between the reader $\mathcal{R}$ and the tag $\mathcal{T}$. The challenge tags $\mathcal{T}_0^\star$ and $\mathcal{T}_1^\star$ must be uncorrupted, which means that no $\mathsf{CorruptTag}(\mathcal{T}_{\{0,1\}}^\star)$ query has been made. Adversaries implicitly pass state.

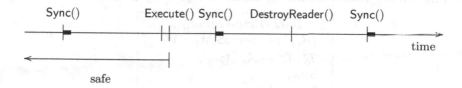

Fig. 3. Self-stabilizing Forward Privacy

Definition 3.7 (Self-stabilizing forward privacy). Let C be a class of adversaries in $\{forward, weak, narrow, reader destructive\}$. An RFID scheme is said to be C-forward private w.r.t. tag corruption and reader destruction if for all probabilistic polynomial-time adversaries $\mathcal{A} = (\mathcal{A}_0, \mathcal{A}_1, \mathcal{A}_2) \in C$

$$
\mathbb{P}[\textbf{\textit{SS-Fwd-Priv-Game}}_{\Pi,\mathcal{A}}(\eta)] - 1/2
$$

is a negligible function of η.

Theorem 3.8. Let Π be a self-stabilizing forward private RFID system. Then, Π is private with respect to Definition 3.5.

Proof. By inspection. Note that the games are the same up to the Execute call. The new adversary just has extra power, namely, the distinguishing capability of $\mathcal{A}_2^{\mathcal{O}^+}$, i.e., a winning adversary against **Priv-Game** is also a winning adversary against **SS-Fwd-Priv-Game**, where $\mathcal{A}_2$ just outputs the bit b chosen by $\mathcal{A}_1$. $\square$

Next we introduce the notion of backward privacy with respect to reader destruction. Backward privacy is the time-transposed analogy of forward privacy, see Figure 4. Therefore, the same limitations on privacy during the time-period

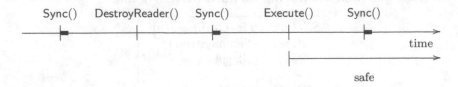

Fig. 4. Self-stabilizing Backward Privacy

where reader destruction takes place still apply. Moreover, since tags lack a timing device, the lapse extends beyond the compromised time slot. From the tag's perspective it is impossible to know that time has passed and therefore when an attacker interacts first with the tag during a later time slot, the tag is in an inherently insecure situation. In such a situation, the best one can hope for is that the tag gets back to a secure state (it self-stabilizes) after interacting with a legitimate reader. The following security definition captures this notion.

Definition 3.9 (Self-stabilizing backward privacy game)

$$
\begin{array}{l}
\boldsymbol{SS\text{-}Back\text{-}Priv\text{-}Game}_{\Pi,\mathcal{A}}(\eta) \ : \\
(sk, pk) \leftarrow \mathsf{SetupSystem}(1^{\eta}) \\
\mathcal{T}_0^{\star}, \mathcal{T}_1^{\star} \leftarrow \mathcal{A}_0^{\mathcal{O}^+}(pk) \\
\mathsf{Sync}() \\
\mathcal{R}^{\star} \leftarrow \mathcal{A}_1^{\mathcal{O}}() \\
b \leftarrow \{0,1\} \\
\mathsf{Execute}(\mathcal{R}^{\star}, \mathcal{T}_b^{\star}) \\
b' \leftarrow \mathcal{A}_2^{\mathcal{O}}(\mathcal{T}_b^{\star}) \\
\boldsymbol{win} \ if \ b = b'.
\end{array}
$$

The challenge tags ($\mathcal{T}_0^{\star}$ and $\mathcal{T}_1^{\star}$) must be uncorrupted, i.e., no $\mathsf{CorruptTag}(\mathcal{T}_{\{0,1\}}^{\star})$ query has been made. Adversaries implicitly pass state.

Definition 3.10 (Self-stabilizing backward privacy). Let C be a class of adversaries in {forward, weak, narrow, reader-destructive}. An RFID scheme is said to be C-self-stabilizing backward private w.r.t. tag corruption and reader destruction if for all probabilistic polynomial-time adversaries $\mathcal{A} = (\mathcal{A}_0, \mathcal{A}_1, \mathcal{A}_2) \in C$

$$\mathbb{P}[\boldsymbol{SS\text{-}Back\text{-}Priv\text{-}Game}_{\Pi,\mathcal{A}}(\eta)] - 1/2$$

is a negligible function of η.

4   Protocol Description

In this section we first recall a slightly modified version of the OSK protocol [OSK03] and prove it narrow-forward private in the random oracle model, as a proof-of-concept. Then, we propose two new protocols that achieve self-stabilizing forward and backward privacy. Both security proves are in the random oracle model.

4.1   The OSK Protocol

The modified version of the OSK protocol is depicted in Figure 5. The protocol uses two hash functions f and g. The state of the tag consists of a symmetric key k that gets hashed with every authentication attempt. The reader has a table T consisting of pairs of tag identities id and keys k. When the reader gets an answer c to a challenge n, it will search in T for any matching key, and will literately hash the keys when no match is found.

	$\mathcal{T}$ state: k		$\mathcal{R}$ state: $T = [id, k]$
0			$n \leftarrow \{0,1\}^l$
1		$\xleftarrow{\quad n \quad}$	
2	$c \leftarrow h(k, n)$		
3	$k \leftarrow g(k)$		
4		$\xrightarrow{\quad\quad c \quad\quad}$	
5			$\exists (id, k) \in T, i < t : h(g^i(k), n) = c$
6			then $k \leftarrow g^i(k)$; return T
7			else return $\bot$

Fig. 5. Slightly modified version of the OSK protocol

Theorem 4.1. *The modified version of the OSK protocol depicted in Fig. 5 is narrow-forward private in the random oracle model.*

Proof. Suppose that there is an adversary $\mathcal{A} = (\mathcal{A}_0, \mathcal{A}_1)$ that wins the **Priv-Game** with non-negligible probability. Then we build the following simulator $\mathcal{S}$. $\mathcal{S}$ initializes the system and then runs the adversary $\mathcal{A}_0$ simulating all oracle calls. The random oracle $\mathcal{H}$ is simulated as usual by having a table $T_{\mathcal{H}}$ storing previous queries and answers. Eventually $\mathcal{A}_0$ finishes and outputs tags $(\mathcal{T}_0^\star, \mathcal{T}_1^\star)$. Let k_0, k_1 be respectively the secret of $\mathcal{T}_0^\star$ and $\mathcal{T}_1^\star$. As in the game, $\mathcal{S}$ will draw a random bit b. Next, $\mathcal{S}$ runs $\mathcal{A}_1^{\mathcal{O}}(\mathcal{T}_b^\star)$ which eventually outputs a guess bit b'. By hypothesis we get that $b' = b$ with probability significantly higher than $1/2$. Now $\mathcal{T}$ rewinds the adversary $\mathcal{A}_1$ until it performs the first call to the random oracle $\mathcal{H}$ of the form k_0, m or k_1, m'. Then runs $\mathcal{A}_1^{\mathcal{O}}(\mathcal{T}_{1-b}^\star)$ and swaps in $T_{\mathcal{H}}$ all occurrences of k_0 and k_1. By hypothesis we get that $\mathcal{A}_1$ outputs $b' = 1 - b$ with probability significantly higher than $1/2$. Since $\mathcal{A}_1$ is narrow, its view is exactly the same as in the previous run, which leads to a contradiction.   □

4.2   A Self-stabilizing Private Protocol

Figure 6 depicts our protocol for self-stabilizing forward and backward privacy. The core of the protocol is the OSK protocol plus some modifications for backward privacy. The state of the tag consists of two keys k and k'. Intuitively, the former key is used for communication with the readers and the latter is used for (indirect) communication with the back office. The state of the reader includes

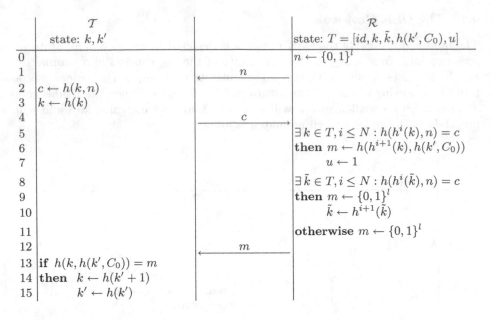

$\mathcal{T}$		$\mathcal{R}$
state: k, k'		state: $T = [id, k, \tilde{k}, h(k', C_0), u]$
		$n \leftarrow \{0,1\}^l$
	$\xleftarrow{\quad n \quad}$	
$c \leftarrow h(k, n)$		
$k \leftarrow h(k)$		
	$\xrightarrow{\quad c \quad}$	
		$\exists\, k \in T, i \leq N : h(h^i(k), n) = c$
		then $m \leftarrow h(h^{i+1}(k), h(k', C_0))$
		$u \leftarrow 1$
		$\exists\, \tilde{k} \in T, i \leq N : h(h^i(\tilde{k}), n) = c$
		then $m \leftarrow \{0,1\}^l$
		$\tilde{k} \leftarrow h^{i+1}(\tilde{k})$
		otherwise $m \leftarrow \{0,1\}^l$
	$\xleftarrow{\quad m \quad}$	
if $h(k, h(k', C_0)) = m$		
then $k \leftarrow h(k'+1)$		
$k' \leftarrow h(k')$		

Fig. 6. Self-stabilizing Forward and Backward Private Protocol

a table T consisting of a tag identity id; the last-known key k; the fist-key-of-the-day $\tilde{k}$; a MAC $h(k', C_0)$ and a bit u that tells whether or not the tag has authenticated during the current time period. The MAC constitutes a proof of knowledge of k' and C_0 is a system-wide constant.

The Sync() protocol gathers the tables $T_{\mathcal{R}}$ from each reader $\mathcal{R}$. Then it computes, for each tag, the latest key k used. If there is a table $T_{\mathcal{R}}$ for which $u = 1$ then it sets $u \leftarrow 0$, $\tilde{k} \leftarrow h(k'+1)$ and it updates k' in the back office by computing $k' \leftarrow h(k')$. Finally, it distributes the updated tables to all readers.

Theorem 4.2. *The protocol depicted in Fig. 6 is narrow self-stabilizing forward private in the random oracle model.*

Proof. Suppose that there is an adversary $\mathcal{A} = (\mathcal{A}_0, \mathcal{A}_1, \mathcal{A}_2)$ that wins the **SS-Fwd-Priv-Game** with non-negligible probability. We build the following simulator S. S first creates system parameters by calling $(\mathrm{sk}, \mathrm{pk}) \leftarrow \mathsf{SetupSystem}(1^\eta)$. Then, it proceeds as in the **SS-Fwd-Priv-Game**, invoking $\mathcal{A}$ when specified. Again, the random oracle $\mathcal{H}$ is simulated by having a table $T_{\mathcal{H}}$ storing previous query-answer pairs. At some point $\mathcal{A}_0$ outputs challenge tags $\mathcal{T}_0^\star$ and $\mathcal{T}_1^\star$. Let $t_0^\dagger$ and $t_1^\dagger$ be respectively the time when $\mathcal{T}_0^\star$ and $\mathcal{T}_1^\star$ initiated the last successful authentication, see Figure 7.

Define $k_i^\dagger, k_i'^\dagger$ as the secret keys of $\mathcal{T}_i^\star$ at time $t_i^\dagger$, for $i = 0, 1$. Let $t_i^\ddagger$ be the time of the last Sync call before $t_i^\dagger$ and let $k_i^\ddagger, k_i'^\ddagger$ be the secret keys of $\mathcal{T}_i^\star$ at time $t_i^\ddagger$, for $i = 0, 1$. Next $\mathcal{S}$ will rewind the adversary $\mathcal{A}_0$ and resume its execution with a modified random oracle $\tilde{h}$. $\tilde{h}$ is defined as h, except for the following four points: $\tilde{h}(k_i'^\ddagger) := h(k_{1-i}'^\ddagger)$ and $\tilde{h}(k_i^\dagger) := h(k_{1-i}^\dagger)$ for $i = 0, 1$. Note that this modification

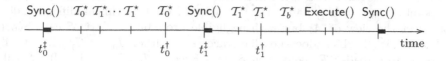

Fig. 7. Timeline of events

does not affect the view of $\mathcal{A}_0$ but with negligible probability. Next, $\mathcal{S}$ calls $\mathcal{A}_1^{\mathcal{O}}(\mathcal{T}_{1-b}^{*})$. Note that $\mathcal{T}_{1-b}^{*}$ has exactly the same state that $\mathcal{T}_b^{*}$ had in the previous execution of $\mathcal{A}_1^{\mathcal{O}}$, therefore the view of $\mathcal{A}_1$ remains unchanged. Finally, $\mathcal{S}$ calls $\mathsf{Execute}(\mathcal{R}_0^{*}, \mathcal{T}_0^{*})$, $\mathsf{Execute}(\mathcal{R}_1^{*}, \mathcal{T}_1^{*})$ and $\mathsf{Sync}()$ followed by $\mathcal{A}_2^{\mathcal{O}+}(\mathcal{T}_{1-b}^{*})$. It remains to show that $\mathsf{DestroyReader}$ calls do not change the view of the adversary. This is easy to see since the internal state of tags and readers at any time are the same, with exception of $h(k_i^{\ddagger})$ and $h(k_i'^{\ddagger})$. For example, the information on the readers about $\mathcal{T}_i^{*}$ at time $\max(t_0^{\ddagger}, t_1^{\ddagger})$ is $id_i, k = h(k_i^{\ddagger}), \tilde{k} = h(h(k_i'^{\ddagger}) + 1), h(k_i'^{\ddagger}, \tilde{d}), 0$ in one view, and $id_{1-i}, k = h(k_i^{\ddagger}), \tilde{k} = h(h(k_i'^{\ddagger}) + 1), h(k_i'^{\ddagger}, \tilde{d}), 0$ in the other. But this is not a problem since the adversary never has access to these values, due to the fact that the $\mathsf{Execute}$ and Sync calls destroy this information.

Note that since $\mathcal{A}$ is narrow, it does not have access to a Result oracle.

This time, $\mathcal{A}$ must output $1 - b$ with probability significantly higher than $1/2$ but since its views are indistinguishable, this leads to a contradiction. $\square$

Theorem 4.3. *The protocol depicted in Fig. 6 is narrow self-stabilizing backward private in the random oracle model.*

Proof. The main idea of the proof is similar to the one of Theorem 4.2. Suppose that there is an adversary $\mathcal{A} = (\mathcal{A}_0, \mathcal{A}_1, \mathcal{A}_2)$ that wins the **SS-Back-Priv-Game** with non-negligible probability. As before, we build the following simulator S. S first creates system parameters by calling $(\mathsf{sk}, \mathsf{pk}) \leftarrow \mathsf{SetupSystem}(1^\eta)$. Then, it proceeds as in the **SS-Back-Priv-Game**, invoking $\mathcal{A}$ when specified. Again, the random oracle $\mathcal{H}$ is simulated by having a table $T_{\mathcal{H}}$ storing previous query-answer pairs. At some point $\mathcal{A}_0$ outputs challenge tags $\mathcal{T}_0^{*}$ and $\mathcal{T}_1^{*}$. Let $t_i^{\dagger}$ be the time when $\mathcal{T}_i^{*}$ initiated the last successful authentication, for $i = 0, 1$, see Figure 8.

Let $t_i^{\ddagger}$ be the time of the last Sync call before $t_i^{\dagger}$ and let $k_i^{\ddagger}, k_i'^{\ddagger}$ be the secret keys of $\mathcal{T}_i^{*}$ at time $t_i^{\ddagger}$, for $i = 0, 1$. Next S will rewind the adversary $\mathcal{A}_0$ and

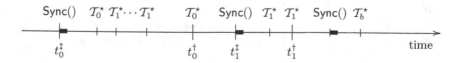

Fig. 8. Timeline of events

resume its execution with a modified random oracle $\tilde{h}$ defined as h except for the points $\tilde{h}(k_0'^{\ddagger}) := h(k_1'^{\ddagger})$ and $\tilde{h}(k_1'^{\ddagger}) := h(k_0'^{\ddagger})$. Note that this modification does not affect the view of $\mathcal{A}_0$ but with negligible probability. Next, $\mathcal{S}$ calls Sync() and then $\mathcal{A}_1^{\mathcal{O}}()$, which does not have access to either T_0^* or T_1^*. Eventually $\mathcal{A}_1$ outputs a reader $\mathcal{R}^*$ and then $\mathcal{S}$ runs Execute($\mathcal{R}^*, T_{1-b}^*$). Finally, $\mathcal{S}$ calls $\mathcal{A}_2^{\mathcal{O}}(T_{1-b}^*)$. Note that T_{1-b}^* has exactly the same state that T_b^* in the previous execution of $\mathcal{A}_2$ and therefore the view of $\mathcal{A}_2$ remains unchanged. This time, $\mathcal{A}$ must output $1 - b$ with probability significantly higher than $1/2$ but since its views are indistinguishable, this leads to a contradiction.   □

Remark 4.4. This protocol suffers from de-synchronization when reader corruption has taken place.An adversary can use the data from a corrupted reader to move forward the key k' both in a tag or in the back office. Throughout this paper we focus on privacy and the purpose of this protocol is to show achievability of our privacy notions. In this protocol there is still a trade-off possible between de-synchronization resistance and privacy. The reader could additionally store the keys $\tilde{k}$ from adjacent time-slots. This, of course, extends the unsafe window from one to three time slots but it allows re-synchronization.

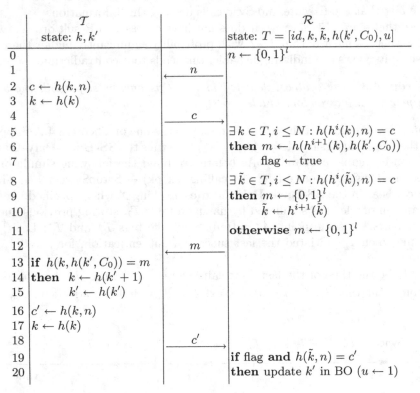

	$\mathcal{T}$ state: k, k'		$\mathcal{R}$ state: $T = [id, k, \tilde{k}, h(k', C_0), u]$
0			$n \leftarrow \{0,1\}^l$
1		$\xleftarrow{\quad n \quad}$	
2	$c \leftarrow h(k, n)$		
3	$k \leftarrow h(k)$		
4		$\xrightarrow{\quad c \quad}$	
5			$\exists k \in T, i \le N : h(h^i(k), n) = c$
6			**then** $m \leftarrow h(h^{i+1}(k), h(k', C_0))$
7			flag $\leftarrow$ true
8			$\exists \tilde{k} \in T, i \le N : h(h^i(\tilde{k}), n) = c$
9			**then** $m \leftarrow \{0,1\}^l$
10			$\tilde{k} \leftarrow h^{i+1}(\tilde{k})$
11			**otherwise** $m \leftarrow \{0,1\}^l$
12		$\xleftarrow{\quad m \quad}$	
13	**if** $h(k, h(k', C_0)) = m$		
14	**then** $k \leftarrow h(k' + 1)$		
15	$k' \leftarrow h(k')$		
16	$c' \leftarrow h(k, n)$		
17	$k \leftarrow h(k)$		
18		$\xrightarrow{\quad c' \quad}$	
19			**if** flag **and** $h(\tilde{k}, n) = c'$
20			**then** update k' in BO $(u \leftarrow 1)$

Fig. 9. Improved Self-stabilizing Forward and Backward Private Protocol

	$\mathcal{T}$			$\mathcal{R}$
	state: k, k'			state: $T = [id, k, \tilde{k}, h(k', b), t]$
0				$n \leftarrow \{0,1\}^l$
1		$\xleftarrow{\quad n \quad}$		
2	$c \leftarrow h(k, n)$			
3	$k \leftarrow h(k)$			
4		$\xrightarrow{\quad c \quad}$		
5				$\exists k \in T, i \le N : h(h^i(k), n) = c$
6				then $m \leftarrow h(h^{i+1}(k), h(k', b))$
7				output id
8				$\exists \tilde{k} \in T, i \le N : h(h^i(\tilde{k}), n) = c$
9				then $m \leftarrow \{0,1\}^l$
10				output id
11				otherwise $m \leftarrow \{0,1\}^l$
12				output $\perp$
13		$\xleftarrow{\quad m \quad}$		
14	if $h(k, h(k', b)) = m$			
15	then $k \leftarrow h(k', b+2)$			
16	$k' \leftarrow h(k')$			
17	$t \leftarrow h(k', k, 4)$			
18		$\xrightarrow{\quad t \quad}$		
19				store t for the BO

On the time slots where reader destruction has taken place, the back office does not update any key.

Fig. 10. Improved Self-stabilizing Forward and Backward Private Protocol

4.3 Improving Synchronization

Figure 10 depicts an improved version of the protocol from Section 4.2. By adding a second authentication it is possible to address the de-synchronization issue exposed in Remark 4.4. This allows the reader to verify whether or not the key update has been successful and only report successful key updates to the back office.

Theorem 4.5. *The protocol depicted in Fig. 10 is narrow self-stabilizing forward and backward private in the random oracle model.*

Proof. The proof closely follows the lines of the ones of Theorems 4.2 and 4.3. Note that authenticating twice does not compromise privacy, otherwise that would be a valid attack against the protocol from Section 4.2, contradicting Theorem 4.2 or 4.3.   □

5 Conclusions

We have proposed a new model for RFID privacy that considers off-line systems and the potential threat of reader subversion. We have elaborated on the privacy notions from the literature and adapted the standard notions of forward and backward security to this setting. We have shown that the straightforward generalization is unachievable. We have proposed the notions of self-stabilizing forward and backward privacy, which are the strongest one can expect to attain.

We have designed two authentication protocols that achieve self-stabilizing forward and backward privacy. We have proven the security of these protocols in the random oracle model. This protocols use only a hash function as a cryptographic primitive, which makes it suitable to be implemented using some of the many lightweight functions proposed in the literature [Sha08, PHER07].

References

[ALM09]   Avoine, G., Lauradoux, C., Martin, T.: When Compromised Readers Meet RFID. In: Youm, H.Y., Jang, J. (eds.) WISA 2009. LNCS, vol. 5932, pp. 36–50. Springer, Heidelberg (2009)

[AO05]   Avoine, G., Oechslin, P.: RFID Traceability: A Multilayer Problem. In: S. Patrick, A., Yung, M. (eds.) FC 2005. LNCS, vol. 3570, pp. 125–140. Springer, Heidelberg (2005)

[Avo05]   Avoine, G.: Adversary Model for Radio Frequency Identification. Technical Report LASEC-REPORT-2005-001, Swiss Federal Institute of Technology (EPFL), Security and Cryptography Laboratory (LASEC), Lausanne, Switzerland (September 2005)

[JW07]   Juels, A., Weis, S.: Defining Strong Privacy for RFID. In: International Conference on Pervasive Computing and Communications – PerCom 2007, New York City, New York, USA, pp. 342–347. IEEE Computer Society Press, Los Alamitos (2007)

[NIBY06] Nohara, Y., Inoue, S., Baba, K., Yasuura, H.: Quantitative Evaluation of Unlinkable ID Matching Schemes. In: Workshop on Privacy in the Electronic Society – WPES, Alexandria, Virginia, USA, pp. 55–60. ACM Press, New York (2006)

[OSK03]   Ohkubo, M., Suzuki, K., Kinoshita, S.: Cryptographic Approach to "Privacy-Friendly" Tags. In: RFID Privacy Workshop. MIT, Massachusetts (2003)

[PHER07] Peris-Lopez, P., Hernandez-Castro, J.C., Estevez-Tapiador, J.M., Ribagorda, A.: An efficient authentication protocol for rfid systems resistant to active attacks. In: Denko, M.K., Shih, C.-s., Li, K.-C., Tsao, S.-L., Zeng, Q.-A., Park, S.H., Ko, Y.-B., Hung, S.-H., Park, J.-H. (eds.) EUC-WS 2007. LNCS, vol. 4809, pp. 781–794. Springer, Heidelberg (2007)

[Sha08]   Shamir, A.: SQUASH - A New MAC With Provable Security Properties for Highly Constrained Devices Such as RFID Tags. In: Nyberg, K. (ed.) FSE 2008. LNCS, vol. 5086, pp. 144–157. Springer, Heidelberg (2008)

[Tsu06]   Tsudik, G.: YA-TRAP: Yet Another Trivial RFID Authentication Protocol. In: International Conference on Pervasive Computing and Communications – PerCom 2006, Pisa, Italy. IEEE Computer Society Press, Los Alamitos (March 2006)

[Vau07]   Vaudenay, S.: On Privacy Models for RFID. In: Kurosawa, K. (ed.) ASIACRYPT 2007. LNCS, vol. 4833, pp. 68–87. Springer, Heidelberg (2007)

Developing Efficient Blinded Attribute Certificates on Smart Cards via Pairings

Lejla Batina[1], Jaap-Henk Hoepman[1,2], Bart Jacobs[1],
Wojciech Mostowski[1,*], and Pim Vullers[1,**]

[1] Institute for Computing and Information Sciences,
Radboud University Nijmegen, The Netherlands
{lejla,jhh,bart,woj,p.vullers}@cs.ru.nl
[2] TNO Information and Communication Technology, The Netherlands
jaap-henk.hoepman@tno.nl

Abstract. This paper describes an elementary protocol to prove possession of anonymous credentials together with its implementation on smart cards. The protocol uses self-blindable attribute certificates represented as points on an elliptic curve (which are stored on the card). These certificates are verified on the reader-side via a bilinear pairing.

Java Card smart cards offer only very limited access to the cryptographic coprocessor. It thus requires some ingenuity to get the protocol running with reasonable speed. We realise protocol runs with on-card computation times in the order of 1.5 seconds. It should be possible to further reduce this time with extended access to the cryptographic coprocessor.

Keywords: anonymous credentials, elliptic curve cryptography, smart card, bilinear pairing, attributes, blinding, protocols, Java Card.

1 Introduction

With the growing use of smart cards in e-ticketing in public transport, huge centralised databases are compiled with detailed travel information of individual citizens. This raises considerable privacy and security concerns [14]. It leads to a renewed interest in anonymous credential systems, offering attribute-based authorisation. With such system a smart card may be personalised, but does not show its identity on entry into a public transport system. Instead it shows an attribute — such as "first class train pass valid in December 2009" — together with a signature on the public key of the card that is linked to this attribute. The corresponding private key is assumed to be stored in protected hardware in the card, inaccessible from the outside. We assume the attribute to be fairly general, and not identifying individual cards/people. The signature, however, is specific, and may be used for tracing. Therefore we are interested in self-blindable signatures as proposed by Verheul [25].

---

* Sponsored by the NLnet foundation through the OV-chipkaart project.
** Sponsored by Trans Link Systems/Open Ticketing.

D. Gollmann, J.-L. Lanet, J. Iguchi-Cartigny (Eds.): CARDIS 2010, LNCS 6035, pp. 209–222, 2010.

Other credential systems exist, see for instance [5,6,8]. They typically require non-trivial computational resources, such that implementing them on smart cards is a serious challenge, see for example [12,21,23]. Of these Danes [12] implements idemix [8] zero knowledge proofs on smart cards, with running times in the order of tens of seconds; Sterckx et al. [21] implement direct anonymous attestation [6] with running times under 3 seconds; Tews and Jacobs [23] describe an implementation of Brands' selective disclosure protocols [5], with running times around 5 seconds. All quoted times refer to the execution time on a smart card.

This paper distinguishes itself through its use of elliptic curve cryptography (ECC). It does so for two (main) reasons.

- ECC supports small key and certificate lengths — compared to RSA — and thus reduces the time and bandwidth needed for transfer (of public keys between card and terminal) and for blinding (via modular multiplication of big natural numbers).
- ECC supports a form of signature via bilinear pairings [20] which is stable under blinding [25].

Actual use of ECC on smart cards is relatively new. The major deployment is probably in the latest generation of European e-passports, using Extended Access Control to protect finger prints [7]. Java Card generation 2.2 smart cards offer support for ECC, through the cryptographic coprocessor, basically via only two primitives, namely Diffie-Hellman key agreement (ECDH) and Digital Signature Algorithm (ECDSA). This is barely enough to implement our protocol on a card efficiently. Crucial in our implementation are the following two points.

- We abuse ECDH to perform point multiplication (repeated addition, or integer scalar multiplication) on the card. Diffie-Hellman does such a multiplication implicitly, however, it only returns the x-coordinate of the resulting (multiplied) point. In principle, we have to reconstruct the corresponding y-coordinate (on the reader-side) by taking a square root, and checking which version (positive or negative) is the right one. However, we show how this reconstruction can be partially avoided via some tricks (see Section 4.2).
- Modular multiplication of two (big) natural numbers is not supported, that is, the Java Card API does not provide access to this operation on the card's cryptographic coprocessor. Therefore we use our own implementation in Java Card, which leads to a significant slow down. It can be mitigated by reducing the number of bits in the blinding factor, for instance from 192 to 96 (or even to 48).

The main contributions of this work are as follows.

- A new protocol for anonymous credentials is described that can be used for various applications which require smart cards, in particular e-ticketing.
- An implementation of this protocol, via several optimisations, on an ordinary Java Card, using bilinear pairings on elliptic curves on the terminal-side.
- A running time on the card in the order of 1.5 seconds.

Our results show that anonymous credentials on smart cards are becoming feasible. Also, they show that increasing access to the cryptographic coprocessor may increase the number of applications of advanced smart cards. Hopefully this perspective stimulates card manufacturers.

This paper is organised as follows. In Section 2 an overview of elliptic curve cryptography and pairings is given. These techniques are used for the protocol given in Section 3. Finally, Section 4 describes the implementation details and gives an indication of times needed for protocol runs, with a number of different parameters.

2   Elliptic Curves and Pairings

In this section we introduce some notation and we give an overview of the mathematical background of elliptic curves and pairings. The finite field containing q elements, where q is a prime power, is denoted by $\mathbb{F}_q$. An elliptic curve E over $\mathbb{F}_q$ is the set of all solutions, that is, all the points $P = (x, y)$ satisfying the following equation

$$E : y^2 = x^3 + ax + b, \tag{1}$$

where $a, b \in \mathbb{F}_q$ and $4a^3 + 27b^2 \neq 0$, together with a special point ∞ called the point at infinity. The set of points $P \in \mathbb{F}_q{}^2$ on the curve is sometimes written as $E(\mathbb{F}_q)$.

Here, a and b are called the curve parameters. The field $\mathbb{F}_q$ is of the form $\mathbb{F}_{p^n}$ for some prime number p and $n \in \mathbb{N}$ ($p \neq 2, 3$). The solutions of equation (1) form an abelian group with point addition as the group operation and the point at infinity as the zero-element. The condition $4a^3 + 27b^2 \neq 0$ is required for E to be non-singular, as required for cryptographic applications. For cryptography we need a finite cyclic group in which the group operation is efficiently computable, but the discrete logarithm problem is very difficult to solve. Elliptic curve groups meet these criteria when the underlying field is finite and p is at least 160 bits.

We write $n \cdot P$, with scalar $n \in \mathbb{Z}$, for repeated group operation, that is, the point addition. Let E be an elliptic curve over $\mathbb{F}_q$ and let $P \in E$ be a point of order k. Let $Q \in \langle P \rangle$ be a point generated by P, that is, $Q = \alpha \cdot P$ for α where $0 \leq \alpha < k$. The problem of finding the logarithm α for given P and Q is called the elliptic curve discrete logarithm problem (ECDLP).

As mentioned above, we are using bilinear pairings on elliptic curves for our protocol. Therefore, a so-called pairing friendly elliptic curve is required, that is, a curve with a small embedding degree and large prime-order subgroup. In 2005, Barreto and Naehrig (BN) discovered a new method for constructing pairing friendly elliptic curves of prime order over a prime field [1]. More precisely, BN curves are defined over $\mathbb{F}_p$ where $p = p(u) = 36u^4 + 36u^3 + 24u^2 + 6u + 1$ for $u \in \mathbb{Z}$ such that p is prime. The order of a BN curve is a prime n where $n = n(u) = 36u^4 + 36u^3 + 18u^2 + 6u + 1$. Hence, a BN curve is constructed by generating integers u until both $p(u)$ and $n(u)$ are prime numbers. The embedding degree of BN curves is 12 and we detail the parameters for our case in Section 4.3.

2.1   DH and DSA for Elliptic Curves

The Diffie-Hellman key agreement protocol (DH) and the Digital Signature Algorithm (DSA) are easily adapted to the ECC case as in [2] and [15] respectively. We recall the protocols, which in this case are called ECDH and ECDSA.

EC Diffie-Hellman Key Agreement (ECDH). Alice (A) and Bob (B) wish to agree on a secret key over an insecure channel. They first agree on the set of domain parameters ($\mathbb{F}_q, E, n, h, G$). Here, E is an elliptic curve over $\mathbb{F}_q$, G is a generating (publicly known) point in the elliptic curve group of order n and the integer h is called the cofactor. For the cofactor we have: $\#E(\mathbb{F}_q) = h\,n$. Due to the security of the ECDLP one usually selects a curve for which $h \leq 4$. Any random point of sufficiently high order on an elliptic curve E can be used as a key.

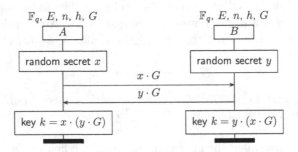

Fig. 1. EC Diffie-Hellman key agreement protocol

Key Agreement. Each time a shared key is required, the following steps, as depicted in Fig. 1, have to be performed.

1. A chooses a random secret x, where $1 \leq x \leq n - 1$, as her private key and sends B the corresponding public key $x \cdot G$
2. B chooses a random secret y, where $1 \leq y \leq n - 1$, as his private key and sends A the corresponding public key $y \cdot G$.
3. B receives $x \cdot G$ and computes the shared key as $k = y \cdot (x \cdot G) = (xy) \cdot G$.
4. A receives $y \cdot G$ and computes the shared key as $k = x \cdot (y \cdot G) = (xy) \cdot G$.

So, they both end up with the same point as the common key: $k = xy \cdot G$. An adversary Eve may have knowledge of G, $x \cdot G$, and $y \cdot G$ but not of x or y. She wants to determine number $xy \cdot G$. This task is called the "(computational) Diffie-Hellman problem for elliptic curves".

EC Digital Signature Algorithm (ECDSA). The ECDSA is specified by an elliptic curve E defined over $\mathbb{F}_q$ and a publicly known point $G \in E$ of prime order n. As above, a private key of Alice is a scalar z and the corresponding public key is $Q = z \cdot G \in E$. The ECDSA requires a hash function in addition and consists of two parts as explained below.

Signature Generation. In order to sign a message m, A should perform the following steps:

1. Select a random integer k, where $1 \leq k \leq n-1$.
2. Compute $(x_1, y_1) = k \cdot G$.
3. Compute $r = x_1 \bmod n$. If $r = 0$, then go back to the step 1.
4. Compute $s = k^{-1}(h(m) + z\,r) \bmod n$, where h is a hash function. If $s = 0$, then go to step 1.
5. A's signature for the message m is the pair (r, s).

Signature Verification. In order to verify A's signature on m, B performs the following steps:

1. Obtain an authenticated copy of A's public key Q.
2. Verify that r and s are integers in the interval $[1, n-1]$.
3. Compute $w = s^{-1} \bmod n$ and $h(m)$.
4. Compute $u_1 = h(m)\,w \bmod n$ and $u_2 = r\,w \bmod n$.
5. Compute $(x_0, y_0) = u_1 \cdot G + u_2 \cdot Q$ and $v = x_0 \bmod n$.
6. Accept the signature if and only if $v = r$.

2.2 Pairings

A bilinear pairing is a map $\mathbb{G}_1 \times \mathbb{G}_2 \rightarrow \mathbb{G}_T$ where $\mathbb{G}_1$ and $\mathbb{G}_2$ are typically additive groups and $\mathbb{G}_T$ is a multiplicative group and the map is bilinear, that is, linear in both components. Many pairings are used in cryptography such as the Tate pairing, ate pairing and the most recent R-ate pairing [24]. For all these pairings one often uses specific cyclic subgroups of $E(\mathbb{F}_{p^k})$ as $\mathbb{G}_1$ and $\mathbb{G}_2$ and $\mathbb{F}_{p^k}^*$ as $\mathbb{G}_T$.

The bilinearity property can be written as follows:

$$e(P + P', Q) = e(P, Q) \cdot e(P', Q)$$
$$\text{and}$$
$$e(P, Q + Q') = e(P, Q) \cdot e(P, Q')$$

As a result, $e(n \cdot P, m \cdot Q) = e(P, Q)^{n\,m}$. Pairings are used for many (new) cryptographic protocols [2], such as short signatures [4], three-party one-round key agreement [16], identity based encryption [3] and anonymous credentials [9].

Here we use pairings of the form $e\colon E(\mathbb{F}_p) \times E(\mathbb{F}_{p^k}) \rightarrow \mathbb{F}_{p^k}$, obtained by taking $\mathbb{G}_1 = \mathbb{G}_2 = \mathbb{F}_{p^k}$ and using the obvious inclusion $\mathbb{F}_p \rightarrow \mathbb{F}_{p^k}$ in the first argument. The number k is known in this context as the embedding degree. As previously mentioned, one uses $k = 12$ for BN-curves.

Pairing-based Signatures. We briefly recall the pairing-based signature approach of Verheul [25], but here in the context of e-ticketing. Assume there is a system-wide public key $s \cdot Q$, for $Q \in E(\mathbb{F}_{p^k})$, with private key s under control of a scheme provider. Let ticket/card c have private key k_c, with corresponding public key $P_c = k_c \cdot P$, for some generator $P \in E(\mathbb{F}_p)$. An interesting form of signature, by the scheme provider, on such a key is simply multiplication with s. Thus, $s \cdot P_c = s \cdot (k_c \cdot P) = (s\,k_c) \cdot P = R$ can be used as signature on P_c. A pairing e can be used to check a claim that a point $R \in E(\mathbb{F}_p)$ really is a signature, namely by checking:

$$e(P_c, \, s \cdot Q) \stackrel{?}{=} e(R, \, Q).$$

Indeed, if $R = s \cdot P_c$ then both sides are equal to $e(P_c, \, Q)^s$, and thus equal. In this scenario the card terminal, and not the card, verifies the signature. Notice that the first argument of the pairing $e(-, -)$ involves a point in $E(\mathbb{F}_p)$ coming from the card. Hence the card does not have to do any of the (more complicated) work in $\mathbb{F}_{p^k}$.

A powerful aspect about these signatures is that they are invariant under blinding. Thus, if a card chooses an arbitrary number b as blinding factor, the resulting pair $(b \cdot P_c, \, b \cdot (s \cdot P_c))$ is again a signature, for the private-public key pair $(b\,k_c, \, b \cdot P_c = (b\,k_c) \cdot P)$. Each time the card is used it can thus present a different (signed) public key, such that the different uses cannot be linked.

Of course, when a card presents a reader with such a pair P_c, R the reader should not only check that R is a proper signature on P_c, that is, R is $s \cdot P_c$, but also that the card knows the private key corresponding to the public key P_c. This can be done via standard challenge-response exchange, for example using ECDSA.

2.3   Elliptic Curves on Smart Cards

The on-card part of our protocol is running on a Java Card smart card [11]. Java Card technology gives us an open environment where we can easily implement our protocols using Java and load them onto a development smart card. A Java Card may be equipped with a cryptographic coprocessor to support a selection of cryptographic algorithms defined by the official Java Card API [22], and possibly some proprietary extensions provided by the card manufacturer [18]. Since version 2.2 the Java Card API offers support for EC based algorithms. When it comes to the implementation of our protocol on a Java Card "EC support" alone is not enough as there are some issues that we need to be aware of, as follows.

Java Card is an embedded and closed device. Internally its cryptographic coprocessor implements all the routines required for a given cryptographic protocol (for example ECDH), but externally we can only utilise what is exported through the API. For example, we may be able to perform the ECDH key agreement protocol on the card (and hence scalar point multiplication), but we do not have access to the point addition or point doubling primitives. The only other EC based algorithms that the card can support are EC key generation and ECDSA signature generation and verification. Extension of the algorithms that the card provides is practically impossible. The cryptographic coprocessor is not accessible through Java code, and implementing EC operations in Java (byte)code hinders performance significantly [23]. As long as we stick to the built-in cryptographic operations the performance is acceptable. For example, a single point multiplication for 192 bit keys/points (using the ECDH operation) takes about 0.10 seconds, ECDSA signature generation about 0.12 seconds, and EC key pair generation about 0.60 seconds. A detailed method to measure Java Card performance and some performance results can be found in [19]. Furthermore, the card may or may not support the compressed point format (and hence point reconstruction) as input for EC based algorithms.

Due to this limited environment and performance requirements we need to *balance* our protocol such that the operations required on the card are minimised and match the cards capabilities. The computationally expensive operations, like pairing, should be performed by the terminal. Ideally, the card should only be asked to perform operations supported natively by the Java Card cryptographic API.

Finally, as all cryptographic support is optional in Java Card, we need a development card that actually does support the EC based algorithms. We used the NXP JCOP31 2.4.1 Java Card based on the SmartMX platform. It supports ECDH and ECDSA with key sizes up to 320 bits, but it does not support the compressed point format.

3   Protocol for Attribute-Proving

This section describes an elementary protocol of how a card c demonstrates in a secure and privacy friendly manner that it possesses some attribute(s) a. This attribute is just a number, with certain meaning that we abstract away.

3.1   The Protocol

System Setup The scheme provider has a public fixed point $Q \in E(\mathbb{F}_{p^k})$ and a finite set of attributes. For each attribute a a secret key s_a, which is a number below the order of Q, and public key $Q_a = s_a \cdot Q$ are generated. The associated pairs (a, Q_a) of attributes and public keys are publicly known, and stored in all terminals together with the fixed point Q. This use of different signing keys for different attributes goes back to work of Chaum on e-cash [10], where for instance an e-coin of 50 cents had a different ("50 cent") signature than an e-coin with a value of 100 cents.

A card c generates a key pair $k_c, P_c = k_c \cdot P$ where $P \in E(\mathbb{F}_p)$ is a fixed system wide generator. The private key k_c of the card is assumed to be stored in a protected manner such that it cannot leave the card. Upon personalisation it receives an attribute together with a certificate $C_a = s_a \cdot P_c$ linking its public key P_c to the attribute a. The attribute a corresponds to a product that the owner of the card has bought.

Before the protocol, as described below, will be run, some form of authentication between the card and terminal should be performed. This is required to protect the card from proving the possession of an attribute to a rogue reader. After this initial authentication phase the card can be sure that it communicates

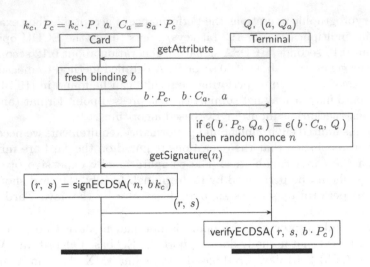

Fig. 2. Protocol for proving self-blindable attributes

with a genuine reader and can proceed with the execution of the protocol. This preceding step will be ignored here.

Protocol Description. The protocol for proving self-blindable attributes, as depicted in Fig. 2, is initiated by a terminal which requests an attribute from the card. The card generates a fresh blinding factor b to blind its public key and the certificate. It responds by sending the blinded values ($b \cdot P_c$ and $b \cdot C_a$) together with the attribute stored on the card.

The terminal can now perform a pairing signature verification, as discussed in Section 2.2, using the card's response, the attribute's public key Q_a and the fixed point Q. Note that the terminal can select the correct public key Q_a to use by matching the attribute returned by the card. If the verification succeeds the terminal generates a random nonce n which is used to challenge the card, that is, to request a signature over n. The card responds with an ECDSA signature (r, s) of this nonce, which is created using its blinded private key $b\,k_c$.

Finally the terminal verifies the ECDSA signature using the blinded public key. This works since $b\,k_c$ together with $b \cdot P_c = (b\,k_c) \cdot P$ is a valid key pair. When the verification succeeds the card has proved possession of the requested attribute.

3.2   Some Issues

Privacy. In this protocol the attribute itself is not hidden, and may thus be used to trace cards/people. This can be overcome to some extent by using only a limited number of fairly general attributes. For instance, as possible validity date one can choose to use only the first day of each month, and not every possible day of the year. Alternatively, one may provide a card with several attributes, stating for instance: "year card valid in January 2009", "year card valid in February 2009", and so on. In this way each card can present the appropriate attribute, after receiving the current date from the terminal.

Efficiency. A drawback of the current protocol is that it only proves a single attribute to the terminal. Consider the situation in which a card holds more than one attribute. The terminal could then perform multiple requests to the card in which an index indicates which attribute is requested. This is, however, not a very efficient solution since the required amount of time for proving grows linearly with the amount of attributes to be proved.

One approach could be to combine all attributes into a single point on the curve, requiring only a single protocol run to proof all attributes. However, such method could lead to new privacy issues since all attributes are disclosed at once. Therefore selective disclosure of these attributes, as proposed by Brands [5], would be preferred. The efficient adaption of these techniques to the elliptic curve setting is a subject for further research.

Revocation. Within various settings, for example e-ticketing for public transport, it is highly desirable to be able to revoke cards, for instance after abuse or after early termination of a contract. However, revocation is non trivial as terminals only get to verify blinded keys and blinded certificates. This blinding makes straightforward black listing impossible. Kiyomoto and Tanaka [17] proposed a solution to this problem that is unfortunately broken. The essence of their idea is that the private key consists of two parts, the second part encoding some personal identifiable information. This second subkey is put on the blacklist, and the protocol checks, in a blinded fashion, whether the subkey occurs on the blacklist. This approach does not work because the user, after getting revoked, can choose new subkeys that, when combined, still match with the original certificate, but where the second subkey is different and no longer occurs on the blacklist.

The solution to this problem can be obtained as follows (to be detailed in a forthcoming paper). The crucial observation is that even though $K_i = k_i \cdot P$ is *called* a public key, there is no reason to actually *make* it public: the proof that you have a certificate for a certain attribute always blinds both the public key and the certificate. So let us assume we keep the public key and certificate *secret*, and only publish it when we want to revoke it. This way, users whose public key is unknown cannot be traced because their key cannot be guessed, breaking out of the assumed paradox.

4   Implementation and Performance Indicators

To understand practical limitations and estimate performance of our protocols, we implemented the protocol from Fig. 2 in Java (terminal-side application) and Java Card (card-side application). Our implementation involves the following components:

Bouncy Castle Library with Extension for Pairings. The Bouncy Castle (BC) library[1] is a collection of cryptographic APIs for Java and C# programming languages. Bouncy Castle provides full support for ECC and an interface to the common Java Cryptography Extension API. However, it does not implement pairings or elliptic curves over fields other than $\mathbb{F}_p$ and $\mathbb{F}_{2^m}$. Thus we have added our own implementations of $\mathbb{F}_{p^2}$ and $\mathbb{F}_{p^{12}}$, and the Tate, ate, and R-ate pairings. To minimise maintenance overhead we strived to keep our extensions purely *on top* of the Bouncy Castle library, that is, we did not change anything in the original library. In future we plan to contact the BC development team to incorporate our extensions into the official BC tree.

Smart Card IO Library. Since version 6.0 the standard Java Development Kit includes support for communication with smart cards by providing the `javax.smartcardio` package. We used it to talk to a Java Card smart card on which our client applet was installed.

A Java Card with the Client Applet. The protocol on the card-side is implemented as a Java Card [11] applet and loaded onto a development Java Card.

4.1 Java Card Applet

In Section 2.3 we described the practical limitations of Java Cards that we have to take into account while programming the card. The actual operations that the card needs to perform are scalar multiplication of points and modulo multiplication of natural numbers. In the end the applet performs the required steps of the protocol in the following way.

An on-card random number generator is used to generate the blinding value. This value is stored in an EC private key structure on the card, which we call the *blind* (not blinded) key. Then two ECDH key agreement operations (effectively two scalar point multiplications) are performed with this blind key to calculate the blinded public key, and the blinded certificate, both of which are EC points. As mentioned in the introduction, the ECDH implementation only returns the x-coordinate of these multiplications, forcing the terminal to reconstruct the y-coordinate (see below).

The second part of the protocol requires the card to sign a nonce with the ECDSA algorithm using a blinded private key $b \cdot k_C$. The modular multiplication of these two large natural numbers has to be performed using hand implemented Java code. That is, for this last step we cannot utilise any of the Java Card API routines, like the key agreement above, to make the coprocessor do the multiplication with high performance. This single modular multiplication is the main bottleneck on the card-side implementation (see Section 4.5).

4.2 Terminal Application

The terminal application needs to cope with the shortcomings of the Java Card applet. This comes down to the fact that the terminal has to reconstruct the

---

[1] http://www.bouncycastle.org

points received from the card, $b \cdot P_c$ and $b \cdot C_a$, before they can be processed any further.

If we know the x-coordinate of a point on the curve, the square of the corresponding y-coordinate is known, namely as $y^2 = x^3 + ax + b$. By taking the square root of $x^3 + ax + b$ we find either y or $-y$. This forms the basis of "point compression", for compact representation of points. This is important for the implementation, because Diffie-Hellman on a Java smart card only produces the x-coordinate of a multiplication, as mentioned in Section 4.1.

This reconstruction is a simple guess work, trying different signs for the two y-coordinates. For the ECDSA signature verification this is not a real issue since this verification is reasonably fast, although this is of course not optimal. For the pairing signature verification simple guessing is not desirable. Therefore we exploit the bilinearity of the pairing to avoid computing more than two pairings, as would be the case without point reconstruction.

First we calculate $e_1 = e(b \cdot P_c, Q_a)$ and $e_2 = e(b \cdot C_a, Q)$ where we take any sign for the y-coordinate of $b \cdot C_a$. If $e_1 = e_2$, which happens if we have two right, or two wrong, signs in the first parameters of the pairing, the verification succeeds. In the remaining case, which means we took one right and one wrong sign, we check whether $e_1 e_2 = 1$ holds. If it holds, the verification also succeeds. This is true because of the following. If $e_1 \neq e_2$, the error is caused by the wrong sign resulting in one pairing being the inverse of the other, that is, $e_2 = e_1^{-1}$. Here we can use that $e_1 e_2 = e_1(e_1^{-1}) = 1$ to avoid an extra pairing calculation for the negated point of $b \cdot C_a$.

4.3 System Parameters

For our test we selected three BN curves for keys of length 128, 160 and 192 bits. The domain parameters p and n are generated by the BN indices $u = 1678770247$, $u = 448873116367$ and $u = 105553250485267$ respectively (see Section 2). The curve E is defined as $y^2 = x^3 + 3$, that is, take $a = 0$ and $b = 3$ in the general form $y^2 = x^3 + ax + b$, with the default generator $G = (1, 2)$.

These key lengths have been chosen to indicate performance for various levels of security, that is, protection against fraud. A key length of 128 bits provides borderline security, whereas 160 and 192 bits provide, respectively, a minimal and a standard level of security [13].

The length of the blinding factor generated by the card is either equal to the chosen key length or a half or a quarter of this length. Reducing this length of the blinding factor is a way to partially compensate for the slowness of the modular multiplication (in Java Card) of big numbers. This way a trade off can be made between privacy and performance.

4.4 Test Results

The results of our tests are summarised in Table 1. These values are the average of ten test runs for each configuration, that is, for each combination of key and blinding length.

Table 1. Test results for various key and blinding lengths

key (bits)	blinding (bits)	getAttribute (ms)	getSignature (ms)	card total (ms)	verification (ms)	protocol (ms)
192	192	545	2202	2748	143	2891
	96	543	1340	1884	136	2020
	48	544	907	1451	130	1582
160	160	442	1417	1860	126	1987
	80	443	912	1355	133	1489
	40	442	670	1113	127	1240
128	128	364	1235	1599	91	1691
	64	363	780	1143	93	1237
	32	362	565	927	86	1014

The table shows the duration (in milliseconds) of the getAttribute and getSignature requests to the card. The total amount of time spent by the card, which is the sum of the durations of the requests, is shown in the 'card total' column. For the terminal we measured the duration of the signature verifications, summarised in the 'verification' column. Finally the total duration of the protocol execution is shown in the 'protocol' column.

4.5   Analysis

We first look at the part of the protocol executed on the smart card. From the results given in Table 1 it can be seen that the duration of the getAttribute request depends only on the length of the key. This is in strong contrast with the getSignature request which also depends heavily on the blinding size.

This contrast can be explained by the available support from the cryptographic coprocessor. For the blinding in the getAttribute request the applet uses the ECDH primitive provided by the coprocessor to perform the required two point multiplications. The blinding in the getSignature request, which requires a modular multiplication, has to be calculated *without* the help of the coprocessor. In theory it is possible to abuse the RSA cipher (and hence use the coprocessor) to do large part of the modulo multiplication by using the fact that $4ab = (a+b)^2 - (a-b)^2$, as in [21,23]. The squares in this equation can be performed by doing an RSA encryption/exponentiation with a suitable RSA public key, that is, one with the exponent 2 and the required modulus. The numbers $a+b$ and $a-b$ are then just messages to be encrypted using the RSA cipher, which is provided by the Java Card API.

We tried this approach, but with no success. The main obstacle is that the RSA cipher on the card operates only within valid bit lengths for RSA keys, starting with 512 bit keys. Although the number to be multiplied (the message) can be any value, the number of non-zero bits in the modulus has to be at least

488 bits for 512 bit keys according to our tests. Since our modulus is only 192 bit long the card refused to perform RSA encryption with such short modulus value. However, we believe that a more flexible RSA implementation on the card would allow this optimisation.

The performance of the terminal application is good, taking less than a tenth of running time on the smart card. The drawback on this side is caused by the use of the ECDH primitive to calculate the blinded value. This results in the problem that the card only responds with the x-coordinates of the blinded values. Therefore the terminal has to reconstruct the actual point from these values as mentioned above. If the card could respond with the actual points, either in compressed or uncompressed format, instead of just the x-coordinate, the duration of the verification phase could be shortened.

A large benefit of our use of ECC is the small amount of data that needs to be exchanged between the terminal and the card. For key lengths of 192, 160 and 128 bits the total amount of bytes exchanged is 168, 152 and 136 respectively. This would allow an implementation to use a *single* APDU pair (command and response) for all communication. This is in strong contrast with RSA-based protocols [21,23] which already require multiple APDUs to transfer a single command.

5   Conclusions

In line with results of others [12,21,23] this paper demonstrates that implementations of anonymous credential systems with smart cards are becoming possible. One important bottleneck (and source of frustration) remains the limited access offered to the coprocessor on current Java Card smart cards. This paper uses elliptic curves (with pairings) and abuses Diffie-Hellman key agreement for (scalar) point multiplication, together with several other tricks, to bring on-card computation times down to around 1.5 seconds. We expect to be able to further reduce this time via additional optimisations.

References

1. Barreto, P., Naehrig, M.: Pairing-friendly elliptic curves of prime order. In: Preneel, B., Tavares, S. (eds.) SAC 2005. LNCS, vol. 3897, pp. 319–331. Springer, Heidelberg (2006)
2. Blake, I., Seroussi, G., Smart, N.P.: Advances in Elliptic Curve Cryptography. In: LMS, vol. 317. Cambridge Univ. Press, Cambridge (2005)
3. Boneh, D., Franklin, M.: Identity-based encryption from the Weil pairing. In: Kilian, J. (ed.) CRYPTO 2001. LNCS, vol. 2139, pp. 213–229. Springer, Heidelberg (2001)
4. Boneh, D., Lynn, B., Shacham, H.: Short signatures from the Weil pairing. Journal of Cryptology 17(4), 297–319 (2004)
5. Brands, S.: Rethinking Public Key Infrastructures and Digital Certificates: Building in Privacy. MIT Press, Cambridge (2000)
6. Brickell, E.F., Camenisch, J., Chen, L.: Direct anonymous attestation. In: Pfitzmann, B., Liu, P. (eds.) Computer and Communications Security - CCS 2004, pp. 132–145. ACM Press, New York (2004)

7. BSI: Advanced security mechanisms for machine readable travel documents – Extended Access Control (EAC). Tech. Rep. TR-03110, German Federal Office for Information Security, BSI (2008)
8. Camenisch, J., van Herreweghen, E.: Design and implementation of the idemix anonymous credential system. In: Computer and Communications Security - CCS 2002, pp. 21–30. ACM, New York (2002)
9. Camenisch, J., Lysyanskaya, A.: Signature schemes and anonymous credentials from bilinear maps. In: Franklin, M. (ed.) CRYPTO 2004. LNCS, vol. 3152, pp. 56–72. Springer, Heidelberg (2004)
10. Chaum, D.: Blind signatures for untraceable payments. In: Chaum, D., Rivest, R.L., Sherman, A.T. (eds.) Advances in Cryptology - CRYPTO 1982, pp. 199–203. Plenum Press, New York (1983)
11. Chen, Z.: Java Card Technology for Smart Cards: Architecture and Programmer's Guide. Java Series. Addison-Wesley, Reading (2000)
12. Danes, L.: Smart card integration in the pseudonym system idemix. Master's thesis, University of Groningen, The Netherlands (2007)
13. ECRYPTII: Yearly report on algorithms and keysizes (2008-2009). Tech. Rep. D.SPA.7, European Network of Excellence in Cryptology II (ECRYPTII) (2009)
14. Jacobs, B.: Architecture is politics: Security and privacy issues in transport and beyond. In: Gutwirth, S., Poullet, Y., Hert, P. (eds.) Data Protection in a Profiled World - CPDP 2008. Springer, Heidelberg (2010)
15. Johnson, D., Menezes, A.: The elliptic curve digital signature algorithm (ECDSA). Tech. Rep. CORR 99-34, Department of Combinatorics & Optimization, University of Waterloo, Canada (2000)
16. Joux, A.: A one round protocol for tripartite Diffie-Hellman. Journal of Cryptology 17(4), 263–276 (2004)
17. Kiyomoto, S., Tanaka, T.: Anonymous attribute authentication scheme using self-blindable certificates. In: Intelligence and Security Informatics - ISI 2008, pp. 215–217. IEEE, Los Alamitos (2008)
18. NXP: Smart solutions for smart services (z-card 2009). NXP Literature, Document 75016728 (2009)
19. Paradinas, P., Cordry, J., Bouzefrane, S.: Performance evaluation of Java Card bytecodes. In: Sauveron, D., Markantonakis, K., Bilas, A., Quisquater, J.-J. (eds.) WISTP 2007. LNCS, vol. 4462, pp. 127–137. Springer, Heidelberg (2007)
20. Smart, N.: Elliptic curve based protocols. In: Blake, I., Seroussi, G., Smart, N. (eds.) Advances in Elliptic Curve Cryptography. LMS, vol. 317, pp. 3–19. Cambridge Univ. Press, Cambridge (2005)
21. Sterckx, M., Gierlichs, B., Preneel, B., Verbauwhede, I.: Efficient implementation of anonymous credentials on Java Card smart cards. In: Information Forensics and Security - WIFS 2009, pp. 106–110. IEEE, Los Alamitos (2009)
22. Sun Microsystems, Inc.: Java Card 2.2.2 Application Programming Interface Specification (2006)
23. Tews, H., Jacobs, B.: Performance issues of selective disclosure and blinded issuing protocols on java card. In: Markowitch, O., Bilas, A., Hoepman, J.H., Mitchell, C., Quisquater, J.J. (eds.) WISTP 2009. LNCS, vol. 5746, pp. 95–111. Springer, Heidelberg (2009)
24. Vercauteren, F.: Pairings on elliptic curves. In: Joye, M., Neven, G. (eds.) Identity-Based Cryptography. CIS, vol. 2, pp. 13–30. IOS Press, Amsterdam (2009)
25. Verheul, E.: Self-blindable credential certificates from the Weil pairing. In: Boyd, C. (ed.) ASIACRYPT 2001. LNCS, vol. 2248, pp. 533–550. Springer, Heidelberg (2001)

On the Design and Implementation of an Efficient DAA Scheme*

Liqun Chen[1], Dan Page[2], and Nigel P. Smart[2]

[1] Hewlett-Packard Laboratories,
Long Down Avenue, Stoke Gifford,
Bristol, BS34 8QZ,
United Kingdom
liqun.chen@hp.com
[2] Computer Science Department,
Woodland Road, University of Bristol,
Bristol, BS8 1UB,
United Kingdom
{page,nigel}@cs.bris.ac.uk

Abstract. Direct Anonymous Attestation (DAA) is an anonymous digital signature scheme that aims to provide both signer authentication and privacy. One of the properties that makes DAA an attractive choice in practice is the split signer role. In short, a principal signer (a Trusted Platform Module (TPM)) signs messages in collaboration with an assistant signer (the HOST, a standard computing platform into which the TPM is embedded). This split aims to harness the high level of security offered by the TPM, and augment it using the high level of computational and storage ability offered by the HOST. Our contribution in this paper is a modification to an existing pairing-based DAA scheme that significantly improves efficiency, and a comparison with the original RSA-based DAA scheme via a concrete implementation.

1 Introduction

An anonymous signature scheme is a special type of digital signature. In common with a conventional signature scheme, an anonymous signature scheme must ensure that only an authorised signer can produce a valid signature. However, given a signature it must also ensure that no unauthorised entity should be able to identify the signer. Another difference is highlighted by the nature of the public keys used to perform signature verification. To verify a conventional signature, the verifier makes use of a single public verification key which is bound to the identity of the signer. In contrast, to verify an anonymous signature the verifier makes use of either a group public key or multiple public keys. In either case the keys are not bound to an individual signer, and the level of anonymity

---

* The second and third author would like to thank the EU funded project eCrypt-2 for partially supporting the work in this paper. The third author was supported by a Royal Society Wolfson Merit Award.

D. Gollmann, J.-L. Lanet, J. Iguchi-Cartigny (Eds.): CARDIS 2010, LNCS 6035, pp. 223–237, 2010.

provided depends upon the size of the group or the number of public keys. The first anonymous signature schemes were group signatures, introduced in 1991 by Chaum and van Heyst [12].

In this paper we shall concentrate on a specific form of anonymous signature that uses a group public key, namely a signature provided by a Direct Anonymous Attestation (DAA) protocol. The security notions of DAA are different from group signatures, e.g., there is no group manager-based traceability in DAA. For the details of the security model of DAA and differentiation between the group signatures and DAA, we direct the reader to [5,7]. In addition to a number of interesting security and privacy features, DAA has a unique property that makes it an attractive choice. In short, the signer role in DAA is split between

1. a principal signer with limited computational and storage capability but high security assurance, and
2. an assistant signer with greater computational and storage capability, but lesser security.

Concrete realisation of these entities is provided by a TPM and a standard computing platform, termed the HOST, into which the TPM is embedded. The TPM represents the principle signer and holds the secret signing key; the HOST assists the TPM in computing a signature, and satisfying the privacy requirement. Note that the HOST is prevented from learning the secret signing key, and hence from producing a valid signature without interaction with the TPM.

The TPM is a physically secure hardware device designed to enable higher levels of security than are possible using software alone. One can view the TPM as a form of coprocessor capable of storing cryptographic keys and performing limited computational tasks in a secure manner; communication with the TPM is typically performed via a low-bandwidth Low Pin Count (LPC) bus interface. From a functional perspective, the TPM is specified by the Trusted Computing Group (TCG); estimates suggest over 100 million standardised TPM devices are currently in existence, mostly within high-end laptops. This deployment is intended to support a wide variety of applications including full disk encryption, Digital Rights Management (DRM) and, crucially for this work, anonymous digital signatures. Crucially, said applications must be designed with great care so as not to expose the constrained nature of both TPM and LPC bus as a bottleneck.

The concept of DAA, and a concrete scheme, were first introduced by Brickell, Camenisch, and Chen [5]; for a historical perspective, we direct the reader to [6]. This RSA-based scheme, which we term RSA-DAA from here on, was adopted by the TCG and included in version 1.2 of the TPM specification [26]; this TPM specification was recently adopted by ISO/IEC as an international standard [23]. Support for RSA-DAA alone represents around 10% of the TPM resources and as such, schemes that retain the same functionality but do so more efficiently remain an interesting and challenging open problem. One option, which has formed the focus of much recent work, is the development of DAA schemes based on elliptic curves and pairings; we generically term such schemes ECC-DAA from here on. The advantage of using these underlying building blocks is obvious: both the key and signature length can be much shorter, and computational load placed on the TPM less severe. As a result, ECC-DAA is typically more efficient in computation, storage and communication cost than RSA-DAA.

MAIN CONTRIBUTIONS: To the best of our knowledge, there are six existing ECC-DAA schemes. Brickell, Chen and Li [7,8] proposed the first such scheme, basing it on symmetric pairings. In order to improve flexibility and efficiency, Chen, Morrissey and Smart proposed two extensions [15,16,17] based instead on asymmetric pairings. Although the security of all three schemes is based on both the LRSW [24] and DDH problems, a flaw in the first extension was discovered by Li and further discussed in [14,17]. Three further schemes were proposed by Chen and Feng [19], Brickell and Li [10], and Chen [13] respectively. The security of these schemes is based on the q-SDH [4] and DDH problems. Using previous work as a starting point, this paper makes two main contributions.

Firstly, we make three modifications to the ECC-DAA scheme described in [17]. In summary, these modifications are:

1. The first modification is purely syntactic and implies no change to the security proof from [17]: we simply move computations which could be performed by the TPM to the HOST, and vice versa. This has the effect of balancing the workloads of TPM and HOST, ultimately reducing the computational load placed on the TPM.
2. Next we replace the public key signature based endorsement key from [17] with a public key encryption based endorsement key, combined with a Message Authentication Code (MAC). This mirrors more closely how the authentic channel is created in the currently deployed RSA-DAA scheme.
3. Finally we replace the root key, used by the ISSUER in generation of the TPM DAA secret key, with a small subset of public system parameters. We also remove the requirement for the TPM to verify a certificate chain (from the root public key of the ISSUER to the current public key) in every join process. This verification was required in all previous DAA schemes, including RSA-DAA, and has two main purposes: firstly to allow the TPM DAA secret key to have a different life-cycle from the ISSUER public key, and secondly to to avoid the TPM accepting an arbitrary key that does not belong to a given issuer. Our modification is based on two facts:
   (a) in our new DAA scheme the TPM operations are strictly limited to the small subset of public system parameters and do not actually use the issuer current public key, and
   (b) the public system parameters can have a much longer life-cycle than the ISSUER public key.
The modification vastly reduces the TPM workload in the Join protocol.

From here on, and unless otherwise specified, one can read ECC-DAA as meaning our modified scheme as described in Section 2.

Secondly, we demonstrate how the ECC-DAA scheme can be implemented and evaluate it via a concrete comparison with the incumbent RSA-DAA. In particular, we present experimental results that illustrate various implementation options and compare aspects of the schemes (e.g., efficiency and communication cost) using a commodity computing platform (that represents the HOST) and an embedded computing platform (that represents the TPM).

2   The Pairing-Based ECC-DAA Scheme

A DAA scheme involves a set of issuers, signers, and verifiers. An ISSUER is in charge of verifying the legitimacy of signers, and of issuing a DAA credential to each signer. A signer, which due to the split role is a pair of HOST and associated TPM, can prove membership to a VERIFIER by providing a DAA signature; this requires the signer holds a valid DAA credential. The VERIFIER can verify the membership credential from the signature, but it cannot learn the identity of the signer. Linkability of signatures issued by a HOST TPM pair is controlled by an input parameter bsn (standing for "base name") which is passed to the signing operation. There is assumed to be a list RogueList which contains a list of TPM secret keys which have been compromised. Based on these definitions, the rest of this section describes our ECC-DAA scheme, which is based on the scheme of [17] and relies on the use of asymmetric pairings.

NOTATION: Throughout the constituent protocols and algorithms, we let $\mathfrak{I}$, $\mathfrak{H}$ and $\mathcal{V}$ denote the set of all ISSUER, HOST and VERIFIER entities; the set of all TPM entities is denoted by $\mathfrak{M}$. The value of bsn will be used by the signer/verifier to link signatures, if bsn $=\perp$ then this implies that signatures should be unlinkable.

If S is a set, we denote the act of sampling from S uniformly at random and assigning the result to the variable x by $x \leftarrow S$. We let $\{0,1\}^*$ and $\{0,1\}^t$ denote the set of binary strings of arbitrary length and length t respectively. If A is an algorithm, we denote the action of obtaining x by invoking A on inputs $y_1, \ldots, y_n$ by $x \leftarrow A(y_1, \ldots, y_n)$, where the probability distribution on x is determined by the internal coin tosses of A. Finally, we use $[x]P$ to denote the scalar multiplication of an elliptic curve point P by some integer x.

NOTE: Before proceeding with the description of our scheme, we note a general issue that needs to be considered throughout. Specifically, every group element received by any entity needs to be checked for validity, i.e., that it is within the correct group; in particular, it is important that the element does not lie in some larger group which contains the group in question. This strict stipulation avoids numerous attacks such as those related to small subgroups. When asymmetric pairings are used, as here, this is particularly important since $\mathbb{G}_1$ and $\mathbb{G}_2$ can be considered as distinct subgroups of a large group $\mathbb{G}$. If communicated group elements are actually in $\mathbb{G}$, as opposed to $\mathbb{G}_1$ and $\mathbb{G}_2$, then various properties such as anonymity and linkability break down. As a result, we implicitly assume that all transmitted group elements are elements of the specified groups: within our scheme, the use of Type-III pairings [20] allows efficient methods for checking subgroup membership as described by [18] and expanded upon in Section 3.

2.1 The Setup Algorithm

To initialise the system, one needs to select parameters for each protocol as well as the long term parameters for each ISSUER. We assume that prior to initialisation each TPM has a private endorsement key $\mathcal{SK}$ embedded into it (e.g., in read-only memory) and that each ISSUER has access to the corresponding public endorsement key $\mathcal{PK}$. We also assume a public key IND-CCA encryption/decryption scheme (ENC/DEC) has been selected for use with these keys, and a MAC algorithm (MAC) with key space $\mathcal{MK}$ has been selected in order to achieve authentication.

As explained previously, this latter point is both a minor departure from the ECC-DAA scheme of [17] (in that there, the TPM endorsement key was a signature/verification key pair) and a minor departure from the TCG developed TPM specification [26] (in that there, message integrity was "achieved" by using SHA-1 in [26] instead of a MAC function[1]).

On input of the security parameter 1^t, the Setup algorithm executes the following steps:

1. *Generate the Commitment Parameters* par_C. In this step, three groups $\mathbb{G}_1$, $\mathbb{G}_2$ and $\mathbb{G}_T$, of sufficiently large prime order q, are selected. Two random generators are then selected such that $\mathbb{G}_1 = \langle P_1 \rangle$ and $\mathbb{G}_2 = \langle P_2 \rangle$ along with a pairing $\hat{h} : \mathbb{G}_1 \times \mathbb{G}_2 \mapsto \mathbb{G}_T$. Next, two hash functions $H_1 : \{0,1\}^* \mapsto \mathbb{G}_1$ and $H_2 : \{0,1\}^* \mapsto \mathbb{Z}_q$ are selected and par_C is set to $(\mathbb{G}_1, \mathbb{G}_2, \mathbb{G}_T, \hat{h}, P_1, P_2, q, H_1, H_2)$. Note that in our scheme, and in contrast with existing ECC-DAA schemes, the TPM operations are strictly limited to $\mathbb{G}_1$. This allows a subset of par_C, namely par_T, to be set to $(\mathbb{G}_1, P_1, q)$ and installed on the TPM in preference to par_C.

2. *Generate Signature and Verification Parameters* par_S. Two additional hash functions are selected, namely $H_3 : \{0,1\}^* \mapsto \mathbb{Z}_q$ and $H_4 : \{0,1\}^* \mapsto \mathbb{Z}_q$, and par_S is set to (H_3, H_4).

3. *Generate the ISSUER Parameters* par_I. For each $i_k \in \mathfrak{I}$, the following steps are performed. Two integers $x, y \leftarrow \mathbb{Z}_q$ are selected, and the ISSUER private key isk_k is set to (x, y). Next, the values $X = [x]P_2 \in \mathbb{G}_2$ and $Y = [y]P_2 \in \mathbb{G}_2$ are computed; the ISSUER public key ipk_k is set to (X, Y). Then an ISSUER value K_k is derived from the ISSUER public values. Finally, par_I is set to $(\{\mathsf{ipk}_k, K_k\})$ for each ISSUER $i_k \in \mathfrak{I}$.

4. *Generate TPM Parameters*. The TPM generates a public/private key pair $(\mathcal{PK}, \mathcal{SK})$ for the associated endorsement key. In addition, it generates the private secret value DAAseed. Finally, par_T is set to $(\mathcal{PK}_\mathfrak{h})$ for each TPM embedded in some host $\mathfrak{h} \in \mathfrak{H}$.

5. *Publish Public Parameters*. Finally, the public system parameters par are set to $(\mathsf{par}_C, \mathsf{par}_S, \mathsf{par}_I, \mathsf{par}_T)$ and published.

---

[1] We place "achieved" in quotes, since it is a well known that a Merkle–Damgård style hash function, when applied to a concatenation of the message and a key, cannot provide secure message authentication.

NOTE 1: In our scheme, the ISSUER value K_k is derived from a representation of par_T; if the same par_T is used by multiple issuers, in order to limit K_k to a single issuer, the issuer value K_k can be set by using both par_T and a unique issuer name. This is an important difference from other existing DAA schemes, including RSA-DAA. In all the previous DAA schemes, K_k is computed to be a representation of the ISSUER root public key. This is used to certify the ISSUER's public key ipk_k so that the ISSUER and TPM can update their keys without synchronising with each other.

However, there may be a long certificate chain between K_k and ipk_k that could result in the Join protocol very inefficient; specifically, the TPM needs to verify said certificate chain. Our modification is based on the fact that the parameter par_T could be used over a longer timescale than the the ISSUER public/private key pair (isk_k, ipk_k). Therefore, the ISSUER could update his key without changing par_T and without requiring each TPM to update its private key synchronously.

NOTE 2: Each TPM has a single DAAseed, but can create multiple DAA secret keys, even associated with a single issuer. To allow this, a number cnt is used as an additional input to DAA secret key generation: the TPM DAA secret key is generated by using DAAseed, K_k and cnt as input.

2.2   The Join Protocol

This is a protocol between a given TPM $\mathfrak{m} \in \mathfrak{M}$, the corresponding HOST $\mathfrak{h} \in \mathfrak{H}$ and an ISSUER $\mathfrak{i} \in \mathfrak{J}$. The protocol proceeds as shown in Figure 1, and it is virtually identical to that of [17]. The difference is the way that the ISSUER and TPM establish an authentic channel between themselves. For simplicity of analysis, in [17] this mechanism was provided by a digital signature algorithm. However, in practice the TPM will not use a signature algorithm, but an encryption algorithm and an integrity check function. For the sake of privacy, the TCG does not want a TPM to provide a piece of evidence for each transaction. Since each endorsement key is bound to a particular TPM, a signature signed under the endorsement key can be used as such evidence in a public manner, (although the public key encryption mechanism still provides this evidence to an issuer). In this paper we follow this approach; the minor difference from the TPM specification [26] is, as mentioned, that we make use of a MAC function to achieve authentication rather than a hash function as in [26].

2.3   The Sign/Verify Protocols

This is a protocol between a given TPM $\mathfrak{m} \in \mathfrak{M}$, HOST $\mathfrak{h} \in \mathfrak{H}$ and VERIFIER $\mathfrak{v} \in \mathcal{V}$ as described in Figure 2. The main difference between this version and the protocol in [17] is the computation of $W \leftarrow [t]D$ by the HOST, as opposed to the computation of $\beta \leftarrow \hat{h}(S, X)$. This avoids a costly pairing operation by the HOST, and an expensive $\mathbb{G}_T$ operation by the TPM. This advantage comes at the expense of the VERIFIER being required to compute more operations in $\mathbb{G}_1$, but less pairing operations and operations in $\mathbb{G}_T$.

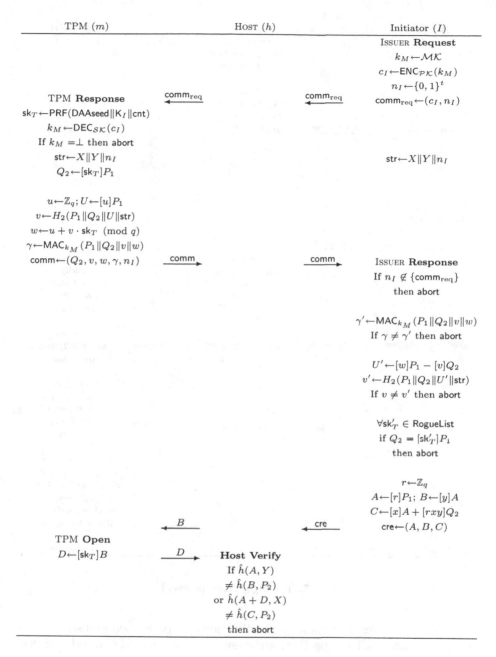

Fig. 1. The Join protocol

It is easy to see that these minor modifications to the Sign and Verify protocols have no affect on the security proof from [17]. Indeed, the VERIFIER still verifies a Camensich-Lysyanskaya credential [11] and a proof of equality of two discrete

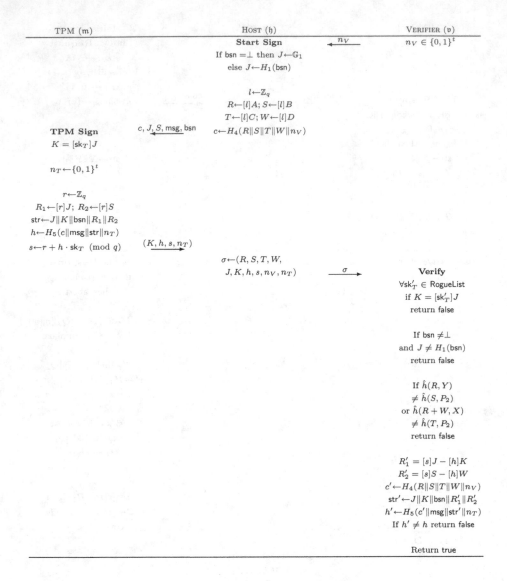

Fig. 2. The Sign/Verify protocol

logarithms. However, now these two verifications are performed in distinct steps rather than being mixed together; we suggested this makes the overall protocol structure simpler to understand. In addition, the modifications produces a more efficient protocol for the HOST, TPM and VERIFIER. In addition, by splitting the proof of equality of discrete logarithms from the credential verification step, we enable the use of batch pairing verification techniques as expanded upon in Section 3.

3 Implementation Details

3.1 RSA-DAA Scheme

Rather than replicate the detail here, we refer the reader to [5] for much of the notation and the RSA-DAA scheme itself. Several implementation details demand some discussion and clarification.

CHOICE OF PARAMETERS: The RSA-DAA scheme was instantiated using the security parameters defined in [5]. That is, the security parameters in [5, Section 4.2] were used to generate public and private ISSUER keys as described by [5, Section 4.3]; pertinent features include the 2048-bit n and 1632-bit Γ.

ENDORSEMENT KEY ALGORITHM: As described in [5, Appendix B], we altered the Join protocol to include the notion of TPM endorsement. Effectively this means the TPM holds a 2048-bit RSA key, and the PKCS#1 RSAES-OAEP primitive is used as the endorsement key algorithm within Step 4 of the Join protocol; we assume the public key of each TPM utilises a "small" exponent (i.e., $e = 65537$) and interleave additional messages to avoid extra communication steps.

IMPLEMENTATION OPTIONS: A central part of each protocol in the scheme is computation of k-term (multi-)exponentiations (i.e., the product of k single-exponentiations) modulo an n and Γ.

Three issues related to this type of computation are worthy of note. Firstly, there is scope for pre-computation based on the "somewhat fixed" bases taken from the per-ISSUER public key (e.g., g', g and h). The value of such an approach relates to the frequency of interaction with a given ISSUER, and therefore we do not pursue it in our implementation. Secondly, there exists a subtle overhead associated with the fact that various exponents for exponentiation modulo n are larger than the group order; no entity other than the ISSUER has knowledge of $\Phi(n)$ and hence they must be used, as presented, in their larger form. Thirdly, we suggest that the diverse range of operand lengths used leads to some natural inefficiency: in short, one must either employ a general-purpose implementation strategy and pay a penalty in terms of performance, or employ a special-purpose implementation strategy and pay a penalty in terms of memory footprint. Depending on the entity (i.e., ISSUER, HOST, VERIFIER or TPM) one or other may be unattractive. Examples of this issue include:

- In various steps, entities perform computation modulo n and Γ which are of significantly different lengths: either one adopts a general-purpose strategy that supports all moduli, or a special-purpose strategy for each.
- In various steps, entities compute the result of multi-exponentiation with 2, 3, 4 and 6 terms with varying length exponents. Either one adopts a general-purpose strategy for any number of terms and any exponent length, or a special-purpose strategy or each. As an example, consider that in step 3.a.i of the Sign protocol, the TPM is required to compute

$$R_0^{r_{f_0}} R_1^{r_{f_1}} S^{r_v} \pmod{n}$$

where r_{f_0} and r_{f_1} are both 688-bit integers and r_v is a significantly larger 2776-bit integer. One could view the resulting mismatch as disadvantageous in the sense that some effort is being "wasted" during a multi-exponentiation,

We opted for general-purpose strategy throughout our implementation, reasoning that this provides a fair comparison given the similar approach in the ECC-DAA case.

3.2 ECC-DAA Scheme

The ECC-DAA under consideration is that described in Section 2; several implementation details demand some discussion and clarification.

CHOICE OF PARAMETERS: To instantiate the ECC-DAA scheme, we use pairing groups based on Barreto-Naehrig (BN) curves [2]. These are elliptic curves of the form

$$E : y^2 = x^3 + b,$$

for $b \neq 0$, where the curve order and the finite field are defined by the polynomials

$$q(s) = 36s^4 - 36s^3 + 18s^2 - 6s + 1,$$
$$p(s) = 36s^4 - 36s^3 + 24s^2 - 6s + 1.$$

To generate such curves, one searches random values of s of the correct form until $q(s)$ and $p(s)$ are both prime; searching for a b that produces a valid elliptic curve over $\mathbb{F}_p$, of order q, is then a simple task. In our implementation we selected $s = -7493989779944505618$ and defined a curve using $b = 18$. This yields roughly 256-bit values for $q(s)$ and $p(s)$ that are hence compatible with AES-128 bit key sizes; alternatively, one could consider the security level as comparable with 3000-bit RSA. Based on this curve, we select

1. The rational points on the curve $E(\mathbb{F}_p)$ as $\mathbb{G}_1$.
2. The order-q subgroup of $\hat{E}(\mathbb{F}_{p^2})$, where $\hat{E}$ is the sextic twist of E available due to the form of BN-curves, as $\mathbb{G}_2$.
3. The order-q subgroup of the finite field $\mathbb{F}_{p^{12}}$, available due to the embedding degree of BN-curves being 12, as $\mathbb{G}_T$.

Elements of the finite field $\mathbb{F}_{p^{12}}$ are represented by a polynomial basis with respect to the polynomial $\chi^{12} + 6$. Using these groups, we implemented the Ate pairing [22], which runs a short full-Miller loop followed by an exponentiation in $\mathbb{G}_T$. We note that more efficient pairing algorithms exist (e.g., R-ate), but made this selection partly based on possible inclusion in the IEEE P1363.3 Identity-Based Public Key Cryptography standard.

ENDORSEMENT KEY ALGORITHM: The choice of TPM endorsement key algorithm was selected to be ECIES defined over the group $\mathbb{G}_1$. The KEM component consists of a single element in $\mathbb{G}_1$. For encryption two point multiplications are required, whilst for decryption one point multiplication is required. The DEM component consisted of AES-128, combined with a CBC-MAC, (actually a variant of CBC-MAC called EMAC was used, which corresponds to MAC algorithm two in the ISO 9797-1 standard).

CREDENTIAL VERIFICATION: In both the Join and Sign/Verify protocols, verification of a blinded Camenisch-Lysyanskaya signature is required. Namely, given $A, B, C, D \in \mathbb{G}_1$ we need to verify whether both

$$\hat{h}(A, Y) = \hat{h}(B, P_2)$$

and

$$\hat{h}(A + D, X) = \hat{h}(C, P_2).$$

To optimise this operation, we use an analogue of the small-exponent batch verification techniques from [3]. Specifically, we select two small exponents $e_1, e_2 \in \mathbb{Z}_q$ whose bit length is half that of q; to verify the two pairing equations we then verify whether

$$\hat{h}([e_1]A, Y) \cdot ([-e_1]B, P_2) \cdot \hat{h}([e_2](A + D), X) \cdot \hat{h}([-e_2]C, P_2) = 1.$$

Thus the verification involving four pairing computations is replaced by one product of four pairings, plus four (relatively short) multiplications in $\mathbb{G}_1$. As surveyed in [21], computing a "product of pairings" is less expensive than computing the pairings independently; the methods improves verification of a blinded Camenisch-Lysyanskaya signature by around 40%.

SUBGROUP CHECKING: Recall from Section 2 that group element accepted by some entity within a protocol needs to be verified, i.e., checked to ensure it is within the correct subgroup. Such checking falls into one of three categories:

- Checking whether $X, Y \in \mathbb{G}_2$ can be done by first checking whether $X, Y \in \hat{E}(F_{p^2})$, and then verifying that $[q]X = [q]Y = \mathcal{O}$.
- Checking whether $r \in \mathbb{Z}_q$ or $Y \in \mathbb{G}_1$ is trivial. In the first case we simply need to check whether x is an integer in the range $[0, \ldots, q - 1]$, and in the second case we check whether Y lies on the curve $E(F_p)$. This simplicity is possible because there is no cofactor of $\mathbb{G}_1$ in $E(F_p)$ as a result of the curve choice.
- We ignore the cost of checking whether $X, Y \in \mathbb{G}_2$ because this is performed once only, by a given entity, on receipt of a public key from some ISSUER. That is, we expect the cost to be amortised across all interactions with the ISSUER.

3.3 Experimental Results

To evaluate the proposed ECC-DAA scheme, and compare it with RSA-DAA, we present some concrete experimental results. We used two platforms where

1. the ISSUER, HOST and VERIFIER entities were represented by a 64-bit, 2.4 GHz Intel Core2 (6600) processor targeted with GCC 4.3.2, and
2. the TPM entity was represented by a (simulated) 32-bit, 33 MHz ARM7TDMI processor targeted with ARM ADS 1.2.

Table 1. Experimental results for RSA-DAA and ECC-DAA. Note that Steps 5 and 6.*c* of the RSA-DAAJoin protocol involve primality testing and, as such, the results have quite a high standard deviation; where operations relate to entries in a rogue list (e.g., Step 4 of the RSA-DAAVerify protocol), the quoted result is per-entry rather than based on an assumed list length.

Join			
Step	ISSUER	HOST	TPM
1	––	13.38ms	––
2	––	––	25.73s
3	1.62ms	––	––
4.a	––	––	30.15s
4.b	0.32ms	––	––
4.c	––	< 0.01ms	––
4.d	––	––	< 0.01s
4.e	––	––	17.26s
4.f	––	––	––
4.g	46.15ms	––	––
5	138.08ms	––	––
6.a	––	< 0.01ms	––
6.b	30.61ms	––	––
6.c	––	72.99ms	––
7	––	––	––
8	––	––	< 0.01s

(a) Performance of the RSA-DAAJoin protocol.

	Sign			
Step	HOST		TPM	
	bsn =⊥	bsn ≠⊥	bsn =⊥	bsn ≠⊥
1.a	2.03ms	13.33ms		
1.b	––			1.28s
2.a	71.69ms		––	
2.b	––			1.27s
3.a.i	––			30.99s
3.a.ii	144.19ms		––	
3.b.i	0.04ms		––	
3.b.ii	––			< 0.01s
3.c.i	––			< 0.01s
3.c.ii	< 0.01ms		––	
4	––		––	

	Verify	
Step	VERIFIER	
	bsn =⊥	bsn ≠⊥
1	175.04ms	––
2	3.99ms	––
3	––	13.31ms
4	1.61ms	––

(b) Performance of the RSA-DAASign/Verify protocols.

Join			
Step	ISSUER	HOST	TPM
ISSUER Request	1.14ms	––	––
TPM Response	––	––	2.77s
ISSUER Response	4.16ms	––	––
TPM Open	––	––	1.12s
HOST Verify	––	46.08ms	––

(c) Performance of the ECC-DAAJoin protocol.

	Sign			
Step	HOST		TPM	
	bsn =⊥	bsn ≠⊥	bsn =⊥	bsn ≠⊥
Start Sign	4.09ms	6.53ms	––	
TPM Sign	––			3.34s

	Verify	
Step	VERIFIER	
	bsn =⊥	bsn ≠⊥
Verify	47.19ms	48.31ms

(d) Performance of the ECC-DAASign/Verify protocols.

One might argue this software-only approach makes little sense because a TPM will typically be equipped with hardware accelerators for primitives such as RSA, SHA1 and a PRNG. As a result, we stress that our results are indicative only: we attempt to model the asymmetry that exists between entities in terms of computational ability, and give a relative comparison of the two schemes that relates move directly to a software-based TPM [27].

Our implementation of both schemes was constructed using vanilla C with assembly language fragments for performance-critical sections. Both use SHA-256 as an underlying hash function with a counter-based iteration extending the digest size where appropriate; rather than a cryptographically secure PRNG, both implementations use the C LCG-based PRNG. Within both schemes we take advantage of persistent state where possible: we avoid re-computation of common intermediate results (e.g., between Step 5 and 6.b of RSA-DAA) via caching. However, the clear advantage that exists in terms of computation is counter-balanced by an implication for memory footprint that we ignore somewhat.

An important difference is the algorithms used for exponentiation (resp. scalar multiplication):

- Within RSA-DAA and with $k = 1$ term, the HOST, ISSUER and VERIFIER use sliding window (with $w = 4$) exponentiation; with $k > 1$ terms they use Strauss' method (or Shamir's trick) for multi-exponentiation. The more constrained TPM platform also uses sliding window (with $w = 4$) exponentiation when $k = 1$, but repeated single-exponentiation for $k > 1$.
- Within ECC-DAA, all entities use (signed) sliding window (with $w = 4$) scalar multiplication and group exponentiation; there are no instances of multi-exponentiation.

We concede that aggressive specialisation and efficient (multi-)exponentiation techniques (e.g., those described in detail by Möller [25] and Avanzi [1]) would yield improved results for both schemes.

The results are given in Tables 1. For each step in each protocol, we give timings in milli seconds on the HOST, ISSUER, VERIFIER or (simulated) TPM platform as appropriate. The names for the different stages for the RSA-DAA protocol are taken from the description in [5]. We again stress that the results are indicative only, and they do not include hidden costs such as communication and random number generation. Even so, one can draw several concrete conclusions:

- Aside from performance, the results highlight that the RSA-DAA scheme is significantly more complicated in terms of the number of steps and interaction between entities; we suggest that this hints at a higher communication cost.
- The performance of RSA-DAA has some significant performance bottlenecks in our software-only approach, particularly in terms of computation on the TPM; the availability of hardware accelerators within makes this point moot however. In contrast, the results indicate that our ECC-DAA scheme *is* feasible using a software-only approach. As such, one can either view it as removing the need for dedicated hardware in the TPM (e.g., for modular arithmetic) *or* potentially being significantly faster should similarly dedicated hardware be available.

- Our ECC-DAA scheme not only provides performance advantages for the TPM, but also for the ISSUER and HOST. What is surprising is that even though the verification in our ECC-DAA scheme requires several pairing operations, it is still faster than the equivalent RSA-DAA verification operation by some margin. In part, this is due to our efficient batching technique, and the specific choice of pairings adopted.
- Finally, we note that the security parameters for our ECC-DAA scheme have been selected to be equivalent to a 128-bit AES security level. Thus, on paper at least, our ECC-DAA scheme has a higher security margin than the RSA-DAA scheme while still delivering the aforementioned performance advantages.

References

1. Avanzi, R.M.: The complexity of certain multi-exponentiation techniques in cryptography. Journal of Cryptology 18, 357–373 (2005)
2. Barreto, P.S.L.M., Naehrig, M.: Pairing-friendly elliptic curves of prime order. In: Preneel, B., Tavares, S. (eds.) SAC 2005. LNCS, vol. 3897, pp. 319–331. Springer, Heidelberg (2006)
3. Bellare, M., Garay, J., Rabin, T.: Fast batch verification for modular exponentiation and digital signatures. In: Nyberg, K. (ed.) EUROCRYPT 1998. LNCS, vol. 1403, pp. 236–250. Springer, Heidelberg (1998)
4. Boneh, D., Boyen, X.: Sort signatures without random oracles. In: Cachin, C., Camenisch, J.L. (eds.) EUROCRYPT 2004. LNCS, vol. 3027, pp. 56–73. Springer, Heidelberg (2004)
5. Brickell, E., Camenisch, J., Chen, L.: Direct anonymous attestation. In: Computer and Communications Security – CCS 2004, pp. 132–145. ACM Press, New York (2004)
6. Brickell, E., Camenisch, J., Chen, L.: Direct anonymous attestation in context. In: Mitchell, C. (ed.) Trusted Computing, ch. 5, pp. 143–174. IEEE, London (2005)
7. Brickell, E., Chen, L., Li, J.: Simplified security notions for direct anonymous attestation and a concrete scheme from pairings. Int. Journal of Information Security 8, 315–330 (2009)
8. Brickell, E., Chen, L., Li, J.: A new direct anonymous attestation scheme from bilinear maps. In: Lipp, P., Sadeghi, A.-R., Koch, K.-M. (eds.) Trust 2008. LNCS, vol. 4968, pp. 166–178. Springer, Heidelberg (2008)
9. Brickell, E., Li, J.: Enhanced privacy ID: A direct anonymous attestation scheme with enhanced revocation capabilities. In: Privacy in the Electronic Society – WPES 2007, pp. 21–30. ACM Press, New York (2007)
10. Brickell, E., Li, J.: Enhanced privacy ID from bilinear pairing. Cryptology ePrint Archive. Report 2009/095, http://eprint.iacr.org/2009/095
11. Camenisch, J., Lysyanskaya, A.: Signature schemes and anonymous credentials from bilinear maps. In: Franklin, M. (ed.) CRYPTO 2004. LNCS, vol. 3152, pp. 56–72. Springer, Heidelberg (2004)
12. Chaum, D., van Heyst, E.: Group signatures. In: Davies, D.W. (ed.) EUROCRYPT 1991. LNCS, vol. 547, pp. 257–265. Springer, Heidelberg (1991)
13. Chen, L.: A DAA scheme requiring less TPM resources. In: Int. Conference on Information Security and Cryptology - Inscrypt 2009 (2009) (to appear)

14. Chen, L., Li, J.: A note on the Chen-Morrissey-Smart direct anonymous attestation scheme (preprint)
15. Chen, L., Morrissey, P., Smart, N.P.: Pairings in trusted computing. In: Galbraith, S.D., Paterson, K.G. (eds.) Pairing 2008. LNCS, vol. 5209, pp. 1–17. Springer, Heidelberg (2008)
16. Chen, L., Morrissey, P., Smart, N.P.: On proofs of security of DAA schemes. In: Baek, J., Bao, F., Chen, K., Lai, X. (eds.) ProvSec 2008. LNCS, vol. 5324, pp. 156–175. Springer, Heidelberg (2008)
17. Chen, L., Morrissey, P., Smart, N.P.: DAA: Fixing the pairing based protocols. Cryptology ePrint Archive. Report 2009/198, http://eprint.iacr.org/2009/198
18. Chen, L., Cheng, Z., Smart, N.P.: Identity-based key agreement protocols from pairings. Int. Journal of Information Security 6, 213–242 (2007)
19. Chen, X., Feng, D.: Direct anonymous attestation for next generation TPM. Journal of Computers 3, 43–50 (2008)
20. Galbraith, S., Paterson, K., Smart, N.P.: Pairings for cryptographers. Discrete Applied Mathematics 156, 3113–3121 (2008)
21. Granger, R., Smart, N.P.: On computing products of pairings. Cryptology ePrint Archive. Report 2006/172, http://eprint.iacr.org/2006/172
22. Hess, F., Smart, N.P., Vercauteren, F.: The Eta pairing revisited. IEEE Transactions on Information Theory 52, 4595–4602 (2006)
23. ISO/IEC 11889: 2009 Information technology – Security techniques – Trusted Platform Module (2009)
24. Lysyanskaya, A., Rivest, R., Sahai, A., Wolf, S.: Pseudonym systems. In: Heys, H.M., Adams, C.M. (eds.) SAC 1999. LNCS, vol. 1758, pp. 184–199. Springer, Heidelberg (2000)
25. Möller, B.: Algorithms for multi-exponentiation. In: Vaudenay, S., Youssef, A.M. (eds.) SAC 2001. LNCS, vol. 2259, pp. 165–180. Springer, Heidelberg (2001)
26. Trusted Computing Group. TCG TPM specification 1.2 (2003), http://www.trustedcomputinggroup.org
27. Strasser, M., Stamer, H.: A software-based trusted platform module emulator. In: Lipp, P., Sadeghi, A.-R., Koch, K.-M. (eds.) Trust 2008. LNCS, vol. 4968, pp. 33–47. Springer, Heidelberg (2008)

Author Index